THE FLIGHT OF THE GARUDA

THE FLIGHT of the GARUDA

THE DZOGCHEN TRADITION
OF TIBETAN BUDDHISM

compiled and translated by

Keith Dowman

REVISED EDITION

WISDOM PUBLICATIONS • BOSTON

Wisdom Publications
199 Elm Street
Somerville MA 02144 USA
www.wisdompubs.org

First edition published 1994

Library of Congress Cataloging-in-Publication Data
   The flight of the Garuda : the Dzogchen tradition of Tibetan Buddhism / compiled and translated by Keith Dowman.—Rev. ed.
      p. cm.
   Includes bibliographical references.
   1. Rdzogs-chen (Rñiṅ-ma-pa) I. Dowman, Keith.
   BQ7662.4.F55 2003
   294.3'420423—dc21

                                                  2003004897

ISBN 978-0-86171-367-7   ebook ISBN 978-0-86171-853-5

18 17 16 15 14
7   6   5   4   3

Cover painting by Terris Temple.
Photography by Lorene Warwick, courtesy of Steve Johnson,
   with thanks to Venerable Carol Corradi.
Interior and cover designed by Gopa&Ted2, Inc. Set in Bembo 10.5/14.

This book was produced with Environmental Mindfulness. We have elected to print this
title on 50% PCW recycled paper. As a result, we have saved the following resources: 3 trees,
1 million BTUs of energy, 293 lbs. of greenhouse gases, 1,592 gallons of water, and 107
lbs. of solid waste. For more information, please visit our website, www.wisdompubs.org.

Printed in the United States of America.

Please visit www.fscus.org.

For Jason and his generation:
May all manner of things be well.

CONTENTS

THE THREE INCISIVE PRECEPTS

PREFACE

IN THE LAST FIFTEEN YEARS since the work that comprises *The Flight of the Garuda* was done, a wealth of Dzogchen texts has been translated and published. This has provided insight into both the breadth and depth of Dzogchen. This revised edition contains only minimal corrections to the original translations so that the integrity of those translations could be maintained.

To the four basic texts I have added a translation of Patrul Rinpoche's *Extraordinary Reality of Sovereign Wisdom*. If it is possible that a Dzogchen meditation manual exists then this is it. Shabkar Lama's *Flight of the Garuda* includes some precepts and meditation instruction on Dzogchen preliminaries, and indeed Dzogchen meditation itself. But *Extraordinary Reality* provides a complete practice including instruction on view, meditation, and action. Simply reading the text may induce the state of nonmeditation that is then to be sustained in the meditation session. In this way it is an initiatory text and, as Patrul Rinpoche asserts, identical to the mind of Garab Dorje himself. Since my first translation of this text was published in 1982 several excellent versions have become available. The improvement of this very important translation over the years is indicative of the increase of our understanding and expression of Dzogchen. My thanks to all who have made it possible.

Keith Dowman
Surendra Bhawan
Kathmandu
April 2003

TECHNICAL NOTE

I HAVE ADOPTED the following conventions in an attempt to make the text as accessible as possible. I have used Tibetan or Sanskrit words in the text only when I have been unable to find an English equivalent. Tibetan words appear in italicized, phonetic form in the text, with their transliterated form in the index. In the notes and occasionally in the text Tibetan words are transliterated according to the Wylie system. Many technical Sanskrit terms have now been assimilated into English (yoga, samadhi, nirvana, mandala, etc.); those that have not appear in italics with appropriate diacritical marks. Whenever the Sanskrit equivalent of a Tibetan word may be of use, primarily in the footnotes and glossaries, I have included it after the transliterated Tibetan word.

PREFACE TO THE FIRST EDITION

THIS BOOK CONTAINS the English translation of four Dzogchen texts belonging to the Nyingma school of Tibetan Buddhism. *Dzogchen,* the Great Perfection, is the quintessence of the tantric paths to buddhahood.

Among these texts, *Secret Instruction in a Garland of Vision* is one of three texts said to have been written by Padmasambhava, Tibet's great guru, who visited Tibet in the eighth century. It belongs to the *lamrim* genre, a stage-by-stage description of the path to buddhahood. *The Flight of the Garuda,* written by Shabkar Lama in the nineteenth century, comprises a series of twenty-three songs composed to inspire and instruct the yogin practicing Dzogchen *tregcho* meditation. The two shorter versified works are extracts from liturgical "revealed texts." *Emptying the Depths of Hell,* revealed by Guru Chowang in the thirteenth century, provides a Dzogchen confessional liturgy, and *The Wish-Granting Prayer of Kuntu Zangpo,* revealed by Rigdzin Godemchen in the fourteenth century as part of an extensive Dzogchen tantra, is a prayer for attainment of the Dzogchen goal.

In the introduction to the book I have attempted to place Dzogchen in a nondogmatic, less abstract, and more human context, by providing a subjective explication of it. Necessarily, Western notions and personal proclivities, needs, and biases have slipped into this interpretation. Insofar as my understanding is imperfect, the result is partial and unorthodox. However, the reader may benefit from this personal commentary if, through inspiration derived from the translations, he fills the gaps, bridges the contradictions, and jumps beyond the verbal inadequacies to a Dzogchen view. But no text or commentary is a substitute for transmission from an exemplar of Dzogchen attainment who demonstrates the Dzogchen path spontaneously and directly.

For my understanding of Dzogchen I have been dependent upon the kindness of many lamas. Kanjur Rinpoche, Dudjom Rinpoche, Khyentse Rinpoche, Jortra Lama, Jatrul Rinpoche Sangye Dorje, Namkhai Norbu Rinpoche, Dodrubchen Rinpoche, Trinle Norbu Rinpoche, and Taklung Tulku Pema Wongyel have all given me crucial insights into the tradition. The merit of any benefit accruing from this book is dedicated to their aspirations. Also, I am very grateful to Martin Parenchio and my wife Meryl for their assistance in editing the manuscript.

INTRODUCTION

I. THE THEORY AND PRACTICE OF DZOGCHEN

The Starting Point:[1] *A Personal Perspective*

"SIMPLICITY" was a word that my lama[2] often extracted from his small store of abstract nouns to express the nature of Dzogchen in English. It is the simplicity of Dzogchen that makes it so difficult to speak about, so elusive, and also, when the mind is veiled by its usual ignorance, somewhat nebulous. But what is implied by simplicity[3] is the key to the lama's mysteries, his power and knowledge, the key to the state of being that would make a world emperor envious. It is the "simplicity" of Dzogchen to which the highest yogin aspires; and it is the reward that the lama proffers his disciples during the frequent discourses upon karmic cause and effect and the precious human body, and during the arduous practice of prostrations at the beginning of the path. The buildup is systematic, prolonged, and intense, but from the very beginning Dzogchen is the goal. This *Dzogchen* of which I am speaking is the highest, most secret, and most direct of the paths to buddhahood in the tradition of Tibetan tantric Buddhism. It is the most sacred of paths, the essence of the mystic wisdom of the East, the most treasured jewel in the sacred treasury of Buddhist Tantra, and it is called the *Great Perfection.*[4]

Before and after shades of the prison-house closed around me, I felt, yet sought reassurance, that a human being is perfectible. Many in the generation that matured during the 1960s found confirmation of this intuition in Buddhism's teaching that there is no limit to the potential of a human being. Later such individuals, becoming the harbingers of a significant social movement, found that the Buddhist Tantra presented this and other essential practical existential theses in a vital and immediate form that exercised the intuition more than the intellect. The bodhisattva path of the exoteric

Mahayana, which teaches without any equivocation beings' perfectibility, demands many successive lifetimes of self-sacrificial devotion before the goal is achieved. The "here and now" ethos of the sixties was not conducive to a long hard slog toward a goal to be achieved after innumerable rebirths. Besides, to the childhood conviction that man was perfectible had been added the post-adolescent belief that the rational, speculative intellect was at best a tool for manipulating reality and was more likely to be a guileful deceiver creating mental miasmas, sometimes in intoxicating forms, but ultimately to be damned by its onanistic nature. Such notions brought into question even the supportive, liberating concepts of both Eastern and Western philosophical and metaphysical systems. Logical, systematic analysis and deductive and dialectical thought were of use in science, but truth was enigmatic, paradoxical, and supra-mental.

Gnosis,[5] compassion, tranquillity, a radiant multidimensional Gestalt, and existential fearlessness were the functions and attributes that I required of my reality. This reality was best expressed in paradox. The reality of the Indian *mahāsiddhas*[6] of the eighth to the twelfth centuries as demonstrated in their songs and legends evinced these characteristics, and the Tibetan lamas were the holders of the lineages the *mahāsiddhas* founded. The Indian sadhus of the Nāth community, for instance, also held lineages originating from the *mahāsiddhas,* and their lifestyles were also attractive and their existential fearlessness self-evident. But to identify a living Eastern tradition that teaches the techniques of awareness and mastery that I desired was one thing; to gain access to the tradition, find a teacher, and obtain initiation was another. What is it that determines which path is followed when we reach a crossroads lacking a signpost? What determines which people we meet and with whom we fall in love? What allows the turtle to win a race with a hare? On the great Indian spiritual quest, or the quest for the Holy Grail in Albion, action taken in the face of imponderables at a crossroads determines whether we are to find, for instance, the Tibetan lama or the Nāth guru, or whether we return the way we came. The quest can rarely begin if the seeker has a round-trip ticket and a home and family awaiting him, or if he runs hither and thither on a preconceived mission with the pretension that he can control his fate. "Nonaction" and "aimlessness"[7] are required to develop the receptivity and tranquillity necessary to take correct action at the point of indecision, to find the teacher—and the tradition.

In the search for a master, the truth of the adage "When the disciple is ready the master will appear" seems fundamental and incontrovertible. There is nothing to do but await in mental silence for recognition of the true guru, the guru within and the guru-buddha outside, when he appears. The holistic laws of synchronicity may consummate the encounter with the guru-buddha immediately, or perhaps the seeker must wait until the moment before the final goal is attained—there is no telling. But the twelve-year *sādhana* the Indian *siddha* Nāropa practiced before his guru Tilopa decided the time was ripe for his initiation, for instance, was as significant a part of his training as the post-initiation period. Thus the teacher chooses the disciple, and the tradition entered upon is determined by the shape of the receptive framework of the mind that allows this guru, rather than another, to embrace it. So when, for example, I say that I came to India to study Tibetan Buddhism, find a teacher, and practice Tantra, the guru knows that actually while roaming aimlessly in samsara I was sufficiently one-pointed in my dissatisfaction, and in my drive to reach existential roots, that emotional attachment along with preconception and strong belief was suffi-ciently neutralized for me to recognize the shape of the guru resident from the first in the simplicity of our original existential condition. The shape of my karmic predisposition led me to the Tibetan Buddhist Tantra, and ini-tiation into a tantric lineage was inevitable after reaching the requisite degree of honesty necessary to face my deepest proclivities without equiv-ocation and without veiling reinterpretation.

So Tibetan Buddhism, the tradition of the lamas, was my own predilec-tion, though at the beginning I had not heard the name of Dzogchen, the yoga that guarantees buddhahood in this lifetime. I had not yet heard expounded any tradition that formalized my untutored and disparate intu-itions about Reality, or the process of realizing it, which seemed to me to be the main purpose of life.

It may be that there was never any doubt about my fate, that nothing I could do would alter my destiny. But in the Dzogchen view destiny and free will are no dichotomy: whatever "is" arises spontaneously as magical illusion in the ground of being, neither coming into existence nor ceasing to be. In the ceaseless dance of yogins and yoginis in the buddhafield of pure pleasure there is neither freedom nor bondage, no awareness nor igno-rance, no coming nor going, no renunciation nor self-development, no self-determination nor predestination; and if such transcendence is not the present actuality, then it is better to keep quiet rather than utter this or that partial, biased opinion. This may appear to be an elitist viewpoint. It excludes those not yet on the path from knowledge of it. But the truth of Dzogchen is applicable only to those in the natural authentic state of total presence *(rig pa)*. For others there is validity and purpose in the truth of karmic inevitability, moral cause and effect, and the progress of self-determined self-development on a relative level to a place where the Dzogchen vision may be glimpsed and nondual precepts given meaning.

There was never any doubt in my mind about the credibility of the tradition or its teachers. The lineage was at least a thousand years old, and before the Communist invasion of Tibet in 1949 the entire culture of the Land of Snows was directed toward the attainment of the Dzogchen goal or a similar formulation of buddhahood.[8] While I was wearing the maroon robe of the Tibetan Buddhist orders, mere mention of the word Dzogchen to the informed layman would evoke respect for the Western student who aspired to it. Acknowledgment of this highest aspiration to a visiting lama invariably provoked amazement that a foreigner had gained access to Dzogchen instruction, leaving one feeling like a worm aspiring to divine rebirth. Perhaps such a lama would indicate in his inevitable circumlocutory style that Dzogchen was so secret that even he had no knowledge of it, and certainly never was his conceit so great that he had ever aspired to attain its goal! If he was prevailed upon to impart precepts, he would announce perhaps an elementary topic and speak about the rainbow body, or maybe he would label a talk on karmic retribution an essential lesson in Dzogchen: the theoretical axiom that Dzogchen cannot be spoken of directly is constantly demonstrated by the lamas in practice. The most potent source of teaching is the *mudrā,* mantra, and tantra of the Dzogchen lama's walking, sitting, talking, eating, drinking, laughing, and meditation, while the most potent exterminator of doubt is the real lama's blessing.[9]

There were few texts pertaining to Dzogchen available in English translation at that time.[10] The lack of available texts in English was filled in part by many literal translations of liturgical texts that gave first indications of the nature of Dzogchen's foundation practices. For myself they also gave the initial encouragement to learn the Tibetan language not only to facilitate practice of the liturgical meditation rites, but also to produce translation that reflected the original as divine revelation, or inspired scriptural poetry, with multilayered symbolic meaning replete with nuance, pun, and paradox. However, unless an art or science—painting, music, poetry, engineering— can be fully integrated into the yogin's *sādhana* in the manner of the *mahā-mudrā siddhas,* like Tantipa the Weaver or Dharmapa the Scholar, the lamas advised that these talents should be abandoned for meditation until the purification phase was complete. This was a lesson that several fellow artists seeking initiation learned with some misgiving.

Then what of the lamas themselves? The mirror-like inscrutability that provides the perfect *tabula rasa* for devotees' mental projection; the unique Tibetan Buddhist sensibility and refinement whereby buddhafields are sim- ulated in every detail of the daily round, even to the extent of transform- ing feces by mantra into liberating nectar for insects; the humility allowed by the complete self-assurance and integrity of a consummate spiritual aris- tocracy who have served as the high priests of Central Asia for centuries with an incomparable magic; and the profound depth of human under- standing and responsiveness, which I will call buddha-compassion, exem- plified by the exceptional lama—these four elements can create a certainty within the seeker that many of these divine beings actually hold the secrets that others claim for them, and that their *tulkus* (incarnations who have undergone unique conditioning) are indeed the tenth or fifteenth reincar- nations of buddha-lamas. In the euphoria and with the high expectations of that time there was no difficulty at all in accepting the elder generation of lamas, those who had completed their training and established themselves as teachers of their peers in Tibet, as accomplished bodhisattvas at the very least. Even the younger generation of lamas, who almost without exception were tulkus whose training had been broken by political turmoil, had a cer- tain conviction and awareness about them, together with the same aura of compassion. This added to the sense that Dzogchen training was like a mir- acle panacea, invariably bringing automatic results.

In the older lamas' formula for success that brought them disciples from all over the world it may be that the unique element was the extraordinary catalyst to their spiritual evolution provided by barbaric foreign invasion, war, rape and pillage of their country, their exile, and that vast welter of suffering. As the legends of the eighty-four Indian *mahāsiddhas* demonstrate, suffering provides the essential motivation for renunciation and meditation practice. In the lamas' pure-land "exile" means "renunciation of homeland and family," a vital precept found in all the texts.[11] Poverty, a practice instituted by Śākyamuni Buddha himself, is a wellspring of experiential learning, particularly if those with whom the beggar interacts perceive him as a mendicant with some ethical integrity. The monastic cloth has the effect on its wearer of intensifying the hells and heightening the heavens.

The wholesale destruction of Tibet's ancient religious culture and the genocidal extermination of "reactionary" monks and laymen during the Cultural Revolution of the sixties can in no way be justified. But a lama whose vision is always a buddhafield remarked that the lesson of impermanence taught by the Chinese Red Guards, the truth of suffering taught by the People's Liberation Army, not to forget the instruction on karmic retribution inculcated by defeat, is worth three lifetimes of meditation in a hermitage. The theocracy that was so abused by Maoism was by no means perfect, and the inflexibility and attachment to the status quo that had ossified parts of Tibetan consciousness cried out for surgery. The radical solution provided by the Chinese to the Tibetans' almost genetically conditioned conservatism was a hellish fantasy made manifest by demonic apparitions. The Red Guard leaders were driven by a "rational" ideal divorced from existential understanding. They pursued a Machiavellian goal justified by a means that mutilated human sensitivity and affection, while their followers were possessed by hungry ghosts, by denizens of hell, and by animal spirits reveling in jungle law. But this grist to the Dzogchen yogin's mill of meditation that history has recently provided, like the stroke of the zazen master's cane on the acolyte's back, can have a highly beneficial effect on the mind's state of awareness. In many ways, experientially, this generation of lama-exiles has been blessed by the silver lining in the disastrous political misfortunes of Tibet.[12]

An existential glow radiated from the pain-lines superimposed upon the wind and sun-worn faces of yogins and monks recently descended from the Tibetan plateau in the winter. This created a strong positive impression upon this cultural exile from the West in quest of the means to deal with his own small burden. Later, the Tibetans' success in establishing themselves in the harsh alien environment of the Indian plains, sustaining communal feeling, maintaining their spiritual practice, building monasteries and temples to reproduce in detail the monastic ambience they had left behind: all this was nothing short of magic, or at least the demonstration of mastery of the skillful means that when applied with flexibility overcome whatever obstacles arise in the adept's path. So it was not only the attraction of the metaphysics, the aesthetics, and the theory of meditation that brought many of us to the lamas, but also their good humor and a demonstrable power and high awareness all fired in the crucible of vast suffering.

In a broader analysis, social and political circumstances were conspiring in Europe, the United States, and Central Asia to create in India and Nepal the conjunction that would fulfill both lamas' and students' destinies. While the Tibetans were arriving in their Indian exile, numbers of Europe's sons and daughters were for the first time in history setting out for India to absorb and practice the practical philosophies and psycho-spiritual arts and sciences of the East—their forebears had come to India to trade and rule. In the middle of the twentieth century, after pursuing rational, scientific dualism beyond their ability to retain connection with their subconscious roots, Western societies were losing touch with the irrational, subjective, nondual foundation of consciousness. The thousands of Western seekers in the East demonstrated the need, and the innumerable Asian-originated sects in the West now show the result.

The lamas' physical need for food, shelter, and clothing, and the imperative to fulfill the prophecy that "when the iron bird flies the Dharma will go to the West," coincided in synchronistic harmony with the needs of Western societies represented by post-sixties seekers. The lamas' needs were fulfilled through their magnetic receptivity. At this point they were mainly unaware of the social pressures and both personal and social neuroses that had formed the minds of the gathering numbers of potential disciples and yogins seeking instruction, but the lamas were nonetheless eager to fulfill their destiny. Individuals who had traveled East for a month or a year, drawn by adventure into India's vast psychic space and personal freedom, frequently found themselves involuntarily pulled within a lama's mandala and appointed to any of many various functions: monk, yogin, scholar, secretary, translator, patron. The legend of Guru Rinpoche, Padmasambhava, the eighth-century founder of Buddhist Tantra in Tibet, who converted the Bonpo shamans and Tibet's gods and demons, extorting vows of service to the Dharma in return for certain powers and awareness associated with a guaranteed status in the nascent spiritual hierarchy, casts analogical illumination upon the relationship between the lamas and their Western acolytes.

Certainly I for one had not gone to India with any intention of devoting my life to the translation of Dzogchen texts, and if anyone had then suggested that I leave England in search of a vocation that promised a life of poverty, I would have responded with incredulity.

The Starting Point: Ignorance

To avoid the unnecessary obstacles that the ego will erect when it is asked to accept its own ignorance as the starting point, ignorance must be clearly defined. In Buddhism ignorance is dualistic perception, the absence of gnostic awareness.[13] It is easier to accept our failure to achieve buddhahood than to come to terms with living in ignorance. Still, insofar as "thinking of the key confirms the prison," any consideration of the means to attain enlightenment asserts our ignorance. At the same time, thinking of the key confirms the possibility of freedom, even if we are ignorant of it. My belief is that everyone at some time has glimpsed a state of beatitude that is liberation from the state of ignorance,[14] or nirvana, although it may not have been recognized as such at the time. Further, I think that the Buddha's liberation is known to us all, familiar like an old friend with whom we have lost contact but whose mind we know intimately. If it were not so, how could the imagery of the Mahayana sutras describing the buddhas' pure lands strike such vibrant chords of recognition and appreciation? How is it that so many of us identify immediately with the events of Śākyamuni's life? Why do we immediately intuit the veracity of the Abhidharma's psychological analysis of the process of enlightenment?

Childhood with its "trailing clouds of glory" can be the most fertile period of gnostic experience, the least "ignorant" period of life, because the preconceptions and preoccupations that form the veil of mental concepts have not yet evolved into rigid mindsets. Chemical psychedelics can, if only temporarily, have the effect of freeing those concepts, and the result is "regression" to a childlike state of freedom from conceptual blocks. In the *mahāsiddhas'* songs of realization the analogy of childhood is employed frequently to evoke the *siddha's* state of enlightenment. Seen in this light "ignorance" is not only ephemeral twin veils[15] obscuring what the sages and scriptures assure us is the natural state of gnostic awareness, it is the means of reaching a fundamental level of reality, omnipresent and indestructible—

vajra-like—that we can know experientially and can learn to abide in constantly and uninterruptedly.

This is not to underestimate the dogged persistence of the proclivities that give rise to emotional clouds and incomplete thoughtforms that obscure reality. One of the most significant features of Dzogchen, an aspect that characterizes it as a "shortcut approach" to buddhahood, is a glad acceptance of the virtual impossibility of eradicating the propensities conditioned genetically, karmically, or in childhood "education" that produce our habitual reaction patterns. This understanding is reflected in the basic meditation precept "Leave alone whatever arises in the mind. Do not seek to change or alter anything. It is all perfect as it stands," and so on. Relaxing the mind, the propensity to evaluate, judge, and react positively or negatively to whatever arises, falls away. Thus detachment evolves. Detachment is the key to penetrating the two veils. In other words, the twin veils are not to be torn down but, rather, penetrated by the eye of perfect insight that perceives the emptiness within through detachment from the form without.

Thus we have a more precise notion of ignorance: it is a function of attachment. The unifying factor of gnostic awareness is the emptiness of both sensory stimulus and penetrating insight. Dualistic perception, ignorant perception, is the tendency to objectify the form of the sensory stimulus due to attachment to it. In a more blunt formulation, for the Dzogchen yogin hatred, lust, and the other passions are not ignorance; they are friendly helpers on the path that create energy and light, and they turn the wheel of life to create the six mental environments that give our lives shape. Thus, although still we may be faced with heaven and hell, the animals' jungle realm, the realm of hungry ghosts, and so on, when we are free of attachment we are exemplars demonstrating the techniques of liberation in the guise of the "hungry-ghost buddha," "*dharmarāja* buddha, "lord-of-beasts buddha," etc. This is one of the meanings of the axiom "The starting point is the goal."

The Starting Point: Initiation

This introduction is structured according to the traditional triad of starting point (or ground), path, and goal. In Dzogchen "The starting point is the path, the path is the goal, and the goal is the starting point." If the mind is dull or meditation unusually bleak, a predictable response to that statement may be "Since there is nowhere to go and nothing to do, what is the purpose of Dzogchen, and why practice any form of yoga?" "The starting point is the goal" refers to the unchanged form of awareness: the forms that arise are the same as ever. The difference lies in the all-important detachment from these forms and the cessation of grasping and clinging. The purpose of Dzogchen is to bring the aspirant to recognition of what is as obvious as daylight; and the blinders to recognition are attachment to the twin veils of emotion and intellect. With a modicum of detachment it becomes evident what happens to emotion and thought. They may not disappear but there is a radical transformation of quality, and motivation becomes that of the bodhisattva vow. Thus, although there may be no striving toward a bodhisattva's state of mind, there is a spontaneous evolution toward it.

However, in a state of ignorance, how do we meditate with detachment? If nothing is to be done, if nothing can be done because all effort is derived from counterproductive attachment, how can we break the continuum of ignorance? The answer is initiation, initiation by direct introduction to the nature of mind. Such initiation induces the state of mind that breaks the vicious circle of moral and mental cause and effect, replacing "horizontal" rational thought processes with a "vertical," creative, muse/ḍākinī-inspired effusion of primal awareness. Meditation upon that state (formless meditation) deconditions consciousness, leaving the original existential condition to arise spontaneously moment by moment.

We are still not out of the woods. If initiation is understood as an enlightenment experience, how can this spontaneous event be induced? Is it simply a matter of formal initiation? This problem should not be glossed over. What error to mistake formal initiation for a real initiatory experience upon which meditation can be based! Initiation implies discovery of the real buddha-lama (in distinction to a human preceptor), and seeking precludes finding. The basis of Dzogchen achievement is not attained without initiation; initiation is the function of the lama; and the "buddha-lama" is a state of acausal primal awareness. The Indian *mahāsiddha* Nāropa, the "Indomitable," with his unflagging quest for the unfindable represented by his guru, Tilopa, is the exemplar in this situation. Without experiential initiation we must practice preliminary techniques and the *tregcho* meditations described in *The Flight of the Garuda*. These are the meditative techniques of Dzogchen, so finely honed by generations of yogic experiment in the laboratory of the mind that inevitably they bring quick results. They prepare the mind for initiation, and initiatory experience can arise during practice of them.

The mainstream Dzogchen schools, the Longchen Nyingtig lineages for example, do not teach the uncompromising dogma of sudden liberation, the doctrine that implies the futility of attempting to condition the relative mind to an absolute reality. Going beyond specious argument there is commitment to a middle path of "absolute relativity" in which the aspirant is induced to accept buddhahood intuitively here and now. In practice, consideration of the dichotomy of sudden and gradual enlightenment should not enter the mind, while at the same time the aspirant practices on the graduated path that may lead to the pith meditations of *The Flight of the Garuda*. But service to sentient beings, generosity, regular offerings of flowers in the temple, prostrations, visualization, and mantra are all skillful means to the attainment of Dzogchen, and any of them can provide the psychic environment in which initiation, or sudden liberation into one's true condition, is achieved. Furthermore, such practices generate vital merit—credit in the karmic bank. On this path the mind may be reconditioned by replacing useless, confused thought processes with merit-generating processes that induce the requisite susceptibility to the buddha-lama's blessing—premonition of initiation—and the ground of initiation is cultivated thereby.

The nature of the ground of initiation can best be understood by introducing the basic concepts and meditations that the Buddha Śākyamuni taught. It may appear at times that Tantra in general, and Dzogchen in particular, are far divorced from the teaching of early Buddhism. On the contrary, it is assumed that the fundamental truisms contained in the four noble truths form the bedrock of the aspirant's mentality: suffering as the nature of existence, desire as the principal human drive, nirvana as the only human goal worthy of aspiration, detachment as the path to happiness. Any progress toward eradication, neutralization, transformation, or full awareness of the twin veils of emotion and mental concepts can prepare the ground for initiation. Discursive contemplation derived from the four noble truths, discussed in the following paragraphs, can be highly efficacious in establishing a receptive attitude to the lama. When such analysis is understood experientially the roots of desire and suffering are severed. If our attachment to thoughtforms can be decreased, gaps in our slavish obedience to the mind's "rational" dictates leaves space for the buddha-lama to make himself known. Since much neurotic or uncontrollable thought is provoked by fear—our insecurities sometimes arise in the most outrageous thoughtforms—fear can be reduced by quietening anxiety about the nature of existence and the purpose of life. Experiential understanding tames our mundane hopes and fears about food, shelter, and clothing, and the eight worldly obsessions[16]— all the rubbish of the mind.

The following questions and answers were the Buddha Śākyamuni's own. The four noble truths arose out of these questions on the nature of existence and reality. The primary question is "What is the principal attribute of existence?" Answer: suffering, the first noble truth. The second question is "What is the cause of suffering?" Answer: desire, the second noble truth. The answer to the first question is reached by equating existence with suffering. Existence consists of birth, sickness, old age, and death. Existence is sustained on every level by desire: desire (including its antithesis) and concomitant attachment and clinging are the dynamics of existence. Any taste of true happiness that we achieve in existence is the result of the cessation of attachment. Happiness is not nonexistence since the same situations (birth, sickness, etc.) still arise; and it is not existence because the quality of happiness is unending, empty, blissful awareness. If happiness does not possess these attributes it is not the buddhas' happiness, but rather, a lesser degree of suffering in which attachment is still operative. Thus, in the buddhas' terms, the happiness of the gods is not true happiness because attachment, as fear of eventual loss of divinity through death, works in the gods' minds like a canker conceived in their spring of seeming contentment to mature in a winter of bile and gall.

Suffering is failure to get what we want; suffering is getting what we do not want; suffering is fear of loss; suffering is losing what we have. After obtaining our desires we suffer the pride of possession; we suffer jealousy if someone else has what we want or something better than we have. In all these situations desire and grasping are the cause of our suffering. To take sexual desire, one universal desire, as an example: we suffer pangs of desire; we suffer the anguish of longing; we suffer unsatisfied lust; we suffer selfish satisfaction; we suffer loss in lust's aftermath; we suffer loss of the object of desire; we suffer the perversions of desire; we suffer unformed adolescent desire, the frustrations of mature desire, and the rage of impotent desire; we suffer lovesickness, falling out of love, and all the neuroses of love and desire; and we suffer sexually transmitted disease. There is some form of pain involved in every stage of sexual desire. Indeed, love and desire are all suffering unless and until there is detachment from this desire. Whatever of the buddhas' happiness there is in desire, and in its corollary love, is the result of transcendence of desire, a state obtained through eradication, neutralization, or intensification of passion.[17] The third and fourth noble truths are the truth of cessation of desire (nirvana) and the truth of the path to cessation, which is practical experience of Buddhadharma, particularly Dzogchen precepts.

The yogin is separated from those who have no knowledge of the four noble truths by his conviction that happiness has nothing to do with satiation of desire. By karmic propensity, by the grace of a teacher, by fortuitous revelation or insight, he has seen that nothing so ephemeral as desire fulfilled is worth the striving. Life is short; death is always at hand; the potential of the human being is far too great to waste on simple psychological, sensual, or physical gratification. He must have had a vision of the greater existential potential, a vision partaken of by yogins, saints, seers, and sages in every part of the world since time began. His definition of happiness begins at freedom from desire. And what remains after desire no longer directs his body, speech, and mind? Simple but pure sensory perception![18]

Such was the Buddha Śākyamuni's insight. Virtually the entire Buddhist canon, both Sutra and Tantra, is concerned in some way with the mechanics of desire and of sensory perception, the part played by ethics and behavioral discipline, and particularly in the Mahayana by selfless giving, which arises simultaneously with the attainment of the primal awareness inherent in unobstructed sensual perception. To comprehend the sophistication and complexity of the various solutions to a problem that in its bold, unadorned, interrogative form seems to be a simple psychological problem, but which upon investigation turns into an insoluble, labyrinthine enigma, we need only look at the mandalas, mantras, and metaphysical equations that constitute a root tantra. Such is the complexity of mind, and it is all in answer to the question of how to sustain pure sensory perception unclouded by thought and emotion.

Sensory perception begins at the moment of birth and continues every moment until death. In sleep our senses are interiorized in dream. What is the constant in this sensory process? It can only be the absolute element of being. Some Hindus call it *satcittānanda*—truth, consciousness, and bliss. In Buddhism, since this constant cannot be located or specified in any way, it is called *śūnyatā*—emptiness.[19] This emptiness, which can also be conceived as a "fullness," is synonymous with "thatness," "the nature of mind," "the womb of buddhahood," and "reality": there is no trace of world denial in the Buddhist tantric view of life. Emptiness does not exist—if it can be said to exist at all—as an independent entity;[20] it is best described as "all-pervasive," "all-penetrating"; and there is nothing that it excludes. Further, since it is identified with the nature of mind, once detachment is achieved it is with emptiness that the yogin identifies, and identifying with emptiness he identifies with the nature of all things. In this way the buddhas' omniscience and omnipotence are a function of simple sensory perception, and simple—pure—sensory perception is the starting point and the goal.

The ground of initiation is laid by absorption of this vision and by any of the innumerable techniques of meditation that facilitate it. The primal awareness, the pure gnostic awareness of sensory perception that is the starting point and the goal, is also the initiation. I have already defined initiation as the enlightenment experience that is the condition *sine qua non* of finding the buddha-lama. The buddha-lama is the agent of the initiation. After initiation the practice of maintaining constant union with him is the essential Dzogchen discipline. Upon initiation, both relative and absolute pledges (the *samayas*) are sworn: the relative pledges of buddha-body, buddha-speech, and buddha-mind support the yogin in action, speech, and samadhi, while the central practice is to condition his being in maintaining the constant primal awareness inherent in each moment of perception until gnostic vision is the irrevocable norm.

The Starting Point: Karmic Acceleration

The Dzogchen yogin consciously entered a dangerous, shortcut, existential path by committing himself to his *samayas* at the time of initiation. It is probable that the wisdom that guided him was the precipitation of a serious trauma, or was it the product of a series of extraordinary events that caused rapid karmic acceleration? Meditation is the most prudent, controlled, and highly tested karmic accelerator. War, rape, a near-fatal accident or disease, or any profound emotional trauma can also give the victim an understanding of his own mortality and bring consequent appreciation of the rare and precious opportunity that human birth affords. Such experiences impress the victim with the significance of the truth of impermanence and with the urgency of making up for time lost, and it involves an awakening to the laws of moral or behavioral cause and effect (karma). Such understanding is vital in accelerating karma to the point where renunciation of the hedonistic world is a necessary prerequisite to continued existence on the planet, and where it becomes evident that one's own best interests are intrinsically bound up with the good of all sentient beings. The *four mindbenders*,[21] discursive contemplations comprising preliminary exercises to tantric meditation, are undoubtedly effective and induce such realization without risking life and limb or sanity, and they may provide other benefits besides. But experiential lessons engraved in consciousness never to be forgotten, informing every impulse, provide the more valuable foundation to Dzogchen practice.

The Path: Entering the Stream

The *streamwinner* is already a yogin. He gains this status by a profound recognition of his own ignorance. *Ignorance,* defined above as an absence of gnostic awareness, is experienced in everyday life as confusion, neurosis, stupidity, sloth, bewilderment, and unfettered emotivity and thought. There are vulgarisms that best describe this state. Recognition of the emotional confusion of our lives and the psychologically negative role of interpretive, judgmental thought is the first positive step in the direction of attaining a higher state of awareness, and our emotions are the most accessible field of experience where, with penetrating insight, emptiness can be perceived. As *The Flight of the Garuda* has it, "How ridiculous to expect to find primal awareness and emptiness after you have suppressed passion!"[22] Thus the Dzogchen precept "Do not suppress thought and emotion" is as valid for the egoist, whose superego refuses to allow him to acknowledge his base self, as it is for the self-righteous, pious, "disciplined" altruist who rationalizes away his fears and inhibitions by invoking the moral code of his order. To deny desire is to kill the goose that lays the golden egg. In this way recognition of our confusion, which is only thought and emotion, is the beginning of the path.

Complete and perfect recognition[23] is initiation itself. But it is a very lucky person indeed who has a moment of sudden recognition of the nature of his entire being and sustains it. Most of us go through a process of self-knowledge gradually unfolding successive levels of the subconscious mental waste that have accumulated since childhood and through many lives. The revelation of this subconscious material can be a very painful experience, exacerbated by the pain inherent in understanding how far we fall short of the view we have of ourselves. Some New Age cults are dedicated to the admirable task of revealing this aspect of the psyche, each cult with its own aims and different degrees of compassion for the initiate. In Dzogchen, recognition of the nature of mind alone is the aim. Once this is achieved, the power of pure perception with its inherent self-originated total presence leads on to perception of the next instant of self-revelation, producing a stream of consciousness that can become a continuum of pure pleasure and delight.

Confession is the ritual formulation of this necessary psychic cleaning. The Dzogchen prayer of confession, *Emptying the Depths of Hell,* shows how the Dzogchen vision must be applied to whatever mental rubbish or conflicting emotions are revealed during the time of self-appraisal. To identify with or reject the contents of one's mental rubbish are both mistakes leading to a false view that escapes the reality of our own being: it is evident that the dangers of departing from a neutral, middle view into extreme, potentially unhealthy reactions and emotional upheavals can produce insanity. Indeed, even if this process of purification is practiced in the light of Dzogchen vision, the dangers are manifold. *The Flight of the Garuda* mentions only the greatest evil, which is identification with the vast psychic power released at the end of the process, creating a malicious demonic force.[24] Another more potent technique in the canon of preliminary Dzogchen instruction teaches the initiate how to evoke the psychic environments produced by the various six basic emotions and how to utilize emotion to fuel this fire.[25] This is instruction in the method of recognition of emotion and thought when they arise in daily practice.

To apply the axiom "the starting point is the goal" to this particular aspect of the path, recognition is the first act of the initiate and the last, and it is the path itself. The ground of the path consists of emotion and thought. The more intense the emotion, and the more fearful and fragmented the thought, the greater the potential for the light and awareness that penetrates to the emptiness of the form: the path consists of a razor's edge that the yogin walks in constant peril of falling into the vajra hell. However, in the mainstream of Dzogchen practice, this razor's edge is internalized. Passion is not to be invoked and exaggerated in any public forum. The uncontrolled yogin is not free of moral cause and effect, and gross literal practice of these precepts will result in a fall as surely as smoke arises from fire. Only if the yogin's karma is such that recognition is insufficient to neutralize gross active manifestation of passion will he fall into the error of taking the meditation into passionate situations outside the retreat hut. The overriding precept is "neither indulge nor reject" in respect to the situations that karma provides, and constant training in this practice modifies karma, as "horizontal" or linear causation becomes subservient to the "vertical" effusion of compassionate energy.[26]

The Path: The Dharma As a Raft

The Dharma is likened to a raft carrying sentient beings across the ocean of life. On the bank of the other shore is the death beyond which is eternal life. In the case of the Dzogchen adept there awaits a rainbow body. The mind of the adept becomes one with the vast field of space that is the ground of being. Out of this ground are emanated all of samsara and nirvana in variegated lightforms, and tulkus are manifest in bodies of light to work for the salvation of all beings. The raft of Dharma is abandoned on the other shore, for here the names of samsara and nirvana are unknown, the path called no more learning begins, and simultaneous with the landing is the realization that the Dharma is as temporal and ephemeral as the rest of creation and that its truth is expedient to accomplishment of its own end. Its purpose is usurped by no-purpose, for the keyword on the other shore is spontaneity. Certainly, a purpose can be discerned by the ignorant conceptualizing mind, and clearly the intent of all movement and quiescence is the enlightenment of all sentient beings. But the acausal, nonoriginated emanations, which comprise the dance of the empty awareness-ḍākinī, arise adventitiously and spontaneously, forming a synchronistic pattern lacking evident linear relationship. However, from the point of view of the devotee at the boarding stage on the near shore, the raft seems to be an absolute.

There must be no doubt as to the efficacy of the method upon which the *sādhaka's* entire life fortune and future lives depend. So the lama and the scriptures make much of the safety of each particular boat, stressing the superior design and construction that allows quick and easy access to the other shore. In Dzogchen the proclivity for doubt is especially potent, and invariably at some point the questions Why meditate? and What use is the Dharma? will arise. Before realization of the nature of reality as emptiness, of form as phantom and illusion, of speech as empty echo, and of the Dharma as an expendable prop becomes a spontaneous and reflexive response, there is danger of the yogin cutting off the hand that feeds him while his appetite is yet unsated. *The Flight of the Garuda* recommends recommitment and reinitiation at the lama's feet in times of doubt and pride.[27]

The Path: Vision

Vision is an unchanging perspective on the nature of reality. The path, the four noble truths, the nature of ignorance, and Dzogchen are all vision. The concept of vision will be discussed in detail in the introduction to the *Garland of Vision* (see p. 160). In the fourfold framework of analysis of the path provided by vision, meditation, action, and the goal,[28] vision or *view* is the first head, and everything that can be written, spoken, or thought is seen from the standpoint of Dzogchen vision. Thus this entire work is a commentary on Dzogchen vision, and the discursive mind is the filter through which the vision is expressed. Another analysis identifies vision as the starting point, meditation as the path, and action as the goal. No doubt such a view teaches a valuable truth about the fundamental but limited use of the intellect, but vision has another meaning, which is best translated as *seeing*. This is the practical aspect of the precept vision as opposed to the theoretical exercise in this verbal explanation of the Dzogchen yogin's perspective. Perhaps the only distinction between these two aspects is the level of clarity of the mind involved. When the buddha-lama writes this introduction his thoughts are the direct expression of his enlightened detachment at the moment of writing. When he rises from his seat of inspiration his vision is sustained. He still "sees" all appearances as buddha-body, all sound as the buddha-speech, and all thought as pure gnostic buddha-awareness. When the buddha-lama thinks "all emptiness is form and all form is emptiness" (if such an absurdity ever crosses his mind) it is so. When we think such a thought we may be affected for good or bad by the degree of our attachment to the words.

There is a dialectic in Dzogchen thought, difficult to catch and analyze, that is effective in detaching the mind from all concepts whatsoever and persuading the intellect that the middle path of perfect detachment is the path to that holistic balance wherein the human potential for power and awareness is maximized. Evidently, this process is not *neti neti* (not this, not that), the process of systematic denial and refutation of whatever concept arises, which has been employed by Hindu schools to great effect. Rather it is an application of Ārya Nāgārjuna's formula of fourfold refutation.[29] The nature of the Dzogchen yogin's reality is frequently described as indeterminable[30] or that which cannot be described by any of the eight extremes: coming into being or ceasing to be, eternal or momentary, existent or non-existent, as appearance or as emptiness. This indeterminable nature of the Dzogchen yogin's reality can be restated in the *anuyoga* metaphor: the energies of the right and the left psychic channels emptied into the central channel, the *avadhūti*. When a perfect holistic balance is obtained, the excluded middle is realized. Guru Chowang's confessional *Emptying the Depths of Hell* is a fine expression of this balancing act.

Since no concept is ultimately valid, every concept is valid to some degree. The validity of an idea is determined by its efficacy. Ideas such as those embodied in the bodhisattva vow and the *Heart Sutra* are universally efficacious, although even these transcendental notions may be poison in the minds of some unbalanced individuals. Every idea has its time and place. From the Dzogchen viewpoint argument as to the ultimate validity of an idea is the occupation of fools.

The Path: Meditation

If vision is the function of pure perception, *meditation* is an unbroken stream of seeing. (*Action* is the dynamic form of the yogin's being.) Dzogchen meditation is a formless meditation, which means that there is no object upon which to concentrate, no visualization to construct and contemplate, no distinction made between subjective cognizer and sensory object. Meditation in the Dzogchen context is the active expression of gnostic awareness. It is outside the realm of cause and effect, so there can be no question of directing the mind toward any form of samadhi. Whatever arises appears spontaneously without coming into existence or ceasing to be, and the awareness from which it is inseparable is likewise an aspect of the continuum of space, color, and name that is beyond the function of the mind to express. Attachment and detachment are perceptual errors in the dualistic realm of sensory object and mental subject: in Dzogchen meditation there is no duality and no problem generated by ignorance.

The Dzogchen meditations described in the translations herein are preliminary exercises. The adjective *Dzogchen* indicates the goal of a lineage of practitioners, but may not pertain to the definition of meditation as given above. The analysis of consummate Dzogchen meditation is a description of the enlightened mind from the standpoint of perfect awareness, total presence *(rig pa),* and it remains unutterable.

The Path: Action

The Dzogchen yogin is first a shape-shifter. No outer or inner form expresses his secret nature, which is emptiness, more than any other; no one specific form of practice is correct practice; and no one outer form of conduct can be adopted as a universal method of service to sentient beings over any other. Insofar as each situation demands a different form of response and expression, the Dzogchen yogin is a chameleon. Just as the chameleon naturally and spontaneously changes color as the chemistry of response works in his body, so the yogin changes his *mudrā* (gesture, posture) and *mantra* (spoken word) as the *bodhicitta* of compassion floods his being at the inception of each new human situation in his sense fields. The entire gamut of emotivity, intellectual stance, and social role comprise his wardrobe; he is as much at home in the temple as in a brothel; and his friends may be found as well among thieves as courtiers. Tinker, tailor, soldier, sailor, the Dzogchen yogin can manifest in any form in any milieu.

However, until he has reached the end of the path, there are certain inner modes that the Dzogchen yogin may find more expedient than others. After all, the bodhisattva vow is an unsleeping master, and some social roles virtually preclude loving one's neighbor on an overt level. So before the drawing of breath also becomes fulfillment of the vow, it may be expedient to seek situations where altruistic aspiration has free play. Later, when the *bodhicitta* arises spontaneously in a constant stream, when transcendent compassion is an integral part of every moment of pure sense perception, the Dzogchen yogin can manifest only as a bodhisattva. Thus the compassionate nature of the Dzogchen yogin's vision and his consequent activity is not systematically cultivated. Rather, compassion is the goal itself under a different name, and having achieved the goal, nothing that can be done is free from compassionate motivation. As Shabkar Lama says in *The Flight of the Garuda*, "Coincident with the development of a happy, glowing, thought-free samadhi is the birth of authentic compassion, which is like the love a mother holds for her only son…This compassion is a very special feature of Dzogchen vision."[31]

Whatever his outer form, the practitioner of Dzogchen is always a yogin, and the yoga he practices is *atiyoga* (sustaining total presence). Any other technique, from simple calisthenic yoga[32] to manipulation of the vital breath with mantra and visualization, is employed as required. The Dzogchen yogin's cave is the cave of emptiness, where Kuntu Zangpo, the Primordial Buddha, sits in eternal meditation. In the realm of radiance and vibration he is the *Yidam* buddha-deity, his bone ornaments the five passions[33] recognized as the five aspects of primal awareness. In the realm of compassionate reflexive action he is Guru Rinpoche; his vajra sceptre, unfailing compassion; and his bell, penetrating insight into the nature of all situations as emptiness; and so forth.

However, in Himalayan Asia many renunciate yogins skilled in yogas besides *atiyoga* are Dzogchen practitioners. My first and most loving Dzogchen teacher was a Khampa yogin named Jortrala, who lived near Darjeeling as his patron's house priest, wore the hair knot, and demonstrated a traditional disregard for personal appearance. Tibetan yogins rarely went naked or wore the single piece of cotton cloth unless they were practicing *tumo*, heat yoga, on the snow line. So, the Dzogchen yogin may also be a priest, and insofar as many great lamas of Tibetan refugee society are priests as well as Dzogchen yogins, the impression is rife that Dzogchen is essentially a monopoly of the hierarchical priesthood of tulkus. Such an impression is false. Many of the great lamas of Tibetan refugee society, including the Dalai Lama and of course many of the Nyingma school lamas, are Dzogchen yogins, but they all would vie to disavow any superiority in Dzogchen over its humblest mendicant practitioner. The role of priest may actually work against progress in Dzogchen, since the tendency to identify the absolute with the sacred, as against the profane, is sometimes present in the priest's work.

Another role expedient in the practice of Dzogchen is that of healer. Since healing is essentially a reimposition of balance and detachment, the Dzogchen yogin who stands identified with the empty awareness and compassion that transcend all sickness (and health) is in a position to transfer the energy and love required to reimpose equilibrium within the patient's unbalanced psycho-organism. Skill in the science of energy-flows in mental, neural, and hemal spheres, in pharmacology and posology, etc., assists the healer's essentially psychosomatic art. A healer may not always be a Dzogchen yogin, but a Dzogchen yogin always has the capacity to heal.

To those ignorant of psychosomatics—and semantics—healing can appear to be magic, and indeed the Dzogchen yogin is always a magician in many senses of the word. The magic of shape-shifting and healing has already been mentioned. The magic of the *mahāsiddhas,* such as materialization, walking through rock, speed-walking, alchemical preparation of the elixir of deathlessness, raising the dead, and so forth, (each of these an ambiguous expression of an equivocal achievement) is attained at the end of the path. The most important magic, the enchantment that is indicative of the supreme *siddhi's* accomplishment, is gnostic awareness of the moment-to-moment spontaneous manifestation of the grand sensory illusion that is *mahāmudrā.* Then besides those powers, called *siddhi,* the Dzogchen yogin has minor powers like extrasensory perception and ability to manipulate "external" phenomena—psychokinesis—that are termed *ṛddhi.* There is no inducement to explain the nature of these powers to the skeptically inclined. The skeptic must make the commitment himself and discover experientially the nature of "magic."

The Dzogchen yogin, however, is not at all a puritan. No vow inhibits him from sensual indulgence or intellectual creativity. No action of body, speech, or mind is forbidden him, and his sainthood is attained by means other than conformity to moral laws. Detachment from every situation and compassion for every sentient being without exception are the signs of his achievement. Again, detachment is not to be understood as distant diffidence or dispassionate indifference. The scriptural definition molds the word as "without identification with or separation from." The actor, the action, and the acted upon are a clear and delightful unitary perception about which the perceiver has an unequivocal attitude of detachment. This prevents involuntary involvement and permits the spontaneous motivating thrust of compassion to determine the tone communicated. The unbroken stream of compassionate detachment is the attitude that outsiders see as sainthood, if the result of the action is perceived as virtuous. To the Dzogchen yogin both socially acceptable and nonconventional acts are equally valid means of transmitting joy and awareness. If his karma is so pure that his activity is restricted to conventional virtue, then he will not only be a saint in the Mahayana sense but to Christian perception as well. From the Dzogchen standpoint his continuous, compassionate awareness is his great achievement.

The Dzogchen yogin in any culture is a traveler, a voyager in psychic spaces. In Western civilization, where adventure to alien shores, with or without weapons, has always absorbed the inclination to delve into the unknown, the age of terrestrial exploration is over. There is nothing left to explore but inner and outer space. This century has seen a radical intensification of interest in the human mind, and particularly to maps of the psyche drawn by Asians, whose introversive aspirations have been given maximal social support for millennia. The Dzogchen explorer faces the most dangerous path and the most rewarding goal. So the predicament of a lone space voyager faced by hostile, disembodied foes on a distant planet may be applied as an analogue germane to the neophyte's career. The Dzogchen yogin's milieu is like space because there is nothing substantial in his universe; there are no concrete points of reference to guide him, no infallible dogma to give his intellect structure or support, and no systematic metaphysical charts to steer him. As in space, there is no upside, downside, center, or circumference to his mandala, and there is no spiritual gravity to pull him down to earth should he fall. The space voyager's fear of the vast immensity that is his environment is similar to the Dzogchen yogin's apprehensive consciousness floating in the endless expanse of inner space. A voyager or explorer he certainly is, because he left all known mental and spiritual territory behind him when he committed himself to his *samayas,* allowing himself to be guided by his spontaneous response to the needs of all sentient beings and the constant imperative to maintain full awareness. He is alone because no matter how close he is to family or Dharma friends, and regardless of the density of other beings around him, he must always take complete responsibility for his own actions and accept the karma of others as if it were his own. At the same time he refuses every offer of complicity and the companionship that shares karmic effect.

The illusion of hostility is a common ambience in which the lone-traveling novice on the path finds himself until he learns how to become invisible and how to transform negative elements into friendly aids on the way. Since public morality must remain subservient to the imperatives that keep his *samaya* intact, if any vicious, socially unacceptable propensities remain, inevitably he will find himself an outsider in the time-honored tradition of the sadhu and mystic. This may entail living an alternative, or perhaps deviant, lifestyle on the fringes of society, forever the scapegoat for the guilty moralist and the self-motivated critic demanding a homogenous and conformist society. Listen to the Western-educated Indian unload his guilt upon the poor Hindu sadhu! Even if his socially negative karmas have been exhausted in past lives, regardless of the success of the shape-shifting stratagems that give him the appearance of conformity, the divergences in the form of the yogin's inner space set him apart. This leaves him open to the paranoias that beset lone individualists. His realization, which maintenance of *samaya* inevitably brings, elevates him above the level where hostile forces are embodied and seen as hostile men and women. He lives in a world of spiritual powers or psychological forces where it is imperative that a mirror-like clarity of mind is maintained, the better to identify and transfix the enemy.

The Dzogchen yogin is also a warrior. This is not a traditional concept in any Buddhist sect of any country (except perhaps Japan), but if the use of such a concept as the spiritual warrior serves to elucidate the Dharma and attract the warrior's mind to the path, then its use is justified. Certainly, on any level of Buddhism other than the inner Tantra the concept would be inimical to the basic precept of *ahiṃsā* (nonviolence); but in the inner Tantra it has some validity. In the past it was not thought anomalous in Hindu Tantra that sadhus should be formed into a fighting force, and indeed specific sadhu orders became the martial protectors of *sanatanam dharam* in the face of Muslim aggression. There is little scope for such crass literality of interpretation in Buddhist Tantra, and certainly for the Dzogchen yogin conflict, war, killing, and slaughter occur only on a metaphysical plain. The

Dzogchen warrior is armed with two highly efficacious weapons, and he maintains some important allies. His principal weapons are the *purbu* and *khaṭvāṅga*.[34] The *purbu* is a *dorje* (vajra sceptre) with the blade of a dagger at one end. The *ngagpa*, the Tibetan Dzogchen warrior, arrayed in the garb demanded by such a highly ritualized society, carries a symbolic *purbu* in his belt, the blades never sharpened, the point as dull as a dog's hind leg. The function of the *purbu* is to transfix demons and spirits, liberating them into the space that is their essence. The *dorje* represents emptiness and awareness, and it is the Dzogchen yogin's penetrating insight into the nature of all things as emptiness that is represented by the point of the dagger. The master's enemies are delusive emotional poisons and thoughtforms, neuroses, and complexes, generated by a dark corner remaining in his own mind or created by another being's ignorant mind. They are psychological functions that appear to have lives of their own to the extent that superstitious human beings propitiate them both ritually and in the course of their daily life and communication with others. Struck by a *purbu* they dissolve into nothingness, while the minds that possessed them, having experienced a taste of the emptiness that liberated the spirit, are freed in catharsis.

A synonym of these spiritual forces that are the yogin's enemies is the evocatively onomatopoeic Tibetan word *gek*,[35] which means literally "obstacle," "hindrance," or "obstruction." In both ritual observance and meditation the yogin devotes considerable time to exercises invoking and destroying *geks*, so that during the periods between meditation he can spontaneously effect the destruction of whatever obstacles of this nature arise in his path. *Geks* arise, complete their pernicious tasks, and vanish with the speed of a changing thoughtform, and there is no time for considered thought and action. Certainly, *geks* are mainly of diminutive size, and mere sight of the *purbu* or *dorje* is sufficient to dissolve them. But phenomena of the same psychological category can possess an individual to the extent that an observer is convinced that the being possessed and the spirit are one, and this perception, by society at large or by even the afflicted being's close friends, can doom the sufferer to the asylum.

It is the Dzogchen bodhisattva's role to exorcise such spirits: his kind alone in society possesses the skillful means. When the nature of the demon or complex is relatively benign but resides continuously in a fragment of the psyche of a person who refuses to acknowledge its presence, it may be the duty of the Dzogchen yogin gently to bring the possessed individual to the recognition that is the prelude to liberation of the spirit. When the spirit is hostile, and the proximity of the insight that can destroy it excites it and its host to aggressive behavior toward the bearer of the awareness, the Dzogchen yogin—the warrior—is forced to engage the enemy with its host as its protector and agent. In such a situation the danger to the Dzogchen yogin lies in the tendency to forget that the host is the sufferer and a victim and so become negatively attached to his own aggression—to take it personally, as we say—thus becoming impotent to exorcise the spirit.

The liberation of spirits is a function of the Dzogchen yogin as exorcist as much as warrior. It must be stressed that although the warrior distinguishes between friend and foe, his attitude toward them both is determined by the same compassion. The compassion toward a friend implies application of a different form of skillful means, but the motivation is identical. Another way of saying it is that the wrathful face that the Dzogchen yogin turns toward hostile beings or spirits is as compassionate as the peaceful mien he shows his friends. The detachment that is neither identification nor separation is the key to this conundrum. So *exorcist* is no mean label; it implies the fully detached skill and compassion of the Dzogchen yogin.

The life stories of the great guru, Guru Rinpoche, are replete with accounts of his successful liberation of petty spirits and his subjugation of gods and demons that would serve the Dharma as guardians and allies. The monk and abbot Śāntarakṣita, invited by King Trisong Detsen to ordain the first Tibetan monks and build a monastery, was unable to suppress the *nāga*-serpents and *yakṣa*-elementals that possessed the ground and building materials. Guru Rinpoche, the warrior-sadhu, subjugated the myriad Tibetan gods and demons as well as their Bonpo shaman devotees whom he encountered as he approached Samye from Nepal before clearing the area around Samye of all aggressive forces. Afterward he visited all the major mountains in Tibet to suppress the powerful mountain gods, and he also made pilgrimage to the lakes wherein dwelt the life spirits of the country.[36] The victorious Indian sadhu traveling alone in the vast empty spaces and treacherous mountains of the Tibetan plateau among nomadic Mongol shamans of an aggressive disposition (these same people were then the conquerors of the whole of central Asia) presents the archetypal image of the Dzogchen warrior and exorcist. The *ngagpas* have maintained the tradition of mendicant Buddhist shamans in Tibet. Since the time of Guru Rinpoche the Tibetans have relied upon the mantric powers of the exorcist to protect them from external danger. Such reliance may not always effect the defeat of an invading army, but it can leave the defenders morally victorious and spiritually unbowed.

The *purbu* is the Dzogchen yogin's weapon against his enemies, while the *khaṭvāṅga* is his weapon against his own ego. The Tibetan Buddhist *khaṭvāṅga* consists of a trident *(triśūla)*, the three-pronged fork carried by Saivite sadhus in India and by the Greek god Poseidon, that pierces the center of a double vajra on a horizontal plane; a "vase of eternal youth" filled with the elixir of immortality; and three human heads below the three prongs. The double *dorje,* or crossed vajras,[37] is the emblem of the karma family (at the northern direction of the mandala), signifying perfect action accomplished spontaneously for all sentient beings. The trident itself by its form indicates the unity of the trinity. The trinity is the three existential modes of the Buddha—*dharmakāya, sambhogakāya,* and *nirmāṇakāya*—and the unity is the Buddha himself, sometimes expressed as a fourth "body" or mode, the *svabhāvikakāya,* or the unity of form and emptiness. The three correspond to secret, inner, and outer planes of being, and also to ignorance, aversion, and desire (although the last two may be transposed circumstantially). Thus the three transfixed heads—the first a blue skull, the second a white dry head, and the third a red head dripping with blood—represent the Dzogchen yogin's recognition of ignorance and sloth, aversion and hatred, and desire and lust as the three modes of buddha-being.[38] It is the *khaṭvāṅga* of emptiness that pierces the nature of the three principal obstacles to clarity and awareness and transforms them into the primal awareness, radiant clarity, and all-embracing compassion of the Buddha's being. Further, it is interesting to note, when Guru Rinpoche was attending Trisong Detsen's court while his consort, the princess Yeshe Tsogyel, was banished, the *khaṭvāṅga* was the form into which the guru transformed her so that he should always have her with him. Thus the *khaṭvāṅga* of emptiness and primal awareness is the Dzogchen yogin's consort, as well as his most potent weapon. In the warrior's perpetual battle to penetrate every obstacle to his enlightenment with emptiness, he has this consort as his constant support.

Transformation, as alteration from an inferior to a superior status, from ignorance to knowledge, and so forth, is not a concept consonant with

Dzogchen *atiyoga*. The reason is that all things from the very beginning are pure and complete in the universal ground of being. *Recognition* is the term germane to description of the awakening process of the Dzogchen yogin. Thus the five poisons are not to be transformed. They are to be recognized for what they are and what they have always been: the five aspects of primal awareness. Furthermore, recognition is achieved by withdrawing consciousness from the stressful mental functions of dualization, relaxing into the original nature of the mind, and getting behind the mindscape so full of objects of potential attachment. If he does not fall into an effective pattern of meditation drawn by the instinct that constantly directs him toward maturing experience, there are various techniques that the Dzogchen neophyte may be taught by his lama to assist recognition of his emotions as aspects of awareness. The recognition can be affected in meditation in the crucible of the mind by provoking emotion and then penetrating its emptiness with the insight that has been developed in insight meditation.[39]

A more direct and forcible method is through the practice called *chod*:[40] here the yogin repairs to a desolate and fearsome power place, such as a charnel ground or the habitation of ferocious demons such as flesh eaters, spirits of disease, malicious ḍākinīs, and so forth. Then preparing his mind with mantra and music, identifying with the Yidam, he invites the spirits to attack him. The four demon spirits[41] are those specifically invoked in the tradition of Machig Labdron, an eleventh- to twelfth-century Tibetan yogini who established the principal chod lineage in Tibet. Machig practiced sexual yoga, and these four demons, particularly, of course, the devil of emotional passion, are the bane of highly sexed yogins. But through exercise in this yoga, the yogin or yogini is rendered safe when he or she must spontaneously respond to the demons evoked in a passionate relationship conducted in the course of *sādhana*. Practitioners of this technique are frequently psychologically and physically mauled, but the greatest warriors of chod become adept in the transformation (recognition or release) of every emotional and spiritual force. Particularly, since the transformation of spirits of disease implies a self-cure, *chod-pas* become immune to illness and learn the art of healing in the process. The lama will emphasize the folly of evoking passion in the mainstream of life, no matter what altruistic motive inspires the bodhisattva neophyte, until one of the practices of cutting attachment described above, or a similar yoga, has been successfully accomplished.

In the initial phase of practice, probably the period immediately following discovery of a buddha-lama, it is most advantageous to spend time in retreat, or better still, as a monk or nun in retreat. In such a space a solid foundation can be laid, beneficial habits can be developed, and the mind can be established in the purity affected by the initiation received from the lama. Most of us must practice no-meditation and no-action in the form of simple purificatory techniques. Further down the path, in freedom from expectation of results, we can assimilate the whole of life's potential into our practice. Intense intimacy, emotional harmony and trust, and spiritual attunement can be developed to an optimal degree in a passionate, sensually interactive relationship, which thus provides one of the most effective situations in which to practice and learn. No better occasion may arise to develop the bodhisattva's responsiveness. The cynic may laugh because the primary universal motivation, sexual pleasure, which he considers all in all to all, including the Dzogchen bodhisattva, is not given primacy here. Of course sexual desire is the starting point. The sexual center is the seat of our vital energy[42] and of *kuṇḍalinī* herself, and the more intense, sustained, and objectless is sexual desire the better. But what must be simultaneous with the arousal of desire is the penetrating insight into desire as emptiness; and the motivation that springs from empty awareness of desire is the bodhisattva's aspiration of selfless service. The pure pleasure, *dewachenpo, mahāsukha,* that is to be found within sexual interaction—which is indeed found if the adept's yoga has been effective and negative karma is not to be gleaned from the encounter—is the inevitable fruit of all our labor; but pleasure must never be the conscious motivation. If this moment is to be prostituted to the next, if a relationship is motivated from the beginning by a selfish desire, if lust is not recognized as emptiness and attachment not destroyed, then the seeds of disaster are sown. Although some physical pleasure is obtained, the result of the relationship may be a break in *samaya* and an eternity in the *dorje nyelwa.*[43] Retribution can take the most violent and sadistic forms; and the negative propensity to repeat the experience, despite the retribution, will become increasingly hard to resist, until a downward spiral destroys all hope of even a human rebirth, let alone a rainbow body. The craving for *mahāsukha, dewachenpo,* pure pleasure, kills all chance of attaining it. The yogin enters a sexual encounter without any hopes or fear, simply enjoying the play of magical illusion, allowing the ramifications of spontaneity to manifest for the sake of all sentient beings.

Nonaction is the key to existential involvement in all passionate situations—a sexual encounter, an angry interaction, a proud stance in competition, or a jealous rivalry. The apparent illogicality of the progression of passionate mental events in the karmic stream is reflected in the superficially structureless nature of the course of the adept's life. When the starting point is a turning around in the seat of consciousness and commitment to the ultimate Dzogchen *samaya,* and the goal is a rainbow body, there is no systematic path. At the starting point, when no doubt the aspirant will first experience the spontaneously arising dictates of responsiveness, karmic cause and effect will still be operative. Even initiation will not necessarily destroy the habits of a lifetime or be changed by an immutable conviction that there is a higher vision. So, at the beginning of the path, motivation will be mixed with nonmotivation. This will lead to some confusion as periods of unsatisfactory horizontal, karmically determined action will seem to dominate the moments of eternal, resuscitating, vertical effusion that seemingly are few and far between.

The Goal

Insofar as buddhahood is inexpressible and inconceivable, it would be best to omit any verbal comment upon it. However the following epigrams, stated or implied in the foregoing commentary, have been useful to me as *koans*—verbal paradoxes—that point directly at the goal.

Only a buddha can recognize a buddha.
The buddha-lama is every moment of perception: all vision is his body,
    all sound is his speech, and all pure awareness is his mind.
Nothing exists that is not a function of mind.
Nothing is evil or undesirable but evil thought makes it so
    (Honi soit qui mal y pense).
The starting point is the path is the goal.
Anything that promotes certainty in the middle way is the only path.
Form is emptiness and emptiness is form.

II. THE LANGUAGE OF DZOGCHEN

If at the beginning there is a viable basis of understanding between lama and disciple on a nonverbal level, still there may be many problems of communication in the conceptual realm. The notion of secrecy can be one such stumbling block. The "secret" or "mystic" dimension is the third in a triadic hierarchy of categories completed by the "outer" and "inner" dimensions. These categories define the relationship between *Hīnayāna, Prajñāpāramitā-yāna,* and *Tantrayāna,* for example. In metaphysical analysis they classify, for instance, buddha-body, buddha-speech, and buddha-mind and the three modes or bodies of Buddha's being: *nirmāṇakāya, sambhogakāya,* and *dharma-kāya.* In Tantra, what pertains to the secret or mystic dimension remains forever secret in the same way that subatomic particles remain hidden from sensory perception. It is impossible to divulge buddha-mind, or the *dharma-kāya,* outside its own frame of reference.

However, in Tantra there are injunctions against the initiate revealing the guru's precepts transmitted at the time of initiation. It may be destructive to the faith and comprehension of the initiate on a different level of practice if he is regaled with precepts irrelevant to his mindstate. For the noninitiate who may be sympathetic to the teaching, it is futile and perhaps destructive to inform his mind with a structure that is significant only after initiation has provided a framework. Last, although no harm can be done to the ultimate truth of Tantra, there is the danger of an outsider, either through honest miscomprehension or through devious twisting of meaning and rearrangement of context, representing what is sublime and intelligent as something vulgar and stupid. At worst this can provoke persecution of initiates, or it can create prejudice and partiality in social consciousness. However, the most important reason for keeping the guru's precepts secret is to maintain the yogin's integrity during the process of realization: exposure of *samayas* outside heart secrecy will inevitably introduce obstacles to their fulfillment.

The *initiate* in the above context refers to an individual who has experiential knowledge of the goal of Tantra. The *outsider* is a person with blinkered vision unable or unready to enter the path, whose spiritual development is limited by mindsets and beliefs labeled as *hedonistic, realistic, nihilistic,* or *eternalistic.*[44] Thus an individual who has had mere formal initiation into the tradition may in fact have a noninitiate's vision and may be negatively influenced by secret revelations. On the contrary, the individual who receives initiation spontaneously and informally outside a practice lineage may gain enormous benefit from fortuitously obtained "secrets." In general, regarding the propagation of Dzogchen instruction outside the framework of a guru-disciple relationship, in the light of the inscrutable level of forever-secret, mystic realities, and insofar as the current social climate is sympathetic to gnostic traditions, most contemporary Dzogchen lamas teach and actively support the public dissemination of their lineages' truths.

This discussion of secrecy has introduced the *secret* or *mystic dimension.* In the context of the highest, inner Tantra,[45] Dzogchen, or *atiyoga,* is the secret level, *anuyoga* the inner level, and *mahāyoga* the outer level. Dzogchen's secrecy is a corollary of its ineffable nature, and, therefore, the adjectives that describe the state of being that is Dzogchen are strained to capture its ambience. In fact, there is little compromise with the statement that the goal is beyond the intellect to comprehend—it is inexpressible. Adjectives employed to evoke this inexpressible existential condition are indicators of the direction in which the yogin must go to attain it. "Naked, stripped, stark"; "direct, immediate, here and now"; and "natural, simple, pure, uncontrived, unelaborated" are three strings of such didactic terms. These words indicate the lack of any conceptual screen between the yogin and his experience, the absence of any judgment about the elements of the situation that confront him, and the absence of preconceptions about the nature of reality in general. Any discursive mental activity obscures pure perception. However, all these statements are examples of the glib, devaluing expression that the precept enjoining the yogin to abhor such attempts at rationalization aims at precluding. There is comfort in these statements, but such intellectual support is to be avoided if the full force of reality is to be experienced in a thought-free state. This point is made here in order to stress that the language of the path is structured with intention to induce transcendence of itself, which is an aspect of the goal.

There is little new in the metaphysical concepts of Dzogchen to the student versed in Mahayana philosophy. One of the best and most accessible sources through which an understanding of the basic concepts of Dzogchen can be obtained is Saraha's *dohas.*[46] Although the concepts are identical, the terminology is different, and the patterns and the angle on the patterns— the way in which aspects are related to create a dynamic and a path—are different. Despite the differences, Saraha demonstrates not only the experiential proximity of the *mahāmudrā siddhas* of the Ganges Valley to the Dzogchen *siddhas* of northwestern India and Tibet, but also the transcultural nature of nondual experience.

In this analysis the traditional structure inevitably formulated as stages of the path is avoided. The nature of the traditional form is inevitable because the structure and its parts gain meaning only in the light of Dzogchen's liberating, soteriological dynamic, the forward drive from ignorance to awareness, from obscurity to light. This continuous awakening progresses along a path of meditation that becomes increasingly formless and inexpressible as experience more and more approximates the ultimate ineffable goal. The analysis by stages with its implication of linear temporal development has its limitation in that the Dzogchen dynamic operates outside time in a field of synchronicity. However, divorced from the graduated structure, Dzogchen terms tend to become dead counters in a futile, spiritually obstructive semantic game, for they describe mystic experience that cannot be exposed to the common light of day without devaluation and dilution of meaning. Nevertheless, this is an attempt to describe Dzogchen terms in a continuing effort to find valid English equivalents, preferably with enriching connotations drawn from the Western tradition. Not that Dzogchen terminology is metaphysically abstruse. The terms that in the context of a Dzogchen song or liturgy are so evocative of the states they represent are found to be prosaic when extracted from their context. *Space, light,* and *awareness* are the three concepts most frequently employed in Dzogchen texts.

The mental activity alienating human beings from immediate, direct experience is referred to frequently in Dzogchen texts as the dualizing function of the mind. First, separation is made between subject and object, the perceiver identifying himself with an egoic consciousness that perceives an isolated, external other. Introversively, in the same way, he alienates himself from aspects of his own being. With a basis in this fundamental dualistic structure, verbal expression gains its meanings from abstract linguistic relationships. In dualistic philosophies, where ignorance is rationalized as an acceptable norm or idealized for the purpose of manipulating an objective reality, valid meaning can be discovered only in the sphere of relativity, in the sphere of objective duality. This statement is framed in the law of the excluded middle. Dzogchen insists unequivocally that on the path of gnostic awareness, meanings informed outside the excluded middle are spurious and deviant and that reliance upon such meanings exacerbates the painful alienation associated with continuous transmigration.

What the excluded middle represents in Dzogchen is described analogically by the mandala. Consider the meaning of nonduality[47] in terms of this mandala. The excluded middle is the nondual space wherein direct, immediate perception is experienced: in a moment of pure perception there is no distinction between the sensory object, the sense organ, and the consciousness that is aware of sensation. Since the consciousness of the psychoorganism is capable of only serial, linear perception (although a subconscious strata constantly synthesizes the streams of data produced by all five senses), when there is full concentration at the door of one specific sense the mental commentary of "the observer" is silenced for a moment. So, in such direct sensory perception, there is intimation of nondual experience. In the next moment this experience becomes less than perfect if the perceiver's clarity of awareness is clouded by either emotivity provoked by the sense object or by mental interference. The mental veil may here be defined as the (muted) chatter of mental apparatus engaged in the preparation of a linguistic definition of the perception. Even at the moment of direct perception when gnostic awareness of emptiness as form and form as emptiness is experienced, the mind is preparing to dualize the situation. Only when there is no emotional attachment to the object of perception and when the mind is still, emptied of all discursive thought, can a legitimate paradigm of nondual, direct perception obtain. The center of the mandala represents the emptiness of the perceptual situation—there is no substantial essence in subject, object, or their interaction. The field of the mandala represents the form—visual, auditory, tactile, olfactory, gustatory, or, indeed, mental. Emptiness and form comprise a unity in the same way that the center and circumference of the circle are inseparable. The indivisible relationship between such polarities is called nondual, and ramifications of this unity that may not be evident are both the beauty of Dzogchen expression and our linguistic hurdle when approaching these texts.

How is this nondual direct sensory experience verbally articulated? Evidently it is not to be done in the manner of ignorant, dualistic expression. But it has to be done with the same vocabulary and grammar. The sacred languages of Tibetan and Sanskrit provide vocabularies sanctified by scripture and the poetry of the adepts of secret cults. The profane language of commerce and science is ill-suited to adaptation to this purpose, although science is increasingly able to provide terminology that compensates for its lack of poetic beauty by a precision of abstract concept. Some commentators retain Tibetan or Sanskrit terms, and some use the typographical device of capitalizing the initial letters of prosaic words to imply a higher order of meaning. Certainly, insofar as grammar and patterns of meanings reflect mind's intrinsic psychological structure, its habits of perception, and its levels of awareness, the Dzogchen vision would ideally require a new form of language. As an increasing number of English-speaking Dzogchen adepts intuitively adapt the material at hand, this language will evolve.

The sacred language of the tantras is mantra. This means that the syllables that comprise a word resonate to a pitch that evokes the prototypical nature of the form that is being articulated. When the master is questioned on this point, he is evasive regarding the specific relationship between sound and form. But there is no ignoring his conviction that sound is intimately related to the realm of form and has the power to affect it. The Indian story of one of the great *uṣṭad* sitarists of an earlier generation, whose instrument burst into flame during a perfect rendition of a fire raga, is explained in terms of the *uṣṭad's* ability to reproduce the sound of the seed-syllable of the element fire precisely, so creating fire itself. However, it is a general principle in many sacred traditions that it is not so much the form of the consonants as the power and thoughtform inserted into the vowel sound by a master, a *siddha*, that is efficacious. That the resonance that vibrates in an inanimate object, such as a fine wine glass, a conch shell, or a singing bowl, is of the nature of vowels rather than consonants supports this notion. Meditative experience indicates that the sacred language of Dzogchen is effective in inducing the states of mind that are evoked. It is imperative that we take great care in selecting the equivalents of these terms in English. Frequently the need to render the form of a meaning exactly takes precedence over aesthetic demands.

A definition of one radical Dzogchen term—nonduality—has already been offered. The paradox of expressing the nondual in dualistic terms is parallel to experience of the relative world in a nondual mode. The next term to be discussed is the synonym of nonduality that indicates that nonduality encompasses duality and that we know nonduality only through a specific mode of awareness that unites polarities and gives the relative world a unity. This term is literally translated as "two-in-oneness," "co-incidence," or "arising as a pair."[48] Since absolute nondual reality itself—emptiness—pervades the relative world and does not exist independent of it, the coincident pair of space and awareness (total presence) is given as the primary level of reality. *Space*[49] is best conceived as the universal, all-pervasive field. Like emptiness itself, it is nothing separate from form, and yet nothing else but it exists. All form is space: thus it is possible for *siddhas* who have dissolved the constituents of their body-mind in space, identifying with it, to walk through walls and eat rock. Space is no cold, vacuous void. It is the richness of the goddess Mahāmāyā, and all the playfulness and energy of the awareness-ḍākinī. *Total presence*[50] is an epistemological synonym of emptiness and the cognitive aspect of space. Again, since the epistemological absolute cannot exist independent of its formal constituent, it is not separate from the sensory fields that constitute ordinary knowledge.

Total presence *(rig pa)* is probably the single most significant term in Dzogchen, and it is peculiar to Dzogchen. It is found in the *dohas* of the *mahāmudrā siddhas,* but generally the term *pure awareness*[51] is preferred there, where it is used as a synonym of total presence. In Dzogchen the phrase "primal awareness of total presence"[52] indicates both the objective and subjective aspects of emptiness as the universe (or *dharmadhātu*) in terms of nondual awareness. Since sensory consciousness is constantly active, the movement of this primal awareness of total presence is referred to figuratively as a dance, and since it is represented figuratively and anthropomorphically as the ḍākinī, the movement within presence is called "the dance of the awareness-ḍākinī." It would be incorrect to characterize the primal awareness of total presence as inherently active, as it is essentially a field coextensive with inner space. Perhaps the best image by which to describe it is that of a whirling firebrand: the body that twirls it remains still, while the whirling flame on the end of the stick creates the impression of a static wheel of fire. Fire is symbolic of dynamic cognition.

If inner space *(dbyings, dhātu)* and primal awareness *(ye shes, jñāna)* are the coincident pair that form the empty essence of reality, the nature of that reality is light.[53] Again, this light is coextensive with emptiness, inner space, and total presence, and insofar as it is inseparable from its forms in the same way that the light of the sun is inseparable from its source, it is best conceived as a field of lightform in potential. It is for this reason that *selwa* can be translated as "luminosity" and "clarity." *Luminosity* is intended to indicate the abstract quality of light before its emanation, and *clarity* indicates the inherent quality of lightform. Although the image of the sun and its beams adequately conveys the relationship between light and its manifest qualities, the image fails insofar as the sun is a substantial entity, whereas the source of lightform is empty space.

The final attribute of emptiness to be mentioned is a quality peculiar to the Buddhist analysis: *responsiveness*. It is the third and final denominator in the list of categories or aspects by which emptiness can be defined: essence, nature, responsiveness.[54] It appears anomalous, an attribute rather than a category. The third logical category is function, or *manifest function,* and the attribute found in its stead is responsiveness and its qualifier is *all-pervasive.*[55] Viewed as a functional attribute of inner space, total presence, and light, the implication is that the dynamic, the intentionality, the purpose of being is compassion, which is a synonym of responsiveness and demonstrable as the responsive aspect of love. It is this compassion that is coextensive with space, the buddha-heart pervading all beings. Viewed as the potential form or manifestation of emptiness, the implication appears to be that every vibration of body, speech, and mind is a form of compassionate energy, nothing excluded. Consider the distinction between responsiveness and compassion. In Dzogchen, compassion is much more than the virtue of loving-kindness.[56] Nor does the word *compassion* in the Dzogchen context denote its English etymological meaning, "suffering together" or "empathy," although both these meanings may be inferred. Essentially, compassion indicates an open and receptive mind responding spontaneously to the exigencies of an ever-changing field of vibration to sustain the optimal awareness that serves self-and-others' ultimate desire for liberation and well-being. The conventional meaning of compassion denotes the latter, active part of this definition, and, due to the accretions of Christian connotation in the West, response is limited to specifically virtuous activity. *Responsiveness* defines the origin and cause of selfless activity that can encompass all manner of response. On this nondual Dzogchen path, virtue is the effect, not the cause; the ultimate compassionate response is whatever action optimizes presence—loving-kindness is the automatic function of primal awareness.

The terms defined above are all synonyms of emptiness and aspects of emptiness like facets of a jewel. If reality is all creation, then just as the universe, the cosmos, all things under the sun, and the totality give inclusive definitions, so do emptiness, space, light, total presence, and responsiveness—they are simply different names for the same ineffable reality. Each indicates a different aspect useful in developing a vision of the path and expressing experience along it. To the yogin they are sacred and secret words that should never be bandied about in idle metaphysical gossip lest the power to evoke their reality is lost. The reality they evoke is to be considered more precious and more worthy of respect than any particular god; the power these words represent is more potent than nuclear fission and more subtly efficacious than all the miracles of the *siddhas*. They describe the ultimate mode of being, the ultimate buddha-body, the *dharmakāya*. There is nothing but the *dharmakāya* to the Dzogchen master, and the paradox, which in itself is a powerful Dzogchen *koan,* is that the Dzogchen master appears as an ordinary human being, and his immediate environment, his mandala, has the same form as our own.

EMPTYING THE DEPTHS OF HELL

by Guru Chowang

INTRODUCTION

GURU RINPOCHE CHOKYI WANGCHUG, or Guru Chowang, is one of the greatest names among the treasure finders or *tertons*. He lived in the thirteenth century (1212–1280) and heralded a major revival in the Nyingma school. His epithet "the second Guru Rinpoche," whence his title is derived, is given to only a small elite of Nyingma school yogins. He was the second of the sovereign treasure finders and the second of the three supreme emanations of Guru Rinpoche.[57] He is also said to be an incarnation of buddha-speech. This array of superior qualifications entitled him to a ḍākinī-consort of similar first-rank attainment, and he found her in the first of the two Tibetan yoginis possessing all the marks and signs of a ḍākinī[58]—Jomo Menmo Padma Tsokyi (1248–1283), an emanation of Yeshe Tsogyel.

Guru Chowang was born in western Lhodrag, midway between the Bhutan border and Yamdrog Lake, where his family had lived for generations. The residence in Layag Village in which he spent most of his life is called Guru Lhakhang. He was a scion of the Pang family. The founder of the Pang lineage, Pangje Tsentram, was honored by King Trisong Detsen for destroying the Bon magician Nyaring, who had attempted to kill the king by hurling meteors at him from the Bon stronghold on top of Hepori, above Samye Chokhor, during the great king's persecution of the Bon shamans. Pangje's son settled in western Lhodrag in Layag, and his seed produced a famous line of bodhisattva *tantrikas*.

Guru Chowang's education was eclectic. His father taught him Dzogchen, Chagchen *(mahāmudrā)*, Zhije, and Chod, the highest meditations of all schools, and he became highly accomplished in the yogas of Dorje Purba

(Vajrakīla) and Shinjeshe (Mañjuśrī Yamāntaka). But apart from his vast formal book learning, he obtained direct experiential knowledge and empowerment from meditative experience and dream vision. The discovery of his principal treasure trove was attended by amazing visions. He had obtained two lists of hiding places, one originating with Drapa Ngonshe,[59] which had caused disaster to many incompetents who had attempted to retrieve the treasure, and a list of twice-hidden books that he had found himself. The nine-headed serpent demon and awareness-ḍākinī protectors took the form of a human woman to give Guru Chowang the keys to the treasure house. As he opened the door a gigantic vulture (*garuda*) emerged, and recognizing it as the essence of the treasure, he mounted it and flew to the thirteenth stage of enlightenment. There he found a tent of rainbow light and Dorje Sempa (Vajrasattva), who initiated him into the "creativity of total presence"[60] and presented him with a flask full of the nectar of immortality. Then from the treasure-house cave he withdrew two large chests containing 108 volumes of secret instruction, and an enormous hollow statue of the protecting serpent-demon containing four sets of general instruction. This treasure of Namkechen,[61] the Dragmar Cave of Chimpu above Samye Chokhor, was the first of his nineteen discoveries made at power places throughout central and southern Tibet: Lhodrag Kharchu, Samye Chokhor, Samye Dragmar Drinzang, Mon Bumthang, Tsang Tsi Nesar, Samye Hepori, Rong Drag, and Kyawo, and many minor sites as well.

Guru Chowang's vision of his spiritual father, demonstrating his clear visionary capacity, is also germane to our text. Two young girls guided him on a winged white horse to the sphere of Guru Rinpoche's present residence—Ngayab Zangdog Pelri, the Copper-Colored Mountain Paradise of Ngayab in the southwest. Here Orgyen Rinpoche transmitted to him the empowerment of the eight *logos* mandates called the consummate secret. He also received specific advice instructing him to follow the bodhisattva path and to teach sentient beings. (At this time, as intermittently throughout Tibetan history, the temptation for Nyingma school yogins to sell their magical power for personal gain was a particularly potent force for negative karma.) Guru Chowang was then returned to his ordinary state of consciousness on a shield of dazzling light.

It appears that the bulk of Guru Chowang's treasure texts have been lost. Jamgon Kongtrul Rinpoche, whose lifework in the nineteenth century included gathering, editing, and ordering the once potent works of *tertons* of centuries past and publishing them in his voluminous compendium called the *Rinchen Terdzo,* found only a few volumes of Guru Chowang's treasures. Among them were *The Consummate Secret of the Eight Logos Mandates* and *Emptying the Depths of Samsara,* which includes *The Peaceful and Wrathful Deities of the Spontaneously Originated Eight Fierce Logos Deities: The Rite of Confession and Restoration of the* Samayā *while Emptying the Depths of Hell.*[62] *The Sovereign Rite of Confession Atoning for Breaches and Breaks of the* Samaya *and Expiating All Errors and Faults,* known by its short title *Emptying the Depths of Hell (Narag Dongdrug),*[63] is a litany written by Jamgon Kongtrul in the nineteenth century based upon the two treasure texts of Guru Chowang mentioned above. Thus, seven hundred years after Guru Chowang's death, his highly potent secret mantra[64] texts are again in full use by the lineal initiates of the eclectic Red Hat lamas. It is a well known and highly respected Nyingma school litany.

The first section of the rite begins with the yogin visualizing in front of him the lama who embodies the hundred Peaceful and Wrathful Deities. The yogin then invokes the Peaceful and Wrathful Deities, calling them by name and offering obeisance with reverence. The great treasure finder assures the practitioner that merely by sounding the names of the buddha-deities with homage and respect, the full effect of the rite is achieved. Verbal acknowledgment of specific faults and breaks in the vow has the same effect. Then relaxing in meditation the yogin recites the hundred-syllable mantra (the *yigya*), Vajrasattva's mantra of confession, with the certainty that eight hundred repetitions in a single sitting confers rebirth as a bodhisattva. There follows acknowledgment of the yogin's failure to maintain the root and branch vows, the tantric *samayas,*[65] thereby restoring these commitments. The next part of the rite is the Dzogchen confession that is included herein. This concludes the litany. As addenda, verses are included to be recited with offering of the butter lamp, the skullcup of grain, the *rakta,* and the *torma* cakes during the eucharistic sacrament when the confession is included as part of the rite of *gaṇacakra.* Again the purpose is restoration of the *samaya.* The entire rite is composed of a series of techniques that guarantee atonement and refulfillment of the *samaya.*

How can admission of error and sin be part of Dzogchen practice? Confession is a process of mental and spiritual purification indispensable to mental and spiritual well-being. On a mundane level the pressures of guilt are released, liberating festering cankers in the subconscious mind. On a transcendental level confession is an acknowledgement of undesirable, repressed mindforms with coincident recognition of their nature as emptiness and liberation. If guilt, errors, and faults are thoughtforms to which the subconscious is negatively attached, then they may be visualized as spirits or ghosts of past experience lurking in dark and murky corners of the mind. Then confession is self-induced exorcism effecting liberation[66] of these spirits. When the mind is completely empty of these spirits—black, grey, or white—and when every experience whatsoever arises fully into awareness leaving no trace, "like the flight path of a bird in the sky,"[67] then the mind is fully liberated. As our text states, the "sin" and the "sinner" are one: when the undesirable thoughtform is released, the mind of the penitent is also liberated. Sin in this context is defined as an action that is not immediately released and dissolved upon its inception. If the mind is innocent, and insight into all experience as emptiness penetrates each moment of the continuum of reality as it arises, then there is no sin and no sinner but a consummate *samaya* and buddhahood. It is our moral and mental preconceptions and biases that obstructs spontaneous insight into events as empty illusion, echo, or bubbles on the surface of the ocean, and that produces what Buddhists call sin. All ignorant sentient beings, and all yogins whose mindflow of pure awareness is broken, even for a moment, need the rite of confession to atone for their sins.

To atone (*at one* in the Buddhist context) means to identify oneself with the guru-buddha, buddha-deity, and awareness-ḍākinī and thus restore the *samaya*. The rites of confession and *samaya* restoration invariably come together in tantric practice, for they are different sides of the same coin. Confession is to remember, and hence to relive, experience that was not fully understood and whose nature was not penetrated to its true reality. *Samaya* restoration is to restore the continuity of release of every experience through penetrating insight into emptiness and thus to restore the *samaya* union with the guru-buddha and ḍākinī, who represent uninterrupted gnostic awareness. On the relative level, where *samaya* means vow or oath, after confession of failure to maintain a vow, the vow is taken again and thus restored.

The root vows of body, speech, and mind are as follows: the vow of buddha-body is to serve and venerate the guru-buddha and to obey his

instruction, to respect the guru-buddha's consorts and the yogin's vajra broth-
ers and sisters, and to maintain a correct vision of the guru-buddha; the vow
of buddha-speech is to practice visualization and recitation in meditation
upon the buddha-deity regularly and frequently; the vow of buddha-mind
is to keep the Tantra secret. The twenty-five branch vows are injunctions
guiding vision, meditation, and action, thus keeping the *samaya* of union
with the guru-buddha, buddha-deity, and awareness-ḍākinī intact.

Emptying the Depths of Hell is a *mahāyoga* text. Virtually all practices associated with the eight logos mandates fall into the *mahāyoga* category. But
since Dzogchen vision is the ultimate perspective on everything that arises,
no matter what the form, Dzogchen practice embraces all the techniques of
the *Hīnayāna, Mahāyāna,* and *Vajrayāna* approaches to buddhahood. The
essential practice of Dzogchen is to penetrate each moment of consciousness with the purifying flame of awareness as it arises, so the successful
Dzogchen yogin has no need of the confessional rites of the gradual
approaches. What is provided for him is confession of lingering traces of
dualistic thought patterns and dichotomous concepts, confession of failure
in vision: this is precisely the nature of the verses extracted from *Emptying
the Depths of Hell* included here.

However, in this liturgy there is no trace of the terminology of penitent
devotee seeking expiation from an external source that would admit a duality of penitent and confessor. The confession is couched in strong affirma-
tive terms strengthening the convictions of Dzogchen vision, and the
confessor is a point instant of gnostic awareness of infinite empty space as
various aspects of the absolute.[68] This point instant of atonement is a
moment in the uninterrupted continuum of naked existential awareness
that is neither within nor without. There is no "I" to be the yogin's own
confessor, nor any external, higher plane of being in which the yogin
bathes. Each dichotomy is resolved in an immediate, unutterable, non-
objectifiable moment of primal awareness. A sense of contrition is assumed,
since contrition is recognition of the absence of continuous buddhahood
and knowledge of the necessity to atone for one's ignorance. It is also
recognition of humility in the face of the divine pride of the moment of
atonement and primal awareness. However, instead of contrition toned
with self-abnegation and abasement, we have a lament for incorrigible
human nature driven by self-destructive desire, ever refusing to see the

insubstantial universe as an enchanting magical web of empty illusion, in which ḍākas and ḍākinīs dance in a constant compassionate display of delight and pure pleasure. Alas! What misery! Thus the self-abasement characteristic of the path of renunciation is replaced with an evocation of the bodhisattva vow. The secret mantra magic of the verses should demonstrate their own efficacy.

EMPTYING THE DEPTHS OF HELL

HŪM! How futile to project notions of being and nonbeing
upon an unformed and inconceivable reality-continuum!
What misery to cling to delusions of a substantial reality!
Atone in the spaciousness of formless, concept-free pleasure.

How pointless to project notions of purity and impurity
upon Kuntu Zangpo,[70] who transcends all moral qualities!
How guilt-ridden are those who cling to moral dualities!
Atone in the spaciousness of Kunzang's pure pleasure.

How exhausting to cling to notions of self and others
in the sameness where superiority and inferiority cannot be!
What anxiety to cling to the duality of success and failure!
Atone in the spaciousness of the pure pleasure of sameness.

How futile to cling to concepts of this life and the next
when the bodhisattva's mind is free of birth and dying!
What anxiety lies in obsession with birth and death!
Atone in the spaciousness of the deathless swastika.[71]

How foolish to project concepts of concrete form and substance
upon the cosmic seed that has no corners or edges!
What boredom lies in the limitations of squares and rectangles!
Atone in the spaciousness of the all-embracing spherical nucleus.

How stupid it is to project notions of beginning and end
in the timeless, unchangeable dimension of past, present, and future!

What misery lies in the duality of transformation and gradual change!
Atone in the spaciousness of unchanging past, present, and future.

How pointless to project causal relationships
upon primal awareness, naturally arising without strain
    or accomplishment!
What grief lies in distinguishing effort from attainment!
Atone in the spaciousness of effortless spontaneity.

How exhausting to cling to concepts of subject and object
in total awareness neither eternal nor temporal!
What misery to separate time from eternity!
Atone in the spaciousness of total awareness.

How futile it is to hold mental and physical pain distinct
in the formless, pristine reality beyond conception!
What anxiety to separate center from circumference!
Atone in the spaciousness of the immaculately real.

How pointless the concepts of inside and out
in the Buddha's boundless palace that has no measure!
What folly to differentiate length from breadth!
Atone in the spaciousness without measure or dimension.

How meaningless are the projections of above and below
in the celestial matrix that has no height nor depth!
What foolishness to dualize high and low!
Atone in the spaciousness of the dimensionless *yoni*.[72]

How exhausting to project notions of inside and out
in the *dharmakāya* that resolves every duality!
What misery to distinguish vessel and contents!
Atone in the spaciousness of immutable *dharmakāya*.

How pitiful are sentient beings, deluded and ignorant,
conceiving fluid, formless events as concrete reality.
Man's bewildered mind—how sadly errant!

In an unborn reality projecting notions of I and mine,
failing to see the illusory enchantment of phenomenal existence,
he hankers after possessions and wealth;
failing to realize the insubstantiality of samsara,
he clings forever to equally deluded friends and relations:
man's imperceptive intellect—how sadly errant!

Forsaking the value of truth, striving in unhealthy activity,
ignoring the Exemplar's injunction, beguiled by irrelevant attractions,
forgetting the primacy of awareness, obsessed by idle pleasures,
how pitiful are sentient beings who have lost their way!
Atone in the spaciousness of nondiscrimination.

THE FLIGHT OF THE GARUDA

by Shabkar Lama Jatang Tsogdrug Rangdrol

INTRODUCTION

THE GENTLE PILGRIM wanders Tibetan trails from power place to power place, sometimes passing over the high Himalayas down to the valley of Nepal. Long dreadlocks are piled on his head, and he wears a ragged patched skirt with a white shawl over his shoulders distinguishing him from most Himalayan monks. At nightfall he can sleep anywhere he finds himself, for he spent his early years in caves in the snow-capped mountains of the Tibetan plateau and cares nothing for comfort. He is vegetarian and he can fast if food is unavailable. Occasionally he may be spurned or ill-treated by bandits, but there is something about him that immediately evinces acceptance and kindness. At the house where he receives hospitality he may offer a healing charm to the sick or aged or an exorcising mantra to banish a malignant spirit. A request for help on the Dharma path is answered in a song composed spontaneously in the moment. He does not stay long in any place but leaves quickly and moves fast down the trail. This mellow yogin, an archetypal figure of the Tibetan plateau, is Shabkar Lama, Tsogdrug Rangdrol, author of *The Flight of the Garuda*.

Shabkar Lama was the scion of a nomad family in a tribal area in the far northeast of the Tibetan ethnic region. In this area there were no aristocratic families ensconced in their hereditary castles producing tulkus for the local establishment monasteries in each generation. His tribal society was democratic and egalitarian. His wonderful life story[73] reflects the humility of a beggar, the magnanimity of a saint without a shred of pretension or affectation, and the good humor and compassion of a man familiar with the hardship of life on the survival line. Lacking the advantages of a princely monastic education, he was a scholar nevertheless, but a scholar who wrote from experience, directly from his heart—he lived what he wrote and taught. Free of political and social bias, following the spirit of Dzogchen, he had no time for sectarian distinctions and took initiation and instruction from not only Nyingma lamas but teachers of every school. It was this impartial ethos that was the foundation of the great nonsectarian revival in eastern Tibet in the nineteenth century. He heralded the great Khyentse Wangpo (1820–92), Jamgon Kongtrul Lodro Taye (1813–99), Patrul Rinpoche (1808–87), and Mipam Jamyang Gyatso (1846–1912), who were the figures most prominent in the full blooming of the eastern Tibetan renaissance.

Shabkar Lama was born in Rebkong[74] in Amdo in 1781. At this time the Gelugpa school dominated Amdo through its great monastic academies; but the Rebkong region, to the north of the Amnye Machen massif, was—and still is—renowned for its Nyingma yogin-*tantrikas (ngagpas)* guided by the Dzogchen tradition. They were respected for their total commitment and devotion, but with their unshorn hair and unkempt appearance, roaming throughout Tibet, they were also feared. Practicing ritual magic for villagers while on pilgrimage, they also taught Tantra and Dzogchen to those ready and willing to learn. Shabkar grew up in this *ngagpa* ambience, receiving transmission from several Nyingma masters before taking full ordination with a Gelugpa lama at the age of twenty. Thereafter the Dzogchen ethos of Rebkong remained his heart practice, indicated by the white and red shawl he wore, while his *gelong* ordination, the outward show, was indicated by the patched lower robe. After ordination he was directed not to monastic discipline but to the lama who was to become his root guru and inspiration throughout his life, whose name was Ngakyi Wangpo.

The Lord of Dharma Ngakyi Wangpo (1736–1807) was a descendant of the Mongol prince Gushri Khan,[75] and his extended family was the ruling family in an area south of Rebkong and the north of the Amnye Machen range. Ngakyi Wangpo was a secular leader and a married lama, a *ngagpa*. We may see this personage as a severe and uncompromising preceptor, like Marpa Dopa, Milarepa's master; but Shabkar paints him only as the most gracious and compassionate of teachers. His principal gift to Shabkar was the initiation, transmission, and instruction upon the revealed cycle of *The Wish-fulfilling Union of Tamdrin (Hayagrīva) and Dorje Pagmo (Vajravarāhī).*[76] This comprehensive cycle of theory and practice provided Shabkar with his personal buddha-deity *(yidam)*—the union of Hayagrīva and Vajravarāhī. It also gave him a manual of meditation and yoga practice that was to sustain him for the remainder of his life.

After initiation Shabkar spent some time in retreat, practicing the preliminary techniques, the creative and fulfillment stages, and Dzogchen—Cutting Through and Immediate Crossing—according to the *Wish-fulfilling Union of Tamdrin and Dorje Pagmo,* his lama's chief practice and now his own. Then after spending more time with his lama, when he received all the initiations of his lineage, he entered a further period of rigorous retreat. In the middle of the Kokonor Lake, the vast Turquoise Blue Lake sacred to Avalokiteśvara, is an island called Great God Heart of the Lake, Tsonying Mahādewa. Since no boat was permitted to sully the lake, the island could only be reached on foot by crossing the ice that covers the lake for a brief period each year. Yogins would provide themselves with a year's provision and isolate themselves in the perfect solitude on the island at the center of the lake mandala. Shabkar remained there three years practicing the *mahā-*, *anu-*, and *ati-* yogas of the Tamdrin-Pagmo cycle. During his sojourn on this island Shabkar wrote *The Flight of the Garuda.* It was an early work of his genius.

Shabkar was known as an incarnation of Milarepa, Tibet's great yogin and composer of divine songs extempore, and his lama, Ngakyi Wangpo, as an incarnation of Marpa the Translator, the patriarchal yogin. Milarepa's talent in composing and singing mystical songs extempore was shared by Shabkar, and so was his propensity for the anchorite's life. But the yogin from Rebkong in Amdo was also a wanderer, roaming on pilgrimage throughout the Tibetan heartland and beyond. Punctuating his pilgrimage with retreats in caves and hermitages, he visited Amnye Machen, Amdo's sacred mountain; he performed the Tsari Rongkhor (the long circumambulation of the Tsari mountain); and he spent a year at Kang Rinpoche, on Mount Kailash. On his pilgrimage to Labchi, to the west of Mount Everest, it was said of him that wherever he traveled he left the people established in the Dharma, and wherever he stepped he converted "black," or tarnished, worldlings into "white," or refined, practitioners. Thus he gained his sobriquet *Shabkar* (White Foot). During his pilgrimage, between retreats, he would continue his instruction at the feet of lamas of every school, particularly the Drugpa Kagyu, with which his own heterogenous brand of yogin-monk mix had a strong affinity. However he was also interested in the Kadampas (the school founded by Jowo Atiśa and assimilated by the Gelugpas), and Je Tsongkhapa himself, whose great work, *The Stages of the Path,* received sustained attention from Shabkar.

Shabkar's study and practice bore fruit in his own writing. He had the gift of speed writing. It was said that he could write a hundred pages daily. If so, he could have spent only a month or so to produce his thirteen volumes of writing, the chief of which concerned his principal practice, the Tamdrin-Pagmo cycle. Other volumes treated the Kadampa School, bodhisattvahood, the Nyingma tantras, and Mañjuśrī, demonstrating the wide purview of his scholarship. Shabkar's rounded personality is evinced also by his meritorious works: the gift of a solid-gold butter lamp to the great monastery of Samye; the gilding of the superstructure of the Boudhanath Stūpa in Kathmandu; the construction of numerous monasteries and temples in his own Amdo homelands. No antisocial, cantankerous hermit, he had the bodhisattva's ability to transform himself into a receptacle of offerings that he used for the good of all sentient beings.

Shabkar passed away in 1851 at the age of seventy-one. On the completion of a long discourse to his disciples, his spirit left his body while he still sat upright in lotus posture. So passed the carefree spirit of the "little anchorite" who, in many ways, both by example and in words, did more to feed the faith and support the spiritual needs of the common people than a multitude of tulkus on brocaded thrones. His spirit returned to inhabit another body, but it did so in the obscurity in which the original Shabkar spent much of his life. His lineage, however, proliferated. Trulshik Rinpoche of Thubten Choling in Solu, Nepal, is the principal contemporary practitioner of his lineage.

That, then, is the Shabkar Tsogdrug Rangdrol who wrote and sang *The Flight of the Garuda.* In his own judgment he was a simple, perspicacious mendicant without a care in the world. The clarity and power of the succinct, simple expression for which he is justly renowned is evident on every page of his work. *The Flight of the Garuda* also demonstrates the writer's eclectic erudition and the fertile memory that allowed him in his extempore compositions to quote or paraphrase verses of Saraha's *Dohakoṣa,* for instance, and passages from Longchenpa's *Dzodun,* among the works that he lists in his colophon.

The Garuda of the title refers to a mythological bird, the Khading, or

Khyung, of ancient Bon legend. It may have been that Khading and Khyung originally represented the powers of light and darkness in the eternal conflict of Manichean Bon myth. The Manichean influence on Bon was derived from countries to the northwest of Tibet. Later, Khyung and Khading were confounded, and the bird came to represent the Bon spirit of fire. It is to be found, for example, in the upper left-hand corner of prayer flags.[77] When the Sanskritic tradition of Buddhism became dominant in Tibet, both Khading and Khyung were assimilated into the Garuda. In the Vedic mythology of ancient Aryan India, it was Garuda who stole the nectar of immortality from Indra, the king of the gods, in much the same way as the cosmic bird Zu stole the Tablets of Destiny from the gods in Babylonian myth. In the later Indian context, Garuda became the vehicle of Viṣṇu, the lord of preservation and order in the cosmos, and particularly Lord Kṛṣṇa's vehicle. Also, in the Purāṇas and epics, as a fire spirit, Garuda features as the implacable enemy of the *nāga* water spirits. In Tibetan Buddhist Tantra, Garuda represents the energy of fire that heals *nāga*-related diseases, particularly cancer.

In the Great Perfection, Garuda is seen to represent the Dzogchen yogin. The nature of the bird is illuminated by the ancient Bon myth that relates how, at the beginning of time, the Khyung manifested spontaneously out of the cosmic egg as a fully mature being. The Garuda can transfer itself instantaneously from one place to another. From the tantric tradition is derived the image of the garuda's wings beating in unison to demonstrate the unitary nature of duality, particularly the simultaneous arising of the gender principles of skillful means and perfect insight.[78] Then from nature, observing the flight of the Tibetan eagle vulture, the Dzogchen yogin can perceive an analog of his own effortless path. The bird in flight is a wonder to behold. Gliding for miles using the wind's currents to support its weight, its instinctual mastery of aeronautics is incomparable. The same kind of natural, intuitive faculty that coordinates the bird's flight governs the Dzogchen yogin's activity.

The two wings that beat in unison in the garuda's poetic flight are form and meaning. Unfortunately the abstract, technical content of *The Flight of the Garuda* does not lend itself to versification and poetic expression in English, so that the balance in Shabkar's songs is not reflected in this translation, in which poetic form and rhythm have been sacrificed to clarity of meaning. Often, several words are required to render a single technical term into

English, and it is impossible to maintain a regular meter. Rather than attempt unsatisfactory versification, I have translated these songs into prose, which is a more suitable medium for their metaphysical and technical vocabulary. Still, the Garuda's flight should appear effortless, its wings beating in unison.

The Flight of the Garuda is a collection of Dzogchen songs compiled to teach *tregcho* meditation. Thus in general the structure of the text shows the evolution of the path. This development is not formulated as an academic treatise on *tregcho,* since the songs are composed in different styles with different thrusts of meaning. The songs can be categorized as songs of introduction (songs 4–7, 10–12, and 14–16); songs of precept (songs 3, 8 and 9, 13 and 14, 16–18, and 21); and aphoristic songs (songs 1 and 2, 16, 17, 19, and 22). Some songs combine introduction and precept in an aphoristic form (e.g., song 16), while others may be an introduction to an aspect of total presence with clear instruction on meditation technique (songs 14–19, and 22 and 23).

Perhaps the most potent songs are the songs of introduction or initiation. Shabkar Lama indicates the purpose of these songs in the final line of each: "Such is my introduction initiating recognition of…the original nature of mind," or "our true existential condition," and so on. The Dzogchen vision that these songs are aimed at initiating and strengthening is not merely an intellectual function but an opening up of a channel for awareness to flow in; or, if it is an intellectual function, then it is the intellect participating in the destruction of its own dualizing propensities and other obstacles to the spontaneous awakening of total presence. Thus these introductions are not philosophical statements but tools inducing a recognition of various aspects of the enlightened mind that is akin to an initiation into total presence. The inspired nature of the Tibetan poetry; the meditative frame of mind during which the songs are sung; the clear, direct, and succinct style of expression; and not least the potency of the metaphysical exposition and formulae all conspire to induce Dzogchen vision spontaneously. In Shabkar Lama's colophon he states explicitly that the songs should be sung during the development process of Dzogchen vision.

The first "introductory" song, initiating recognition of the original nature of mind, or our original existential condition,[79] is preceded by the first "preceptual" song giving instruction on experiential discovery of the nature of mind. It is only on the basis of failure to discover any entity that is mind that this verbal initiation into the original face of mind is effective. Our ingrained, conditioned assumption that the brain as a substantial entity is the mind, or its seat, is destroyed by the failure to find anything substantial that can be called *mind*. Mind immediately becomes something enigmatic, mystical, transcendental, and magical, and an intellectual void. This void is filled by the songs of introduction, which establish the Dzogchen vision. The cynic's view, that this is an example of religious conditioning with less reality than the preconceptions it replaces, is countered by the assertion that the Dzogchen vision has no intellectual structure and that the labeling of attributes performed by these introductions is not so much a labeling process of substantial objective qualities by the subjective mind as the attachment of verbal symbols to actual experiences of gnostic awareness.

Searching for the nature of mind has pointed awareness in the right direction. Practicing the instructions described in the successive songs of precept matures this awareness, and as the state of total presence grows its attributes become focused. What is essentially an inconceivable unutterable gnostic condition is seen to be susceptible to analysis by a metaphysical imagination that serves to direct or guide this unitary, gnostic awareness. Thus Shabkar makes a point of stressing that the three modes of being—the three buddha-bodies—are in truth a single undifferentiated reality. These three modes of being relate to the essence, nature, and responsiveness of the unitary state. The unitary state of being, like the universe expanding from a point of origin, contracting into that point, and expanding again, *ad infinitum,* is represented by the mandala, and the mandala's center, diameter, and circumference relate to the essence, nature and responsiveness that are the three modes of being. The essential insight is recognition of the original nature of being in its ontological aspect as introduced in song 6. Shabkar names this the main practice. This insight precedes the introduction to the "structure" of this original nature, which is Buddha and his five modes representing five aspects of primal awareness.

A second series of songs of precept give instruction in meditation upon the form of emptiness, teaching that all phenomena are mind created. The introductions that follow confirm the insights that arise by applying those precepts. Song 10 introduces the initiatory recognition of all forms, the product of dualizing thought processes, as mind. Song 11 gives a complete series of introductions initiating recognition of the empty nature of mind, the emptiness of phenomena, the indivisibility of appearances and emptiness, and finally the inevitable result of these previous insights—recognition of natural, spontaneous gnostic liberation. It also defines the Cutting Through phase of Dzogchen practice as a twenty-four-hour-a-day meditation.

Song 12 is not a song of introduction, but it has the same force. It defines the three modes of being from two different angles: as the *dharmakāya* and as the *rūpakāya,* as emptiness and as form, as primal awareness and as the forms of awareness that are not separate from it. As Shabkar affirms, this differentiation has the power to initiate recognition of the pure lands of the three modes of being. The projections of total presence, the flow of spontaneously originated appearances pure from the beginning, are the buddhas' pure lands since they are identical to the indivisible light and space that is the *dharmakāya*. In terms of the crystal metaphor that Shabkar employs in this song: according to the static definition, the *rūpakāya* consists of the crystal's natural glow *(sambhogakāya)* and the medium of whatever appears in that dancing glass *(nirmāṇakāya).* According to the dynamic definition, the *rūpakāya* consists of inner radiant light *(sambhogakāya)* and unobstructed manifest diversity *(nirmāṇakāya).* The chief point in this subtle distinction appears to be that in the latter, dynamic aspect, the *nirmāṇakāya* is the diversity of form itself, the contents of the vessel of consciousness rather than its medium, the empty space of the vessel. Thus this distinction is confirming the absolute emptiness of form while focusing upon the form itself—buddhafields!

Song 14 introduces the yogin to recognition of spontaneous release of the six sense fields by means of precepts instructing him in meditation on the one taste. Song 15 introduces recognition of the identity of quiescence and movement in the state of total presence.[80] This paradox is best explained by means of the metaphor Shabkar employs: the quiescence of the ocean bottom is likened to an inactive, thoughtless mind, while the rollers and breakers of the ocean's surface are the active mind. The active and inactive are part and parcel of the same awareness—total presence. For this reason it is impossible to recognize a Dzogchen yogin by his external display: no action of body, speech, and mind can ever be divorced from the ocean of primal awareness. Later Shabkar discusses the folly of identifying a quiescent mind as a realized state. The attainment of quiescence in meditation is an accomplishment of the gods of the formless realm of conditioned existence. This may be useful in controlling the mind while seeking to help sentient beings on the relative plane, and it may be the source of some divine pleasure, but it is not a direct means to the buddhas' enlightenment, which is liberation from all the polarities of existence.

The first part of song 16 is the last song of introduction and in one sense the climax of these verbal initiations: it is an introduction to recognition of Dzogchen itself. A verse describing the resolution of various seeming dualities in the Dzogchen domain removes many obstacles of doubt. Then Shabkar assures us that there is a reflexive responsiveness here, implying the redundancy of a manipulative *siddhi*-ridden mind, as body, speech, and mind function spontaneously to fulfill the bodhisattva vow. In fact, the compassionate aspect of the realized mind is a special quality of Dzogchen practice.

Song 16 ends with a warning in the only verse touching on danger in any of the songs. This danger is the bane of Dzogchen. It explains why Dzogchen precepts are so difficult to obtain. For this reason, a lama who teaches Dzogchen without first ascertaining the moral proclivities of his students risks producing a lineage of demon-yogins. Shaman magicians may seek Dzogchen instruction with the aim of harnessing demon energy for their own dark purposes. With love or money, a student may purchase Dzogchen initiation from an inferior Dzogchen yogin with the sole intention of turning his knowledge to selfish purposes of power and domination. Even though the Dzogchen yogin maintains his bodhisattva vow unbroken and his motivation is unblemished, it appears that negative effects may still result. In the biographies of even great lamas it is recorded that Dzogchen precepts were withheld from them until the end of their preceptor's life, not out of fear that the disciple may turn black, but that selfless, benevolent bodhisattvic motivation could be blunted. Even Yeshe Tsogyel, Guru Rinpoche's consort, was no exception, and precepts were withheld from her until the last moment of the guru's stay. When Shabkar himself was intent upon obtaining a rainbow body, he was warned in a dream by Senge Dongma, the lion-headed ḍākinī, that he could certainly obtain it but that his ability to assist others would be vitiated thereby. The longer the student spends in developing and refining the skillful means of implementing the bodhisattva vow before Dzogchen initiation, the more effective will be the compassionate forms he manifests spontaneously after Dzogchen realization.

How is it that at the threshold of the buddhas' realization the practitioner can be possessed by the "antibuddha"? How is it that at this stage "a demon of intense and infinite evil" can possess the mind and turn the Dzogchen yogin into a black magician? There appear to be several factors at work. The resolution of the duality of virtue and vice can cause a shrinking from virtue and the embracing of vice, as Shabkar indicates. Since all acts are empty illusion, there is no moral reason to prefer one over the other, and since guilt, sin, and karmic retribution are empty illusion, they are no cause for alarm. Further, it seems that the deviant yogin's power is derived from a false identification of the Buddha with the most subtle residue of his ego. He is convinced that he is the Buddha, "the one taste of the *dharmakāya*."[81] If the yogin is well founded in the karma of virtue, with this warning in mind he avoids the destruction of the supports of a virtuous life even though both virtue and vice are equally the illusory play of the mind.

The importance of a firm foundation in the lower approaches becomes evident at this point. A strong foundation in the four noble truths will obviate the danger, and if the lessons of Śākyamuni's three excursions out of the pleasure palace into the city of sickness, old age, and death were the cause of an original turning around in the seat of consciousness, then *bodhicitta* need not be diminished or overwhelmed by demonic perversions. It is not only an article of faith but a fact of peak experience that compassionate responsiveness arises coincident with a samadhi of genuine emptiness. But on the approach to Dzogchen initiation this statement must be predicated by prolonged and profound purification practices before Dzogchen precepts are requested, so that there is no hitch when the goal is in sight. This crucial warning ends the part of song 16 that initiates recognition of Dzogchen, and it ends the songs of introduction.

The songs of precept are straightforward meditation instruction. Shabkar Lama's poetic genius shows itself here, for the content does not naturally lend itself to poetic treatment. The first song of precept is song 4, which instructs in the exercise of discovering the nature of mind. "Discovery of the nature of mind" epitomizes the purpose of Dzogchen. In Dzogchen meditation there is nothing but this imperative to find the mind. But in this discursive form the meditation belongs to the internal preliminary stage of Dzogchen. Shabkar Lama provides the answers in the same song as the questions, assuming that we are intellectually familiar with the answers and that experiential revelation of them is all that is necessary. However, a Western neophyte will gain important insight into the differences between basic oriental and occidental assumptions about the nature of mind if he forgets the Dzogchen answers until all his own preconceptions have emerged.

Song 8 describes another exercise experientially confirming basic Dzogchen hypotheses about mind. "Mind is like the sky"; "the radiance of mind is like sunlight"; "mindforms are ephemeral and capricious"; "all appearances are like reflections in a mirror"; "there is no distinction between appearances and emptiness"; "everything whatsoever is an illusory magical display of mind." All these statements are self-evident, says Shabkar, and the principal difference between the Dzogchen yogin and the anxious, bewildered worldling is that the former has experiential knowledge of these facts while the latter is unable to recognize them due to the partiality and bias inherent in a mind split by subject-object dichotomy. The instruction in song 9 guides the yogin through a partly discursive analysis of appearances in order to convince him of the insubstantiality of all sensual stimuli. This is not an objective scientific analysis of phenomena. It is an examination of our actual experience, which, according to Buddhist thought, is all we can know about the universe.[82] To all intents and purposes, from the point of view of human consciousness, phenomena are mind created, and these precepts convince the yogin of this verity.

Song 13 describes a wonderful meditation that cuts attachment to emotion and uses passion as the source of primal awareness in its five aspects. The mechanics of the technique are clearly described in this song. The pure nature of transcendental awareness inherent in the various emotions is better described like this:

> [This] set of realizations is based in the reflex intuition that every moment of experience is perfect in its ultimate identity.[83] Sloth is undiscriminating and nonjudgmental in vision and nonprejudicial in action; indiscriminate lust is unfocused compassion [love with the infinite universe as a lover]; anger, which burns up discursive thought, is the intrinsic awareness of total presence;[84] coincident with the vanity and pride that bring no fall is a *siddha's* vision of universal sameness; and as for jealousy, there is no room for its passionate attachments and paranoic thought in the reality-continuum of its ultimate sameness.[85]

This meditation is to be performed during formal sessions and in the meditative state at all times. As Shabkar affirms, once the accomplishment has become a habit, once the recognition of the purity in passion has become a conditioned response of mind, reflex intuition takes over. There is no question of transformation of passion here: the term germane to this process is "recognition of what already exists waiting for revelation." Then at the end of this song there occurs the statement that logically emerges from practice of this meditation: "The greater the passion and the greater the intensity of discursive thought, the greater the *dharmakāya.*" In this way samsara itself is the buddhas' throne. This song is also an initiatory introduction into spontaneous release of the five poisons.

Song 14, an initiatory introduction to the spontaneous release of the six sense fields, contains explicit instruction on a technique to reveal the one taste of all things. This song scotches any residual impression an outsider may have that the one taste of emptiness, the fruit of Dzogchen, is a single feeling of innocuous pseudo-equanimity, that the goal is a constant stream of sensory sameness. On the contrary, the vast variety of sense impressions are heightened, despite, or indeed because of, insight into the one taste of emptiness. Since empty awareness and the form that is the sense-impression are inseparable, where the yogin is enjoined to "observe the mind" in this song he cannot but become aware of his detachment and the pure pleasure that accompanies every perception, whether it be pleasure or pain, happiness or sadness. No word in English is adequate to translate the feeling tone of the one taste. The "pure pleasure" of pain, however, is not a sado-masochistic ecstasy; perhaps the feeling tone of detached enjoyment best conveys the nature of this pleasure.

Songs 16, 17, and 18 treat the essence of Dzogchen meditation. Sixteen begins with an initiatory introduction to Dzogchen itself, and each verse is a complete revelation. "'Buddha' or full awareness is the one taste of reality"; "the compassionate responsiveness that arises coincident with thought-free samadhi is the special characteristic of Dzogchen vision"; and then "amorality is a demonic perversion." The latter part of this most significant song 16 includes vital advice on the treatment of doubt and equivocation on the path. Shabkar mentions the most virulent and destructive doubt, namely the thought that meditation is redundant because no relative cause can effect the ultimate, acausal, spontaneous Dzogchen goal. His answer to doubt is the true lama's grace. It is beyond the power of ordinary words to explain or describe to a faithless outsider the nature of the buddha-lama's blessing, and it is totally unnecessary to convince a yogin of the power of his lama's mind. Pray, relax, and remain aware is Shabkar's formula, and he suggests that profound affirmation and renewed conviction will inevitably result. He implies, further, that peak or initiatory experience implanting the Dzogchen vision can be attained through the lama's blessing. The dynamic of this phenomenon is described in the *Garland of Vision* (p. 151), and the point to remember here is that it is the all-pervasive buddha-lama who is the source of blessings, not a human entity perceived as a separate, superior, external being. The yogin's attitude of supplication and his focus upon the goal as embodied in the lama assist this process.

Song 17 is another treasury of precepts. It begins with the ineluctable injunction to leave home, family, friends, and native country. At the beginning so much can be accomplished in the mind by a physical movement away from the objects of the mind's attachment. The remainder of this long song provides detailed instruction upon Dzogchen vision, meditation, and action. It describes the meditation of nonmeditation, and nothing can be said here to clarify Shabkar's aphorisms on this topic, although volumes have been written on the topic of each verse.

Song 18 provides instruction on the methods of removing obstacles on the path. Since at no time are thoughts to be suppressed or neutralized but rather viewed as allies in meditation, if they arise as obstacles a fault in vision has been revealed. Correct vision is accompanied by the relaxed recognition of the nature of obstructing thought, which Shabkar here defines as "the naturally accomplished Great Perfection." This leads into instruction on nonaction. *Nonaction* cannot easily be defined, but one can say that it is accompanied by a sense of perfect balance and poise, even if the nonaction is an extreme of action. Perhaps this is the place to quote Shabkar on intellectual analysis: "It is certain that the intellectual with an analytical view of reality has no connection with the Heart Essence of the Great Perfection (Dzogchen Nyingtig)."

Song 21 is another song of explicit meditation precepts. It begins with more instruction in Dzogchen meditation and continues with various techniques for Cutting Through designed for practitioners of lesser capacity. Yogins with lesser capacity are those who have not attained the essential initiation from the lama or who have not sustained the initiatory state with spontaneous, effortless ease, practicing the foregoing precepts reflexively. The techniques described here are but a few from the vast store of Dzog-chen prescription. These are methods that do not require eons of practice but which immediately cut through the dualities of mind and the propen-sities that block recognition of intrinsic awareness. They are all simple but highly efficacious techniques with the exception of the last one, which requires preparation, detailed visualization, and special conditions for its per-formance. It is a simple version of the technique called *severance (chod)*. The final exercise, involving simulated lunacy, is one of the standard, internal, extraordinary preliminary Dzogchen practices. Such a technique has appeared in various forms in the synthetic new-age "spiritual development" cults that have a tantric flavor, as well as in popular humanistic psychology. The value of such an exercise is self-evident, but it must be performed within a supportive context, such as that of the lama's precepts, or mental damage can ensue.

Songs of the third type are aphoristic songs, those consisting of apho-risms. The Sanskrit *śloka*, a two-line metrical verse, is an ideal vehicle of expression for scripture, epic poetry, and so forth. In Tibetan scripture a four-line verse serves the same aphoristic purpose—a literary device to assist the memory. Yogins going into retreat learn by heart such texts of precept as *The Flight of the Garuda* so that the verse required at any moment is ready on the tip of the tongue. Thus some of the songs of precept are couched in aphoristic verse, and some songs consist entirely of this form—songs 1 and 2, for example. Each verse is complete in itself, and there need be no relationship in content between one verse and the next. The *mahāsiddha's* treasuries of *dohas* are very similar to songs 1 and 2, a similarity strengthened by sameness in meaning and even in vocabulary and syntax. No doubt Shabkar Lama was familiar with either the *mahāsiddhas'* songs themselves or some potted Tibetan plagiarism.

In the context of the path of the supreme inner Tantra, the part of *The Flight of the Garuda* discussed and translated here belongs to the level called *Cutting Through,* which is the penultimate phase of *atiyoga* when Dzogchen is divided into the two levels of Cutting Through *(tregcho)* and Immediate Crossing *(togel).* There is a second part to *The Flight of the Garuda* that treats

Immediate Crossing in a similar manner. Immediate Crossing is a more dangerous vehicle than Cutting Through, and its precepts are never divulged except within the framework of a lama-disciple relationship when they are about to be practiced. However, it is permissible to generalize about this most secret vehicle insofar as it sheds light on the nature of Cutting Through. These two phases of Dzogchen practice are both complementary and serial in relationship. The primal purity that qualifies Cutting Through and the "spontaneous origination" that qualifies Immediate Crossing are different sides of the same Dzogchen coin, and at the same time events are of the nature of primal purity, the foundation from which they spontaneously originate. Thus Cutting Through is the technique of dissolving all appearances, all emotion, and all thought into their original nature of primal purity. Vision, meditation, and action work together to produce spontaneously originated awareness of all things as perfect and complete, as space and light. Experience becomes a continuum of reality, where reality is space and transparent rainbow-colored light.

THE SONG OF THE VISION OF CUTTING
THROUGH TO THE CLEAR LIGHT OF THE GREAT
PERFECTION WITH THE CAPACITY TO TRAVERSE
QUICKLY THE PATHS AND STAGES

THE FLIGHT OF THE GARUDA[86]

NAMOGURUJO:
Homage and reverence to Lama Chokyi Gyelpo,[87]
whose seven-horsed mandala of all-illuminating wisdom and love
radiates all-embracing beams of boundless compassion,
instantaneously enlightening beings of the three realms.

Homage and reverence to Ngagchang Dorje:
From clouds of loving kindness and compassion piled high
in the vast expanse of his radiant, empty dharmakāya,
a downpour of Dharma descends upon the earth
upon his fortunate disciple vessels.

The winds of diligence blowing into the unfurled sails of high aspiration,
the ship of vision carries all beings drowning in the ocean of existence
to the Island of Jewels, the buddhas' trikāya:
Homage to the captain of that ship, Jamyang Gyatso!

The sun of wisdom and love of these my three lamas,
radiating warming rays of potent grace,
struck the white lotus of this lucky vagrant,
and the bud of total presence fully opening
a thousand petals of mystical experience and insight were exposed.

Piled high on the pistils of intelligence
lies nectar that liberates by taste,
the ambrosial nectar of these songs of vision:
This I offer to my lucky disciples, the swarm of bees,
to drink in devotion to their hearts' content.

Song One
The Miraculous Nature of Being[88]

EHMAHO! This carefree and free-speaking vagrant with the deep intelligence now sings *The Flight of the Garuda,* a song of vision, facilitating fast ascent of all the stages and paths.[89] Listen attentively, my beloved sons and daughters!

Like the roar of the dragon, the great name of Buddha resounds throughout the universe, in samsara and nirvana. Constantly vibrating in the minds of the six types of sentient beings, how wonderful that this resonance is not silent a moment!

They may be ignorant of the Buddha's existence within, but how amazing that fools search for him outside! Clearly visible like sunshine, bright and radiant, how surprising that so few can see him!

The Mind, the Buddha himself, having neither mother nor father, how wonderful it is that he knows neither birth nor dying! Suffering all our multifarious feelings, how marvelous that he is unaffected for better or worse!

The original face of the mind, unborn and primally pure—how wonderful its authenticity and natural perfection! Intrinsic knowledge itself, our naturally liberated nature—how marvelous it is that no matter what occurs it is released by letting it be!

Song Two
The Fundamental Meditation

EHMAHO! Noble, beloved sons and daughters, listen without distraction! All the victorious buddhas of the past, present, and future have taught eighty-four thousand books of scripture, teaching as boundless as space itself, but all to one end: how to realize the nature of mind. The buddhas taught nothing more than this.

If the principal root of a tall tree is severed, its ten thousand branches and leaves will wither and die all together; likewise, when the single root of the mind is cut, the leaves of samsara, such as dualistic clinging, perish.

The empty house that has stood in darkness for millennia is illuminated instantly by a single lamp; likewise, an instant's realization of the mind's clear light eradicates negative propensities and mental obscuration inculcated over countless eons.

The brilliance and clarity of sunlight cannot be dimmed by eons of darkness; likewise, the radiance of the mind's essential nature cannot be obscured by eons of delusion.

Indeterminate is the color and shape of the sky, and its nature is unaffected by black or white clouds; likewise, the color and shape of mind's nature is indeterminate, and it cannot be tainted by black or white conduct, by virtue or vice.

Milk is the basis of butter, but the butter will not separate until the milk is churned; likewise, human nature is the ground of buddhahood, but without existential realization sentient beings cannot awaken.

Through gnostic experience of the nature of reality, through practice of these precepts, all beings can gain freedom; regardless of the acuity of his faculties, even a cowherd attains liberation if his existential experience is nondual realization.

When you realize the clear light of mind's nature, the pundit's words of wisdom are redundant. How relevant is another's description of the taste of treacle when your mouth is full of it?

Even the pundit is deluded if he has no existential realization. He may be skilled in comprehensive exposition of the nine approaches to buddhahood, but he is as far distant from buddhahood as the earth is from the sky if he knows of it only from secondhand accounts.

You may keep your strict moral discipline for an eon and patiently practice meditation for an eternity, but if you have yet to realize the clear light of the mind's immaculate nature you will not extricate yourself from the three realms of samsara. Diligently examine the nature of your mind!

Song Three
Instruction in the Essential Meditation

EHMAHO! Now listen further, all my best beloved sons and daughters! No matter what system of mind training you practice, unless you realize the nature of your mind, severing its root, you miss the point of Dzogchen.

The errant aspirant blind to this imperative is like the archer who places his target to the front only to shoot off his arrow in another direction. He is like the householder who searches outside for a thief who is still in the house; like the exorcist who sets his spirit-trap at the west door when the demon lives to the east; like the poor man who begs, blind to his hearth-stone of gold.

Therefore, my beloved children, you who wish to resolve life's frustrations and anxieties by the direct method of discovering the nature of mind, examine your minds in the following way:

What we call "mind" is an insistent chatterer, hopping, skipping, and jumping about. Try to catch it and it slips away, changing shape or vanishing; attempt to focus it and it will not be still, proliferating and scattering; try to pin it with a label and it resolves into unutterable emptiness. But it is this same mind that experiences the gamut of human feeling, and this is the mind that must be scrutinized.

First, what is the origin of this mind? Is it a function of external phenomena—mountains, rocks, water, trees, and celestial breezes—or is it independent of them? Asking yourself where the mind comes from, investigate this possibility thoroughly.

Alternatively, consider whether or not the mind originates from the reproductive fluids of our parents. If so, inquire into the process by which it emerges. Continue this inquiry until it is exhausted and you admit the mind has no origin.

Then second, answer the question Where is the mind now? Is it in the upper or lower part of your body, in your sense organs, in your lungs, or your heart?[90] If it lodges in your heart, in what part of the heart? What is its color and shape? Thoroughly investigate the present location of the mind and its characteristics until you are certain that they are not to be found.

Finally, examine the movement of the mind. When it moves, does it pass through the organs of the senses? In its momentary embrace of external objects, is there physical contact? Is it only a mental function, or are both body and mind involved together? Investigate the process of perception.

Further, when a thought arises with its attendant emotion, first, investigate its source. Second, find its present location, its color and shape and any other attributes. Look long and hard for the answers to these questions. Last, when thought has subsided into itself and vanished, where has it gone? Examine your mind closely for the answers.

At the time of death, what occurs to the mind? How does it leave the body? Where does it exit? Consider these questions and all their ramifications in detail.

Persevere in your careful inquiry, examining the mind until you reach a positive conclusion that it is empty, pure, and utterly inexpressible, that it is a nonentity and free of birth and death, coming and going.

The arid assertions and metaphors of others—statements such as "Mind is emptiness!"—are worse than useless. Until you know the answer yourself, such statements tend to bring doubt and hesitation to the mind. It is like a dogmatic assertion that tigers do in fact live in a country where it is generally supposed that tigers are extinct. It leaves doubt and uncertainty on the subject. After attentively examining your mind and having established its nature, it is as if you have explored the valleys and hills where the tigers are said to exist and, having seen for yourself whether tigers live there, are fully informed. Thereafter, if the question of tigers' existence in that place arises, you will have no doubt as to the truth of the matter.

Song Four
Initiation into the Nature of Mind

EHMAHO! Again, my beloved sons and daughters, gather round and listen! During the analysis and examination of your minds in the manner described above, when you failed to find a mind that you could point to and say This is it! and when you failed to find so much as an atom that you could call concrete, then your failure was supreme success.

First, mind has no origin; since it is originally emptiness its essence is insubstantial. Second, it has no location, no color, and no shape. Finally, it does not move: without moving, it disappears without a trace; its activity is empty activity, its emptiness, empty appearances.

Mind's nature[91] is not created by a cause in the first place, and it is not destroyed by an agent or condition at the end. It is a constant quantity: nothing can be added to or taken from it, it is incapable of increase or decrease, and it cannot be filled or emptied.

Since mind's nature is all-pervasive, the ground of both samsara and nirvana, it is without bias or partiality. No form demonstrates its actuality more clearly than another, and it manifests all and everything equally without obstruction.

Mind cannot be established or defined as anything at all specific, since it goes beyond the limitations of existence and nonexistence. Without coming and going, it is without birth and death, without clarity and obscuration.

The nature of mind in its purity is like a stainless crystal ball: its essence is emptiness, its nature is clarity, and its responsiveness is a continuum.

In no way whatsoever is the nature of mind affected by samsara's negativity. From the first it is Buddha. Trust in this!

Such is my introduction initiating recognition of the original nature of mind, the ground of our being, our true existential condition.[92]

Song Five
Admission of Delusion

EHMAHO! Again, my beloved heart sons, listen! Hear how Dharma-kāya Kuntu Zangpo is free without need for so much as an instant of meditation, and how the six types of beings wander in samsara without having performed even the slightest negative or vicious act.

In the beginning, before anything was, nameless samsara and nirvana were pure potential in the original ground of being. This is how total presence arose from the ground at that time: in the same way that the natural light of a crystal shines out when a sunbeam strikes it, when the primal awareness of total presence was vitalized by life-force, the seal of the vase of eternal youth was broken, and spontaneously originated clear light shone in the sky like the light of the rising sun, as pure lands of pure-being and primal awareness.[93]

Then Dharmakāya Kuntu Zangpo understood this to be his spontaneous manifestation, and instantaneously the outer light of pure-being and primal awareness dissolved into the inner clear light. In the original ground of being, pure from the beginning, he attained buddhahood.

We unenlightened beings, however, did not understand that the nature of spontaneously originated appearances was our own natural radiance, and unmindful perception and bewilderment were the result. This is called "the ignorance that accompanies every perception."

Also at that time the clear light and the appearances arisen out of the ground of clear light were perceived as two. This is called "conceptual ignorance." It was at this juncture that we fell into the trap of ignorant dualism.

Thereafter, as the potentialities of our experience proliferated with the gradual widening of the scope of our activity, the entire gamut of samsaric action emerged. Then the three emotional poisons appeared together with the five poisons that evolved from them, the eighty-four thousand forms of passion developing from the five poisons, and so on. Since then, until this very moment, we have endured the pleasure and pain of the wheel's constant revolutions. We spin endlessly in this samsaric existence as if tied to a water wheel.

If you need elaboration of this topic, consult Kunkhyen Longchenpa's *Treasury of the Supreme Approach* and the *Dense Cloud of Profound Significance,* among others.[94]

Now, although your lama's profound personal instruction has made you aware of the self-deception and delusion harbored in the dark cave of your mind, you have also recognized your mind as Buddha. You have encountered the original face of the Original Lord, the *Ādibuddha,* and you know that you possess the same potential as Kuntu Zangpo. My spiritual children, contemplate this joy from the bottom of your hearts!

Such is my introduction initiating certain recognition of delusion.

Song Six
Initiation into Our True Existential Condition

EHMAHO! Again, beloved children of my heart, listen! *Mind,* this universal concept, this most significant of words, being no single entity, manifests as the gamut of pleasure and pain in samsara and nirvana. There are as many beliefs about it as there are approaches to buddhahood. It has innumerable synonyms.

In the vernacular it is "I"; some Hindus call it the "Self"; the śrāvaka disciples say "selfless individual"; the followers of Mind-only call it simply "mind"; some call it "perfect insight"; some call it "buddha-nature"; some call it the "magnificent stance," some call it the "Middle Way"; some call it the "Cosmic Seed"; some call it the "reality-continuum"; some call it the "universal ground"; some call it "ordinary consciousness."[95] Since the synonyms of mind, the labels we apply to it, are countless, know it for what it really is. Know it experientially as the here and now. Compose yourself in the natural state of your mind's nature.

When at rest the mind is ordinary perception, naked and unadorned; when you gaze directly at it there is nothing to see but light; as total presence,[96] it is brilliance and the relaxed vigilance of the awakened state; as nothing specific whatsoever, it is a secret fullness; it is the ultimacy of nondual radiance and emptiness.

It is not eternal, for nothing whatsoever about it has been proved to exist. It is not a void, for there is brilliance and wakefulness. It is not unity, for multiplicity is self-evident in perception. It is not multiplicity, for we know the one taste of unity. It is not an external function, for presence is intrinsic to immediate reality.

In the immediate here and now we see the face of the Original Lord abiding in the heart center. Identify yourself with him, my spiritual sons. Whoever denies him, wanting more from somewhere else, is like the man who has found his elephant but continues to follow its tracks. He may comb the three dimensions of the microcosmic world systems for an eternity, but he will not find so much as the name of Buddha other than the one in his heart.

Such is my introduction initiating recognition of our true existential condition, which is the principal realization in Cutting Through to the Great Perfection.[97]

Song Seven
Assertion of Intrinsic Buddhahood

EHMAHO! Once more listen attentively, my noble sons and daughters. The three modes of buddha-being—essence, nature, and responsiveness— and the five modes of being, as well as the five aspects of primal awareness, are all completed and perfected in the naturally luminous intrinsic awareness of the here and now.

The essence of total presence, indefinable by any term such as color, shape, or other attribute, is the *dharmakāya;* the inherent radiance of emptiness is the light of the *sambhogakāya;* and the unimpeded medium in which all things manifest is the *nirmāṇakāya.*

The three modes are explained figuratively like this: the *dharmakāya* is a crystal mirror; the *sambhogakāya* is its nature—brilliant clarity; and the *nirmāṇakāya* is the unobstructed medium in which the reflection appears.

From the first, people's minds have existed as these three modes of being. If they are able to recognize this spontaneously, it is unnecessary for them to practice even so much as a moment of formal meditation—the awakening to buddhahood is instantaneous.

In this introduction to the three modes they are defined separately. In truth, my heart-children, do not fall into the error of believing them to be separate, belonging to different continuums.

From the beginning, the three modes of being are empty and utterly pure. Understanding them as a single essence that is the union of radiance and emptiness, conduct yourself in a state of detachment.

The triad of essence, nature, and responsiveness, again, corresponds to *dharmakāya, sambhogakāya,* and *nirmāṇakāya.* Understanding these three as the mystic union of emptiness and radiance, conduct yourself in a state of detachment.

Further, since the primal awareness of self-existing total presence manifests everything whatsoever, this awareness is the pure-being[98] of the Creator, Vairocana; since it is unchanging and unchangeable, it is the pure-being of Immutable Diamond, Akṣobhyavajra; since it is without center or circumference, it is the pure-being of Boundless Light-form, Amitābha; since it is also the gem that is the source of supreme realization and relative powers, it is the pure-being of the Fountain of Jewels, Ratnasambhava; since it accomplishes all aspiration, it is the pure-being of the Fulfiller of All Ambition, Amoghasiddhi. These buddha-deities are nothing but the creative power of total presence.[99]

The primal awareness of total presence is mirror-like awareness because of the manifest clarity of its unobstructed essence. It is awareness of sameness because it is all-pervasive. It is discriminating awareness because the entire gamut of diverse appearances is manifest from its creativity. It is the awareness that accomplishes all actions because it fulfills all our ambition. It is awareness of the reality-continuum, the *dharmadhātu,* because the single essence of all these aspects of awareness is primal purity. Not so much as an atom exists apart from these, which are the creativity of intrinsic awareness.

When a pointed finger introduces you directly and immediately to the three modes—essence, nature, and responsiveness—and the Five Buddhas and the five aspects of awareness, all together, then what is experienced is brilliant, awakened total presence unaffected by circumstance and uninfluenced by clinging thought; it is cognition of the here and now, unstructured and unaffected.

All the buddhas of the three aspects of time arise from this total presence. Constantly identify yourselves with it, beloved sons and daughters, because this is the spirituality of all the buddhas of the three aspects of time.[100]

Total presence is the unstructured, natural radiance of your own mind, so how can you say that you cannot see the Buddha? There is nothing at all to meditate upon in it, so how can you complain that meditation does not arise? It is manifest total presence, your own mind, so how can you say that you cannot find it? It is a stream of unceasing radiant wakefulness, the face of your mind, so how can you say that you cannot see it? There is not so much as a moment of work to be done to attain it, so how can you say that your effort is unavailing? Centered and dispersed states are two sides of the same coin, so how can you say that your mind is never centered? Intrinsic knowledge is the spontaneously originated three modes of being, which is achieved without striving, so how can you say that your practice fails to accomplish it? It is enough to leave the mind in a state of nonaction, so how can you say that you are incapable of attaining it? Your thoughts are released at the moment of their inception, so how can you say that the antidotes were ineffective? It is cognition of the here and now, so how can you say you do not perceive it?

Song Eight
The Method of Attaining Conviction

EHMAHO! Once again, beloved sons and daughters, listen with devotion! "Mind in its insubstantiality is like the sky." Is this true or false, my children? Confirm it by relaxing completely and looking directly at the mind, gazing with your entire mind, free of all tension.

"The emptiness of the mind is not just a blank nothingness, for without doubt it is the primal awareness of intrinsic awareness, radiant from the first. Self-existent, natural radiance is like sunlight." Is this indeed true? To confirm it, relax completely, looking directly at the nature of your mind.

"There is no doubt that it is impossible to objectify or grasp thought or the movement of memory. This capricious, changeable movement is like the cosmic wind!" Is this indeed so? To confirm it, relax completely, looking directly at the nature of your mind.

"Without doubt all appearances whatsoever are our own manifestation. All phenomena, whatsoever manifests, is like reflection in a mirror." Is this indeed so? To confirm it, relax completely, looking directly at the nature of your mind.

No experience is possible anywhere but in the mind, so there is nothing to see other than that seen at the moment of vision. No experience is possible anywhere but in the mind, so there is nothing to meditate upon other than mind. No experience is possible anywhere but in the mind, so there is nothing to do other than what is done in the mind. No experience is possible anywhere but in the mind, so there is no *samaya* to be sustained outside the mind. No experience is possible anywhere but in the mind, so there is no goal to be reached that is not in the mind.

Look, look, and look again. Look at your own mind!

Project your attention into external fields of space, and, attentively watching the nature of your mind, see if it moves. When you are convinced by observation that the mind does not move, retract your attention and concentrate upon the mind within, and look carefully for the projector of diffused thought. When you have decided that there is no entity responsible for thought patterns, look carefully for the color and shape of the mind. When you arrive at the emptiness that has no color or shape, look for a center or circumference. Certain that middle and margin are the same, search for an inside and an outside. Finding no distinction between inside and outside, you arrive at total presence, which is as vast as the sky.

"By virtue of its all-penetrating freedom this total presence that has no center or circumference, no inside or outside, is innocent of all partiality and knows no blocks or barriers. This all-penetrating intrinsic awareness is a vast expanse of space. All experience of samsara and nirvana arises in it like rainbows in the sky. In all its diverse manifestation it is but a play of mind."

You need only look out from the motionless space of intrinsic awareness at all experience, illusory like the reflection of the moon in water, to know the impossibility of dividing appearances from emptiness.

"In a state of total presence there is no separation of samsara and nirvana." Look out from the motionless space of intrinsic awareness at all experience, illusory like the reflection in a mirror, and no matter what manifests it can never be tasted, its existence can never be proved. In this dimension samsara and nirvana do not exist and everything is the *dharmakāya*.

All beings wandering in the three realms of samsara remain trapped in dualism until they realize that within their own perception resides the primal awareness that is the ultimate identity of all experience of samsara and nirvana. Due to the power of the delusive subject/object dichotomy, they hold samsara and nirvana to be different states of mind. They remain bound because, where in truth there is nonduality, they see a duality.

In reality no distinction between samsara and nirvana can exist in anybody's mind. However, when the worldly fool rejects some things and indulges in others, avoiding the "bad" and cultivating the "good," despising one while loving another, then due to partiality, prejudice, and bias, aimlessly he wanders through successive lives.

Rather than attain the spontaneously accomplished three modes of intrinsic awareness without striving, thick-headed aspirants explore the techniques and stages of many time-consuming methods of "self-improvement," leaving them no time to reach the seat of the Buddha.

"Emphatically, all phenomenal appearances whatsoever are one's own vision."[101] Look out from the state of motionless intrinsic awareness and all lightform and animate existence is like reflection. Appearances are empty, sound is empty, and indeed one's own nature is originally empty.

Similarly, turn your attention inward to the mind that is the viewer, and your thought processes, naturally subsiding, are empty like the sky, unstructured, free of conceptual elaboration, utterly indeterminable, beyond description, concept, and expression of any kind.

All events whatsoever are an illusory magical display of mind, and all the magical display of mind is baseless and empty. When you have realized that all events are your own mind, all visual appearances become the empty *dharmakāya*.

Appearances are not binding. It is through attachment to them that beings are fettered. Sever all delusive attachments, children of my heart!

Song Nine
Mist, Dream, and Optical Illusion

EHMAHO! Best beloved, fearless sons and daughters, without applying the spur, the horse will not gallop; without thorough churning, the butter will not separate; without detailed explanation, you will not be convinced of my meaning. So, while I sing my long but lyrical songs, listen in comfort, relaxed, without drooping ears!

Until you perceive all appearances as mind you will never realize the meaning of emptiness. To facilitate this understanding, you favored children must apply yourselves fully to a diligent analysis and thorough search. First, where do appearances come from? Second, where are they now? Last, where do they go?

During your examination you will see that just as mist arises out of the sky and dissolves back into the sky, appearances are the magical display of your mind, arising in the mind and vanishing back into it.

Take as an example the shimmering effect seen by a man with an impaired sense of vision when he gazes ahead. Although the shimmering appears to exist in front of his eyes, nothing is there—it is an optical illusion.

In the same way, when mental functions are impaired by negative propensities that cause clinging to apparently external objects as discrete and substantial entities, then visual and auditory phenomena appear to exist where not so much as an atom can be proved to have ultimate reality. Everything is a figment of mind.

All these figments of mind are baseless and empty. They are nonexistent lightforms, apparition, and magical illusion, like the reflection of the moon in water. Compose yourself in the reality of inseparable appearance and emptiness!

Now, in our sleep we may dream of our native country, our parental home, and our relatives or friends, as if they were actually present, and an appropriate strong feeling may arise. Although our family and friends are not actually present and we have not stirred an inch from our beds, we may experience a face-to-face encounter with them of the same vivid intensity as in the waking state.

Each and every sensual experience of our lives is an experience similar to last night's dream. Just as we attach labels to dream entities, objectifying and clinging to them as substantial entities, so appearances are modified and apprehended by mind in the waking state. In the same way that dreams have no substance, so the figments of the mind, all appearances whatsoever, are also empty.

Song Ten
The Mind-Created Universe

EHMAHO! Only children of my heart, most well-beloved! All appearances are indeterminate and equivocal, so much so that what some can see, others cannot.

Further, regarding the sentient beings of this world, some conceive of the world as earth, some conceive of the world as fire; some conceive of the world as wealth, and some conceive of the world as suffering.

Some sentient beings conceive of water as water, some conceive of water as fire, some conceive of water as nectar; some conceive of water as their home, while others conceive of water as earth.

Some sentient beings conceive of fire as fire, some conceive of fire as wealth; some conceive of fire as their home, while others conceive of fire as food.

Some sentient beings conceive of space as space, some conceive of space as their home, while others conceive of space as earth.

Thus, insofar as appearances are equivocal, they appear as they do through the power of the karmic proclivities of the perceiver. The four elements conceived as the four elements are human perceptions.

Other beings conceive of the earth as the fires of hell, as the farmers' wealth, or as the misery of the racially oppressed.

Likewise, the fire gods conceive of fire as enjoyment, hungry ghosts with bodies of fire conceive of it as their home, and fireflies conceive of it as food.

Likewise, regarding water, denizens of hell conceive of it as fire, hungry ghosts see it as pus and blood, elephants conceive of it as earth, the gods know it to be nectar, shape-shifting gods[102] conceive of it as jewels and a shower of flowers, and *nāgas* conceive of it as their home.

Finally, regarding space, all the gods conceive of space as earth, since they are made of space.

Furthermore, all phenomenal appearances manifest in whatever manner they have thus been perceptually defined.

When Devaputra asked Śākyamuni, "Who made Mount Meru, the sun, and the moon?" the Buddha himself said with his own lips: "In answer to that, surely no creator exists other than the karmic potentialities and habitual patterns and conditioning of our thought processes. These define and label appearances, reifying and objectifying them, forming them accordingly. All things are created by our own minds."

Again, Devaputra asked the Buddha, "Our habitual thought patterns and conditioning may inform the nature of appearances, but from whence comes the solidity and density of Mount Meru, the sun, the moon, and so on?" And the Buddha replied:

"In Benares there once lived an old woman who visualized herself as a tiger and transformed her human body into the body of a tiger, and the people of Benares, having set eyes upon her, fled, and the city was deserted. If in a very short time an old woman can effect such a transformation by visualization, is it indeed not probable that appearances have been created in the same way, when the mind has been conditioned by karmic propensities instilled from beginningless time?"

Thus all things are created by mind.

Further, Hindu sadhus are wont to visualize themselves in a solitary place in order to prevent distraction from the mundane hustle and bustle and diversions round about them, and after they have achieved living in a tangible solitude, even other people can recognize and appreciate it.

One Hindu yogin is alleged to have visualized a rock in the sky, and after it became as stone it impeded passage of the human body.[103]

Therefore, since all appearances are modified by conceptualization, they are the mind's self-manifest display, and all such manifestation is in reality empty.

Further, denizens of the short-lived hells conceive of their bodies as doors, pillars, ovens, ropes, and so on, and suffer the pain of it. In whatever way appearances are conceived in the mind, inevitably in that form they manifest.

All the pleasure and pain of all sentient beings of the six realms is created only by their own minds. On account of this, while you remain absorbed in equanimity, strive for conviction that all things are your own mind's illusory magical display, insubstantial appearances with an empty essence.

Further it is said in the scriptures that the three dimensions of microcosmic world systems of suffering beings exist in a single speck of pollen on a pistil of the lotus that Saint Mountain Lake, Muni Himavatsara, holds in his hand.

The scriptures also assert that when the yogin adept on the path of Immediate Crossing[104] has fully potentiated his vision of reality as total presence, he sees boundless buddhafields, and also boundless fields of residence of sentient beings of the six types, in each and every pore of his body. Into each of the six realms he projects emanations to transform the different beings, and the ultimate purpose of all those beings is served as in a dream.

In such ways all experience of samsara and nirvana is the natural and spontaneous manifestation of one's mind, and the ground of this spontaneous display is emptiness. You must cultivate and sustain conviction in the dimension of emptiness and radiance, remaining free of all attachment to it.

Furthermore, it is said that in a single speck of dust there are as many buddhafields of infinite dimension, and also innumerable realms of sentient beings of the six types, as there are motes of dust on the earth. The victorious buddhas have said that none of these buddhafields and realms of sentient beings intermingle, affect each other, or produce any ill omen.

And again, people say that in the stomach of every insect there is an infinite number of hives of microscopic insects. People also believe that in the reaches of space there are an infinite number of cities constructed upside down, and, likewise, innumerable other cities built on their side or right side up. If you question who made these cities in this way, the answer given by the victorious buddhas is that they were all conceived in the minds of the sentient beings who perceived them.

You must understand that the nature of mind, from the beginning, is like space, and that all experience is also, necessarily, like space. All relative visual and auditory experience is only the natural and spontaneous manifestation of mind in itself.

Although, indeed, there are changes in the mindstream at death, it is the mind's projections that change—there is no external change.

Since all experience is the manifestation of mind, all manifest appearances are baseless and empty. Sustain the experience of the state of total presence where there is no duality between radiance and emptiness, where there is luminous appearance without substance, like the reflection of the moon in water.

All visual appearances, everything that you see, are the spontaneous manifestation of mind. The chalice, the inert phenomena of the world that form a receptacle, is mind; the elixir, the animate existence of the six types of sentient beings that inhabit the world, is also mind; the blissful phenomena of gods and men of the upper realms are mind; the painful phenomena of the three lower realms are mind; the loss of awareness and the passion that manifests as the five poisons are mind; the noumena of total presence and primal awareness, self-existent and spontaneously arisen, are mind; the manifestations of negative thought processes created by cyclical mental habit patterns that potentiate transmigratory tendencies are mind; the manifestation of positive thought patterns, buddhafields, are mind; the phenomena of obstacles erected by hostile forces, spirits, and demons are mind; fully manifest divinity and spiritual powers are mind; the manifest diversity of discursive thought is mind; the phenomenon of one-pointed thoughtless trance is mind; the phenomena of apparent concrete entities with color and shape and other attributes are mind; that which is indeterminate and without specific characteristics is mind; phenomena in which there is no duality of unity and multiplicity are mind; phenomena that cannot be established in any way as either existent or nonexistent are mind.

There is no noumenal or phenomenal manifestation whatsoever that is not mind. The mind is like an artist. The body is created by mind, as are all the many worlds existing in the three dimensions of microcosmic world systems: all of them are also drawn by the mind. All beings possessing this puerile mind are seduced and inveigled by the pictures drawn by their thought processes.

Thus it is of crucial importance to cultivate absolute conviction that all things are the illusory, magical display of mind.

Such is my introduction initiating recognition of mental projections, the concepts of dualistic thought processes,[105] as mind.

Song Eleven
The Natural State of Gnostic Freedom

EHMAHO! Listen further, noble beloved sons and daughters of my heart! The Buddha taught that the creator of all these appearances mentioned above, mind in itself, has no knowable essence and neither color nor shape nor any other characteristic. From the beginning empty and intangible like the sky, the nature of mind is unquestionably empty and baseless.

However, although we may use the sky as a metaphor indicating the nature of mind, it is only pointing at mind's emptiness. Mind is also cognitive, its emptiness manifesting everything; the sky is noncognitive, an empty, blank nothingness. The sky, therefore, does not illustrate the nature of mind.

Such is my introduction initiating recognition of the nature of mind as empty.

The spontaneous efflorescence of the empty radiance of mind's nature manifests the infinite diversity of all and everything. Whatever arises seems like the reflection in a mirror, but there is no duality of viewer and vision—they are one in the space of emptiness.

Such is my introduction initiating recognition of emptiness as appearances.

From the very beginning appearances and emptiness are indivisible: because the mind is empty, appearances are unimpeded, and ungraspable phenomena arise in the dimension of emptiness as variegated radiance. Appearances, on the other hand, do not obstruct or fill emptiness: although they are manifest, their nature is originally empty.

For the yogin who realizes the indivisibility of phenomena and emptiness like a rainbow in the sky or the reflection of the moon in water, every experience of samsara and nirvana is a play of magical illusion. Watching the play of indivisible appearances and emptiness, the yogin whose intellect and mental processes are still is content.

Are your minds still, my beloved children? Look to see if the emptiness and appearances of your mind can actually be divided. Appearances and emptiness are indivisible.

Such is my introduction initiating recognition of indivisible appearances and emptiness.

It follows, then, that naturally indivisible appearances and emptiness, the inherent radiance of self-existent total presence, clear and alert, constitutes the three modes of buddha-being that are a spontaneously originated dynamic.[106]

Therefore, children of my heart, without regard for sessions and intervals of formal practice, in constant meditation sustain this recognition day and night.

Such is my introduction initiating recognition of natural, spontaneous gnostic liberation.

Song Twelve
The Crystal Metaphor and the Dynamic of Being

EHMAHO! Listen again to this vagrant's song! There are two ways of defining the three modes of being: in terms of total presence as the universal ground of being, and in terms of the process of appearances emanating from the total presence that is the universal ground.

Clearly understanding these two definitions you will intuitively recognize samsara and nirvana as pure lands of the three existential modes.

This is the definition of the three modes of being that structure original total presence. I have used this metaphor previously,[107] but here it is again:

Original intrinsic awareness is like a crystal ball: its emptiness is the *dharmakāya's* nature; its clear and natural glow is the *sambhogakāya;* and, as the unimpeded medium of whatever appears, it is the *nirmāṇakāya.*

That is how the three modes of being are defined as original total presence, and although they are not identical to it, neither are they separate from it.

Just as the five colors of the spectrum arise out of a crystal, so the manifestations of the ground of being arise out of original total presence. In the process of manifestation the pristine emanations of the buddhas' pure lands and the bewildering emanations of phenomena and of beings, all things whatsoever, are empty in essence, and this emptiness is the *dharmakāya;* their nature is radiant light, which is the *sambhogakāya;* and their unobstructed manifest diversity is the *nirmāṇakāya.*

That is how the three modes of being are defined as the process of manifestation of appearances in the universal ground of being.

The distinction between these two definitions is rarely made, but it is vital that it be clearly understood. It was made clear to me through Longchenpa's generous explanations.

If you understand this, then you know that the entire universe of phenomena and noumena and the energy that animates it is, and has been from the beginning, the spontaneously originated mandala[108] of the three modes of being, and that it is futile to look for the pure lands of the three modes anywhere else.

If people were capable of spontaneous reflexive recognition of just the six types of sentient life as the three modes of being, then without the necessity to perform even the slightest practice of meditation, they would all attain the buddhas' awakening.

Further, since the three modes of the ground of being are ultimately the *dharmakāya,* do not regard the three as different. Since the three modes of the process of manifestation in the ground of being are the *rūpakāya,* do not regard them as different either. Ultimately the *dharmakāya* and *rūpakāya* are also not different: in the dimension of the *dharmakāya,* emptiness is the one taste.

Finally, reaching the end of the path, after appearances manifesting in the ground have spontaneously dissolved back into the ground, when the dynamic of the universal *dharmakāya* is revealed, the ultimate goal is attained. Thereafter, without stirring from the space of the *dharmakāya,* the two aspects of the *rūpakāya (sambhogakāya* and *nirmāṇakāya)* are displayed like a rainbow, and there is an uninterrupted stream of activity for the sake of all beings.[109]

Song Thirteen
Instruction in Creative Emotivity

EHMAHO! Now listen once again to this vagrant singing! At one time or another all of you have been injured by others. Conscientiously recollect in detail how others have wrongfully accused you and victimized you, humiliating you and grinding you into the ground, and how you were shamed and deeply mortified. Brood on these things, letting hatred arise, and as it arises look directly at its essence, at hatred itself. Then discover first where the hatred comes from, second, where it is now, and finally where it goes. Look carefully for its color and shape, and any other characteristics.

Surely the vision of your anger is ultimately empty and ungraspable. Do not reject anger! It is mirror-like awareness itself.

Then, all you lovers, think of the beautiful man or woman in your heart. You gluttons, consider the food you crave—meat, cake, or fruit. You strutting peacocks, recall and dwell on the clothes you like to wear. You avaricious traders, think about the form of wealth you desire—horses, jewelry, or cash. Carefully considering these matters, allow desire to arise, and when it arises, look directly at its essence, at the greedy and lustful self. Then discover first where it comes from, second where it is now, and finally where it goes. Look carefully for its color and shape and any other characteristics.

This vision of your desire is ultimately empty and ungraspable. Do not reject it! It is discriminating awareness.

When you are tired, depressed, and dull, accept your sloth, and as it arises gaze directly at its essence. Who is it that is slothful? First, where does it come from? Then, where is it now? And finally, where does it go?

This vision of your sloth is ultimately empty and ungraspable. Do not reject your stupidity! It is awareness of the vast plenum of space, the reality-continuum.

Then think about your class and status, your race and influence and your wealth. Consider how handsome or beautiful you are, and how pleasant and effective your voice. Recall to what extent you are virtuous and successful in study, contemplation, and meditation, in reading and writing, in learning in the sciences and arts, and also in the ritual arts, and in converting and controlling others, and so forth. After considering your talents and virtues, thinking that you are a little superior to others, allow pride to arise. As it appears, look directly at its essence, at pride itself. Discover first where it comes from, then where it is now, and finally where it goes. Look carefully at its color and shape, and for any other characteristics.

This vision of your pride is ultimately empty and ungraspable. Do not reject your pride! It is awareness of sameness.

Then consider how others are much more influential and wealthy than you. Recall their talent and success, their large numbers of followers, their wisdom and ability in the arts and sciences, their superior singing, oratory, and effective speech, their superior knowledge of life and how to live it, and their worldly wisdom and persuasiveness. After you have considered all the talents and virtues of others, allow the fear that they are superior to yourself to arise, together with envy and jealousy. Upon its arising gaze directly into the essence of jealousy, at jealousy itself. From where does it come? Where is it now? And finally where does it go? Look carefully at its color and shape and at any other characteristic.

This vision of your envy is ultimately empty and ungraspable. Do not reject your jealousy! It is all-accomplishing awareness.

If you intuit the nature of your passions in this way, emotional defilement becomes primal awareness. How ridiculous to expect to find primal awareness and emptiness after you have suppressed passion! How tragic to spend your life searching for something in a place where it is inconceivable that you should find it!

After you have realized the five poisons as emptiness by this method, it is unnecessary to examine every passion that arises as described in this introduction; there is no need to search for the seat of the passion, its present location, its eventual destination, its color and shape, and so on.

Once you have understood the five poisons as emptiness, avoid pursuing the passion from the moment it arises. Relax into your own nature, into the nature of mind, and without doubt the emotion will naturally subside and vanish.

Such is my introduction initiating recognition of transformed emotional expression, and such also is my instruction in purification through creative emotional efflorescence.[110]

If you have practiced purification through creative emotional efflorescence by the method described above in the past, henceforth whenever the five poisons—defiling passions—arise, by virtue of your habitual reflexive recognition of their hidden core, emptiness and primal awareness will arise as one. Then, the release and arising of appearances are simultaneous—the release and arising of appearances are simultaneous!

In the biographies and teaching of the lamas of the past, the axiom "The greater the passion and the greater intensity of discursive thought the greater the *dharmakāya*" occurs frequently. Know that it means exactly what it says!

For beginners, when powerful and intense emotion arises it is best to examine the passion and then to rest in equanimity.

This is the lama's personal advice, so keep it in your heart.

Such is my introduction initiating recognition of spontaneous release of the five poisons.

Song Fourteen:
Instruction in the One Taste of Sense Impressions

EHMAHO! Once more listen to me, beloved sons and daughters who I treasure like my heart! Wrap soft, silken clothes around your body and observe the mind that thinks How soft! Wrap coarse yak wool or sheepskin around your body and observe the mind that thinks How coarse! When observing the mind, emptiness is the one taste in both perceptions.

Look at the form of a beautiful statue or a great painting and observe the mind that thinks How beautiful! Look at the form of a hideous frog and observe the mind that thinks How repulsive! When looking at the mind, emptiness is the one taste in both perceptions.

Put something sweet like molasses or honey in your mouth, and observe the mind that thinks How sweet! Then taste something like ginger and look at the mind that thinks How pungent! When observing the mind, in both perceptions emptiness is the one taste.

Smell something aromatic like sandalwood incense and look at the mind that thinks How pleasing! Then smell something repugnant like asafetida or wild garlic and look at the mind that thinks How foul! When observing the mind, emptiness is the one taste in both perceptions.

Listen to the sound of a bell, a lute, or flute, and observe the mind that thinks How lyrical! Listen to the sound of stones grating or hands clapping and look at the mind that thinks What cacophony! When observing the mind, emptiness is the one taste in both perceptions.

Imagine that you are reborn as a world emperor ruling the lands of the four continents, that you are surrounded by an entourage of queens and ministers, in a palace constructed out of the five types of precious substance (gold, silver, turquoise, coral, and pearl), where you are eating a feast of a hundred tastes. When such a vision arises in your mind, watch the mind that thinks How delightful! Then imagine yourself a beggar without even a single companion, with nowhere to lay your head but a cowshed, where rain drips in from above and moisture seeps up from below, your body afflicted by many diseases, your hands and feet rotting off from leprosy, tormented by so many troubles that truly you know the meaning of suffering. When such a vision arises in your mind, watch the mind that thinks Oh, the pain! Observing the mind, in both happiness and sadness, emptiness is the one taste.

After you have realized the emptiness of the six sense fields in this way, whenever any positive or negative feeling arises from any of these fields, you need not examine them as in this introduction. Every perception is without foundation, released from the beginning and empty; and refraining from pursuing any of them at the moment of their inception, relax into your own space, into the nature of your mind. Undoubtedly every sense impression is spontaneously released.

Such is my introduction initiating recognition of the spontaneous release of the six sense fields.

Song Fifteen
The Nonduality of Quiescence and Movement

EHMAHO! Again listen attentively, my noble sons and daughters! Relax, let yourself be at rest in the free space of mind's original nature, and observe the quiescent state of the mind. Gazing into the mind at rest, you abide in the infinite space of total presence. Know, therefore, beloved children of my heart, that a quiescent mind is an empty mind in a state of total presence.

Such is my introduction initiating recognition of quiescence as an adornment of mind.[111]

Then, as thought moves in the mind, observe how it is manifest: it moves not the slightest degree out of the space of empty and radiant total presence. Know, therefore, that an active mind is still an empty mind in a state of total presence, beloved sons and daughters.

Such is my introduction initiating recognition of the movement of mind as its play.

No matter how large or violent the rolling wave, it cannot escape the ocean for a moment. In the same way, mind, passive or active, cannot escape total presence and emptiness to the slightest degree. If it is quiescent, it is in a state of total presence, so you can relax. If it is active, whatever arises is the radiant glow of total presence itself, so again, relax.

The assertion that mind in quiescence is in meditation and that an active mind is out of meditation signifies failure to understand the inherent emptiness of both quiescence and activity, and it indicates that quiescence, movement, and total presence, these three,[112] are not yet fused into one.

Therefore, best beloved sons and daughters of my heart, because quiescence and movement are both states of total presence, and because in the past you have fully comprehended both these states separately, now in your existential praxis you should condition yourself in the experience of quiescence, movement, and total presence as one.

Such is my introduction initiating recognition of nondual quiescence and movement.

Song Sixteen
Introduction to Dzogchen—with Cautions

EHMAHO! Listen, only beloved children of my heart, listen with your ears attentive and calm! Set the sweet melodies of this vagrant minstrel, Tsogdrug Rangdrol, upon the white peaks of your heart with the Sweet-Voiced Maiden![113]

When we have established that all experience is the one taste of emptiness, we have no attachment or aversion to samsara or nirvana. The error of apprehending external entities either as aliens or allies, as enemies or friends, is precluded. No "self and other" dichotomy arises in any situation: all things are known as the one taste of emptiness.

The following is a complete exposition distilled into aphorisms. In the pinnacle of approaches to buddhahood,[114] the Great Perfection, known as *Dzogchen*, the whole of samsara and nirvana has been realized as unfounded and acausal.

From the beginning *Buddha*, or full awareness, is the one taste of reality. In the Dzogchen dimension there is no distinction between gods and demons. In the land of Dzogchen there are no buddhas and no sentient beings. In the ground of Dzogchen there are no moral dualities. There is no near or far on the Dzogchen path. There is no attainment or nonattainment of the Dzogchen goal. There is no correct or incorrect behavior in Dzogchen. There is no meditation or nonmeditation in the reality of Dzogchen. Such is Dzogchen vision.

When we realize this Dzogchen vision, all constructs pertaining to the gross and subtle planes of the three doors subside, and thereafter, like tangled wool made manageable by moistening, the three doors—body, speech, and mind—reach a state of quiet, self-directed responsiveness.

Coincident with the development of a happy, glowing, thought-free samadhi is the birth of authentic compassion, which is like the love a mother holds for her only son, except that here the love is directed toward all beings roaming in samsara who lack the Dzogchen vision. This compassion is a very special feature of Dzogchen vision, and this you must know.

After you have resolved that all things are empty, if then in your conduct you abandon virtue and no longer shrink from vice, you have fallen under the spell of a demon of infinite and intense evil. It is crucial to avoid this demonic pitfall.

Such are my introductions initiating recognition of Dzogchen, the Great Perfection.

The following introductory advice about Dzogchen is crucial. While you have yet to realize that all visual and auditory experiences of the relative, external world are totally empty, when you contemplate Dzogchen vision you will tend to ask Why meditate? In order to counteract this tendency, remember to perform these exercises:

While making supplication to the lama, observe your mind. From time to time, when you are in a relaxed state of concentration, observe your mind intently. At these times you will feel totally contented, and appearances will arise as emptiness so vividly that you will think, Although I can touch those things out there with my hand, there is really nothing there! Profound affirmations and confident thoughts will certainly follow, like, This is definitely the Dzogchen vision! At such times you will gain confidence in your vision. But do not spoil it by clinging to it. Just relax in spacious detachment.

Even if you do not practice what is transmitted in this introduction, if you have understood that everything manifests from your own heart center as reflexive forms of emptiness, at the time of death, no matter what fears arise in the *bardo,* you will attain the buddhas' awakening in the universal ground, pure from the beginning.

He who practices the substance of this introduction without having received the transmission is like someone who starts in error on the first day and remains in error until the fifteenth. To say, I have realized emptiness! when you have not yet understood that there is no reality in any experience of the relative world is a great falsehood.

In order to avoid such pitfalls at the outset, as described above, sit at your lama's feet, and having established the nature of your original existential condition through direct transmission, you will avoid any deviation, double binds, and pitfalls that may arise later on. Therefore, my dearest children, keep this advice in your hearts.

Song Seventeen
Aphoristic Instruction on the Dzogchen Path

EHMAHO! Once more, most beloved sons and daughters, listen! After you have fully intuited and established the original existential condition of the Dzogchen vision, you must utterly sever the ties of attachment and aversion to your family and homeland.

Go alone to the forest or to a mountain hermitage. Abandon all physical work and dwell at ease; cease all verbal expression and remain in silence; transcend all objects of thought and let your mind merge with space. In this state, relax, without attempting to change anything, and without diffusion or fixation of your consciousness.

When the mind is free of all ambition and all belief supports, that is Dzogchen vision. Abide in a state of nonmeditation. Realize Dzogchen's goal of nonattainment.

Further, when you are composed in equanimity, living the vision, do not become entangled in any web of judgmental thought by saying to yourself Now I've arrived at a state of total presence! or Now I'm caught in manic depression! No, stay wakeful in the continuum of reality without any notion of present or future attainment, flexible and responsive in unobstructed freedom.

You cannot perceive nonconceptual truth with your structured intellect, and you cannot reach the place of nonaction through temporal activity. If you want to attain the nonconceptual goal of nonaction, rest in naked total presence free of dualistic grasping.

The supreme vision is free of all conceptual duality. Supreme meditation is freedom from the cultivation of some attributes and rejection of others. Supreme action is beyond all striving and effort. The supreme goal is ever immanent, beyond aspiration.

Looking for *it,* the vision cannot be seen: cease your search. *It* cannot be discovered through meditation, so abandon your trance states and mental images. *It* cannot be accomplished by anything you do, so give up the attempt to treat the world as magical illusion. *It* cannot be found by seeking, so abandon all hope of results.

Do not be biased or partial, thus spoiling your free and easy uncontrived consciousness of the here and now by clinging attachments. This radiant insubstantiality, total presence of the here and now, this is the *summum bonum* of all vision. This all-pervasive, all-embracing object of mind transcending the intellect, this is the *summum bonum* of all meditations. This unforced, detached, free, and easy spontaneity, this is the *summum bonum* of all behavior. This unsought, spontaneous accomplishment, present from the beginning, this is the summit of all attainments.

The matrix of vision is observation of emptiness and radiance without clinging to it. The matrix of meditation is maintenance of reflexive release without clinging to it. The matrix of action is relaxation with a free and easy response to the six sense fields. The matrix of the goal is collapse of all expectation and apprehension.

When the mind has no limitations, we see the sovereign vision. When it has no point of reference, we practice sovereign meditation. When we are free of all inhibition and indulgence, we perform sovereign activity. When mind is free of hope and fear, we have attained the sovereign goal.

As there is nothing to see, abandon all fixed ideas, all preconceived notions, and all parameters of vision. As there is nothing upon which to meditate, let be whatever arises adventitiously. As there is no particular way to behave, give up evaluation, judgment, and criticism. As there is nothing to attain, forsake all expectation of results.

Whatsoever can be is total presence, so do not cling to any one thing. Nothing is *it*, so do not judge and criticize. No intellectual concepts are valid, so do not presume.

Primally pure intrinsic awareness, naturally radiant, transcends the intellect and objects of mind, so there is nothing to see. As its essence has no root or ground, there is nothing to meditate upon. As its reflexive release is beyond all limitations and extremes, there is nothing to do based on conscious and rational design. As it is beyond striving, accomplishment, and ambition, there is no fruition.

Its essence is emptiness, so abandon self-denial and self-improvement. Its nature is empty radiance, so let your diligent effort drop away. Everything is unobstructed, so forget your preferences. Just as phenomena arise, let them be, and do not cling to them.

The yogin's perception is like the flight path of a bird in the sky. The bird's flight path vanishes without trace: each previous perception vanishes without repercussion—do not attempt to prolong a perception by pursuing it and clinging to it. The bird's future flight path is as yet nonexistent: do not anticipate the next perception. The present bird print in the sky is colorless and shapeless: the present perception has an ordinary, unremarkable form— leave it alone and refrain from contaminating it or modifying it by applying antidotes.

Just as phenomena arise let them be and do not cling! This is the radical, essential practice during the daily round. If you do not cling to whatever, or however, phenomena appear, emotional defilements, naturally freed, are sublime, primal awareness.

The vision is unoriginated, nonconceptual, capable of any departure whatsoever, for in intense concentration the vision has no specific content. Meditation is a natural, innate process of being free, for in intense meditation there is nonmeditation. Conduct is a performance of magical illusion, innocent of any distinction between giving and taking, abstinence and indulgence, for intense activity is purposeless. The nature of the goal is absence of both hope of attainment and fear of failure, for with intense practice the goal vanishes.

In past, present, and future the mind is acausal and baseless. Its spontaneous manifestation of vivid appearances is a constant wonder. From the first to the last, the nature of all experience is pure! miraculously arisen! eternally free! completely free! effortlessly accomplished! This ordinary consciousness, unforced and authentic, is the buddhas' dynamic, a vast space without limitation.

What is more, with effort, examining and contemplating the mind, you do not see its intrinsic original nature. In the unthinkable, inscrutable, ordinary nature of reality there is neither meditation nor nonmeditation, neither distraction nor nondistraction. Many are liberated through natural no-meditation.[115]

In the unthinkable, inscrutable, ordinary nature of reality there is no difference between freedom and bondage. No matter what arises, when you perceive your original nature the joy arises automatically—and what joy!

Trapped by the thought of desiring thoughtlessness, conflicting thoughts multiply, and in mounting frenzy you run aimlessly hither and thither. Relax and merge into the primal space of total presence, which is free of coming and going. Cut loose and just let it be. Then, ready for anything, you remain firm and stable, as solid as rock.

Grasp this paradox,[116] my sons and daughters! There is not so much as a mote of dust upon which to meditate, but it is crucial to sustain unwavering attention with presence of mind.

Song Eighteen
Obstacles to Dzogchen Practice

EHMAHO! Once more gather round and listen, my children! It is absurd to try to purify external objects, which are insubstantial appearances, the natural forms of emptiness. They are empty from the beginning, like the reflection of the moon in water.

It is absurd to apply forceful antidotes to thoughts and concepts, to internal objects. They vanish by themselves without trace. It is absurd to try to improve mind's manifestations with your renunciation, your practice of self-improvement, or your hopes and fears. They are free from the beginning and primal awareness by nature.

Do not dress up total presence, which is naked clarity itself, in the clothes of elaborate intellectual analysis. Rather, rest in relaxation in that magnificent sameness that is without partiality. Stay free and easy, without a care in the world, in the place where there is no residue to perception.

No matter what thoughts arise in that space, know them to be the natural radiance of impartial and spontaneously existent total presence. Then we are able to let go of the mental residue of perception. Abandoning the manifestations of mind to vast all-embracing space as the play of elusive, effervescent, shimmering reality, we immediately reach the plenum of Kuntu Zangpo's dynamic mind.

The foregoing is called the universal, self-liberating yoga of the naturally accomplished and originally liberated Great Perfection.

Although we do not move, we arrive at the buddhas' seat. Although we do not practice, the goal is spontaneously accomplished. Although we do not abandon emotional defilements, they are purified as they stand. Thus our mind is the same as the dynamic minds of the great lamas, and following in their footsteps our karma is exhausted.

You should understand the enormous significance of this, my sons and daughters. By the generosity of the wise old man Chokyi Gyelpo, I, Tsogdrug Rangdrol, attained the spontaneously originated, dynamic mind of Vagrant Nonaction.[117]

This nonaction may be crucial, but it is not understood by some. Everything is already done, but they say, "I must work hard!" Everything has been liberated from the beginning, but they say, "I want to be free!" Everything is at rest from the beginning, but they say, "I want peace of mind!" The mind is in meditation from the beginning, but they say, "I must meditate!" The vision exists from the beginning, but they say, "I must see it!" The goal is attained from the first, but they say, "I must reach it!"

People who trust in an analytical view are learned, but they know only the taste of dead words and divisive concepts. They claim understanding, but it is an idle boast. They meditate, but their meditation consists of mental structures. They examine the mind, but cling to duality. They are successful, but it is all in samsara.

It is certain that the intellectual with an analytical view of reality has no connection with the Heart Essence of the Great Perfection, the Dzogchen Nyingtig.[118] No specific activity is necessary, for action does not lead to the exhaustion of karmic activity. It is beyond reckoning in terms of action and inaction.

In the nonmeditation beyond meditation, meditation is detrimental. Beyond vision, where there is nothing to see, upon what can you focus? Beyond seeking, where there is no seeking, there is no finding. Total presence is direct recognition of the here and now.

How ridiculous that someone should have this explained and not listen. Such a person has no connection with Dzogchen.

When you observe something that is arising in a dynamic mind of immense space, utterly pure from the beginning, then there is no duality of samsara and nirvana.

To have taken this mind as the subject of my song will indubitably please the victorious buddhas of the past, present, and future.

"However," you may ask, "although at first I may rest free and easy when perceiving external, delusive objects of mind, later will I not again regress into bewilderment?"

The answer to your question is that ordinary individuals attached to their ego will certainly go astray. But as for the yogin who understands all appearances as causeless and baseless and who refrains from attempting to change himself or phenomena, rejecting some things and cultivating others, he will not err because he is naturally composed in detached equanimity.

"Are there no potential traps or dilemmas in this dimension?" you may further inquire.

There is no pitfall or trap possible on this path. Dilemmas and traps are caused by clinging and attachment. If there is no attachment to anything that may arise, what can possibly be the cause of downfall?

However, when total presence arises coemergent with an object, looking at the essence of the thought of what has arisen should not be considered the meditation. The crucial practice is to constantly sustain the aspect of total presence that is naked radiance.

Furthermore, when total presence is quiescent, neither diffused nor concentrated, the lack of concepts and thoughts associated with the quiescent aspect is not the central point of the meditation. In that state you should sustain clarity and strength of mind, crystal clear and acutely awake.

If you fail to understand this vital point and think, "Observing either diffusion or quiescence of mind is the essence of meditation," you will go astray, my sons. Mere quiescence is a trance state of the gods and mere diffusion is ordinary conceptualization. You may meditate on these, but you will not attain buddhahood.

In short, until you realize your goal, at all times whatsoever you should sustain the aspect of total presence that is naked, unobstructed clarity, maintaining a vivid awareness of it as a crystal ball. After your goal is attained, continue to sustain constant identification with that state.

It is said that the central reality of the vision of Cutting Through[119] is total presence, and that total presence should be sustained in all its radiant clarity by stripping the mind naked. This point is of unique importance. It is an aphorism reduced from a hundred words, so remember it well, beloved sons and daughters.

Song Nineteen
The Four Infallible Guiding Stars and the Four Unshakable Bolts

EHMAHO! Once again, sons and daughters of my heart, listen with devotion and respect! Here is instruction on the four infallible guiding stars. The infallible guiding star of vision is called a guiding star because of its unfailing radiance: it is vivid perception of the here and now. The infallible guiding star of meditation is called a guiding star because of its unfailing radiance: it is vivid perception of the here and now. The guiding star of action is called a guiding star because of its unfailing radiance: it is vivid perception of the here and now. The infallible guiding star of the goal is called a guiding star because of its unfailing radiance: it is vivid perception of the here and now.

Here is instruction on the four Unshakable bolts. The Unshakable bolt of unchangeable vision is vivid perception of the here and now, and it is called an Unshakable bolt because of its permanence throughout past, present, and future. The Unshakable bolt of unchangeable meditation is vivid perception of the here and now, and it is called an Unshakable bolt because of its permanence throughout past, present, and future. The Unshakable bolt of unchangeable conduct is vivid perception of the here and now, and it is called an Unshakable bolt because of its permanence throughout past, present, and future. The Unshakable bolt of the unchangeable goal is vivid perception of the here and now, and it is called an Unshakable bolt because of its permanence throughout past, present, and future.

There are a vast number of different visions, but in the self-existent intrinsic awareness of the here and now, which is pure awareness, there is no duality of vision and viewer. Do not look at the vision but look for the viewer. Looking for the creator of the vision, if you fail to find him, then your vision is at the point of resolution. This vision in which there is nothing at all to see, but which is not a blank nothingness of ultimate void, is vivid and unalloyed perception of the here and now: this is Dzogchen vision.

There are innumerable dissimilar methods of meditation, but in the unobstructed clarity, which is ordinary perception of the here and now, there is no duality of meditation and meditator. Do not perform the meditation but look for the meditator. Searching for the meditator, if you fail to find him, then your meditation is at the point of resolution. This meditation in which there is no meditating whatsoever, free of depression and elation, free of cloudy vision and sluggishness, is the natural radiance and unalloyed perception of the here and now—it is meditation fixed in uncontrived sameness.

There is an infinite variety of different modes of behavior, but in the cosmic seed of intrinsic awareness and pure awareness there is no duality of action and actor. Do not perform the action but look for the actor. Searching for the actor, if you fail to find him, then your conduct is at the point of resolution. This conduct, in which there is no activity whatsoever but which is not governed by delusive habit patterns, is the unforced, natural radiance of perception of the here and now—this is immediate, immaculate action, where nothing whatsoever is contrived or forced and nothing is inhibited or indulged.

There are innumerable goals, but in the spontaneously originated, effortlessly accomplished intrinsic awareness of the three existential modes, there is no duality of accomplishment and he who achieves the goal. Without striving for the goal, seek the *sādhaka,* the yogin on the path. By looking for he who is accomplishing the goal and failing to find him, you are at the point of achievement. This goal in which there is no striving for accomplishment, completely free of renunciation and cultivation, hopes and fears, is the spontaneously natural radiance of total presence that is perception of the here and now: this is empty, natural radiance of the three existential modes of the Buddha manifest. It is the ultimate goal of buddhahood.

Song Twenty
Signs of Nonduality

EHMAHO! And again, beloved sons and daughters, listen well!

If you sustain this practice unwaveringly from the beginning until you abandon yourself totally in complete freedom, there will be no stirring from the supreme truth and no departure from the here and now.

When there is no distinction between appearances and emptiness, then perfect vision is realized. When there is no distinction between dream and the waking state, then perfect meditation is realized. When there is no distinction between pleasure and pain, then perfect conduct is realized. When there is no distinction between this life and the next, then your original existential condition is realized. When there is no distinction between your mind and the sky, then the *dharmakāya* is realized. When there is no distinction between your own mind and buddha-mind, then the goal is realized.

Song Twenty-one
Supportive Exercises and Advice

EHMAHO! Once again, beloved children, listen to me! Regard this corporeal body like the reflection of the moon in water. Perceive all vocal expression as echo. Dissolve the multitude of your mental concepts in the purity of their own nature.

Live all visual and auditory experience without attachment, as hallucination, a dream, the reflection of the moon in water, a fairy palace in the sky, a distortion of sight, an apparition, a bubble, and an echo. Perform all your daily activity in this state. Without making any division between sessions of meditation and the intervals between them, practice constantly, day and night.

Do not seek to alter your thoughts in any way. Leave them in their natural state, without forcing them or adulterating them. Let them alone as empty radiance, without clinging to them, and thus allow self-expression to release itself by itself. Let them be, without reification, without meditation, without any effort, and leaving no trace whatsoever.

Treat all past thought as the trackless path of a bird in the sky, all present perception as clear dustless space, and all future thought as the water in a mill with its sluice gate closed. Without cultivating or modifying any thought, with a free and easy attitude, leave thoughts alone in their natural state of open space.

Treat all gross and subtle concepts, the three poisons, the five poisons, and so on, like thieves entering an empty house. Treat external appearances of the six sense fields, which leave no residue in the mind, like a city of magical illusion.

In short, regarding creation, existence, and cessation; the ground, the path, and the goal; vision, meditation, conduct, and fruition; time, place, and verbal expression; the disposition and the disposer; liberation and the liberator; and so forth: when the innate radiance of all these events is unaffected by evaluation and judgment and one is free of effort and striving, without clinging or any partiality, then moment by moment every single experience is brought to a final and certain resolution, without attachment, in the ultimate purity of the empty continuum of mind—like droplets of water merging in the great ocean.

So do not be disheartened when during meditation many thoughts disturb you and you think, This is not meditation. The mind may be actively generating thought, but because mind is empty, thought is also empty. Since whatever arises is a state of total presence, do not attempt any alteration based on judgment and evaluation, but leave it alone in its natural, authentic, uncontrived state. In that way, thought will certainly be released into its own natural purity.

◊ ◊ ◊

If you are a practitioner of lesser capacity, unable to stay in the natural state, you should practice a combination of examination followed by rest in equanimity, as described in the introductions.[120]

Alternatively, you can force thought to its own demise: provoke relevant or irrelevant thoughts and then pursue them, one after the other, in various ways, prolonging each thought until the mind is exhausted. Finally, when you have no more grasping, rest in ease.

Another method is to meditate upon the real lama in the center of your heart. Keep your mind fixed on him for as long as possible, and then, finally, letting go, rest in the state of total presence.

Or again, meditate upon a tiny point of bright light[121] in the center of your heart. Imagine it descending until it reaches the seat of Indra (the navel center). This method will certainly destroy diffused or rampant thought. When agitation is stilled, rest in the state of total presence. When torpor is present, sharpen your gaze, and after stripping total presence naked, sustain the radiance.

Or, as a further option, imagine your mind as a light-seed, and when the image is still, shout "PHAT!"[122] Instantaneously the mind shoots from the fontanel like an arrow, and you should imagine it mixing with the clarity of the sky. Then identify your intellect with the nature of the sky. It is impossible that your torpor will not be eliminated by this method. When it has vanished, rest in a state of detachment.

Since this advice is the result of personal experience, remember it well.

Without being trapped by thought of desire for thoughtlessness, increasing the dimensions of total presence, abandon yourself to it smoothly, and be happy and free in that vast, open space.

Initially (in your practice of meditation), thought is like a rushing river at the bottom of a gorge. In the middle, it flows calmly and majestically like the river Gaṅgā. Finally, just as all rivers become of one flavor in the ocean, so thought is resolved in the state where the mother-light merges with the son-light.

In particular, whatever disease, hostile spirits, or apparitions afflict you, do not make any attempt to ward them off by magical rites. Rather, practice the following meditation that attacks the problem directly and reduces the affliction to the same taste as all other experience.

Go to a spot that tends to breed fear—to a forest, a burning ground, or an island—or to an isolated garden, a rock cave, or an empty house, or go sit under a tree, for instance, and visualize the following. Transmute your own body, the vessel and its contents, all phenomena and noumena, into elixir. Then offer the elixir to all the buddhas and bodhisattvas of the ten directions. After they have been satisfied, they dissolve into light with a disposition of loving-kindness, and the whole of samsara and nirvana is completely filled with the elixir of clear light. Then, with your elixir that liberates by taste, you satisfy all beings under the sky. The oath-bound spirits and Dharma protectors, who are qualities and talents, become your guests, and then the supreme field of compassion consisting of the sentient beings of the six realms, as well as all karmic creditors, hostile spirits, obstructive forces, and elementals—all are satiated.

Then, with the conviction that samsara and nirvana are of one taste, in the unalloyed nature of mind that is the *dharmakāya,* walk and sit, run and jump, talk and laugh, cry and sing. Alternately subdued and agitated, act like a lunatic. Finally, abide in a state of peace and happiness.[123]

At nighttime, sleep peacefully and naturally, free of all discursiveness, free of diffused or concentrated thought. Sleep in the space inherent within, maintaining perfect attention to pure potential.

When you practice in the above manner, disease and hostile spirits are automatically assuaged and pacified. Your view and meditation are then brought to resolution, your realization is like the sky, your meditation is naturally radiant, and you act like a child. Without any frame or points of reference you act spontaneously, like a madman. Making no distinction between self and others, you are a saint. Detached from whatever you say, your speech is like melodious echo. Without desire for anything at all you are like a garuda soaring aloft; you are like a fearless, intrepid lion. All is free from the beginning, like bright clouds in the sky. Such a yogin is a real *sugata*, a *vidyādhara*. He is worthy of enormous respect and homage. He is even far superior to the wish-fulfilling gem.

Song Twenty-two
Interiorization of the Mandala

EHMAHO! And yet again, my beloved sons and daughters, listen to the song of this vagrant! Vairocana is not outside; he exists within. He is the reality-continuum *(dharmadhātu),* the nature of mind free of movement, the true nature of sloth, pure as it stands. That is the real Bhagavan Vairocana.

Vajrasattva is not outside; he exists within. He is the mirror, the unobstructed medium of creative total presence, the true nature of anger, pure as it stands. That is the real Bhagavan Vajrasattva.

Ratnasambhava is not outside; he exists within. He is the sameness that rejects nothing and indulges nothing, judges nothing and evaluates nothing, the true nature of pride, pure as it stands. That is the real Bhagavan Ratnasambhava.

Amitābha is not outside; he exists within. He is sensory discrimination, where pleasure and emptiness vanish into the continuum of space, the true nature of desire, pure as it stands. That is the real Bhagavan Amitābha.

Amoghasiddhi is not outside; he exists within. He is total accomplishment, total presence arising unimpeded and naturally liberated, the true nature of jealousy, pure as its stands. That is the real Bhagavan Amoghasiddhi.[124]

Song Twenty-three
Exteriorization of the Mandala

EHMAHO! Once again my best beloved heart sons, listen with rising joy to my vajra song! When you realize that the Five Buddhas are inherent in the mind's nature and in emotional defilement, then the whole of phenomenal creation and the life therein is a book of instruction and is itself the ultimate mandala. On the parchment of diverse red and white phenomena,[125] the bamboo quill of self-existent primal awareness and total presence inscribes baseless, unattached ciphers liberated from the beginning, creating images to be read in the space of coemergent appearances and emptiness.

This spontaneously accomplished mandala, which is the entire three dimensions of microcosmic world systems, is consecrated by the natural sprinkling of rainwater; its streets and alleyways form the natural lines of its design; our footprints are the dots of colored powder; our own bodies of apparent emptiness are the existential mode of the Yidam buddha-deity; our speech of auditory emptiness is vajra recitation (of mantra); our thought, detached and naturally liberated, is the buddha-deity's spirit; and all the movements of our limbs are the buddha-deity's *mudrā*.

Food and drink are offerings of the nature of reality, and all phenomenal form is the buddha-deity's body; the expression of all articulated sound is music. There is nothing to protect and nothing to be impaired in this natural *samaya*.

Whatsoever the yogin who practices in this manner does, he need not rely upon a path of cause and effect and diligent striving, because in the space of clear-light reality, his instruction, the creative stage of meditation, and the *samayas* are naturally fulfilled. To attain quickly the great miracle of the ultimate power, without striving, is the special characteristic of the Great Perfection, my heart sons and daughters.

When we practice like this consistently, just as clouds vanish into the sky, the welter of thoughts and concepts of samsara and nirvana dissolve into the primal ground of being.

After the *dharmakāya* is revealed as the clear light of intrinsic awareness like the radiant, unobscured solar mandala, we are able to raise the dead and comprehend the mysteries, and demonstrating various miracles we can direct beings.

After perfecting all the qualities of the ten stages and the five paths without exception, individuals of superior capacity are liberated into the pure ground of being in this lifetime, individuals of middling capacity at the moment of death, and those of lesser capacity in the *bardo* (the after-death state). Thereafter, remaining forever inseparable from the pure awareness of the three modes of being in the continuum of reality, emanating apparitional bodies to transform all beings in whatever way is required, we work unremittingly to give ultimate meaning to all sentient beings.

Keep the significance of these words in your mind, and surely the inner sun of happiness will shine upon us.

He who has expressed such aspiration in song is the vagrant Tsogdrug Rangdrol. Through its virtue may all those many aspirants who have such good fortune swiftly dissolve all the defilements inherent in loss of awareness, and in emotion and thought, in the primal continuum of purity. May they attain the goal of buddhahood in this lifetime.

Colophon

This song of the vision of Cutting Through to the clear light of the Great Perfection, which has the potential of leading us quickly through the stages and paths, is called *The Flight of the Garuda*. It is based on many scriptural treasures of Dzogchen: *Introduction to Direct Vision of Total Presence* by Orgyen Rinpoche; *Seven Treasures; Three Chariots; An Afterword on the Great Perfection: The Three Cycles of Space; The Vast Cloud of Profound Truth; Heartdrop of the Dzogchen Ḍākinī;* and *Buddha in the Palm of the Hand,* all by Longchenpa.[126] The secret instruction of my lamas and my own meditation experience decorate its margins. It is written by Jatang Tsogdrug Rangdrol for the sake of many devoted disciples. May it cause boundless advantage to the tradition and to sentient beings.

Since these vajra songs were composed for all those concerned with liberation, they should be sung by yogins when they are focusing upon Dzogchen vision. As the knowledge-bearer Śrī Siṃha[127] said regarding the purpose of such songs:

> *Buddha-mind is all-pervasive; sentient beings' awareness is fragmented:*
> *To create openness like the sky is of great advantage.*

So, just as Śrī Siṃha advises, identify total presence with the vast space of the sky, infinitely increasing its height and depth, and out of this space, which embraces all sentient beings, sing these songs to benefit your meditation on vision.

Samaya! Sarva maṅgalam!
Maintain the commitment! May all beings be happy!

THE WISH-GRANTING PRAYER
OF KUNTU ZANGPO

A Revealed Text of Rigdzin Godemchen

INTRODUCTION

AMONG THE THOUSANDS of incarnations of Guru Rinpoche emanated to reveal initiatory visions, the knowledge-bearer Godemchen has a unique reputation. He discovered a corpus of texts called the Northern Treasure,[128] which had a widely felt and potent effect on the yogin community of his day. Unlike the treasure texts of many other *tertons,* the Northern Treasure has retained its attraction until our own time. It is difficult to characterize Godemchen's revelations in contradistinction to other *terma,* except to say that it is couched in extremely clear and succinct terms and has an overall unity of content and style. It has an affinity to the Dzogchen tradition known as the *Vimala Nyingtig* of the Indian *paṇḍita* Vimalamitra, a contemporary of Padmasambhava in Tibet. The most important texts of the Northern Treasure treat *mahāyoga* and *anuyoga.*

Godemchen was born in Upper Tsang, in the high, wide, inclement valleys of the Tibetan plateau to the north of the highest peaks of the Himalayas. Tsang was the center of Tibetan culture during the fourteenth century when Godemchen (1337–1409) lived, and since he was born into a noble family that traced its lineage to Mongolian royalty, his family seems to have had standing in the community. His father was a priest and mystic of the Nyingma school, an adept in the yoga of Dorje Purba. The young Ngodrub Gyeltsen, as he was named, grew up under the tutelage of his learned father and as a student showed promise at a very early age. The apocalyptic events that earned him his sobriquet *Godemchen,* Master Vulture Feather, occurred in his youth. When he was eleven years old three feathers of the eagle vulture magically appeared on the crown of his head, and when he was twenty-three the three feathers increased to five. The vulture[129] is a sacred bird, sacred in Tibet from time immemorial; a single vulture feather ornamented Guru Rinpoche's victory hat. As to his spiritual lineage, Godemchen was an emanation of Nanam Dorje Dudjom, the disciple of Guru Rinpoche depicted wielding a *purbu*.

His epithet Rigdzin Chenpo, the Magnificent Knowledge-Bearer, signifies the success of his meditation as a Nyingma school yogin living in the mundane world, maintaining Dzogchen vision. The Three Supreme Emanations[130] of Guru Rinpoche, of whom Godemchen was one, were all yogins of this type. His activity as a treasure finder began when he was given a list of hiding places by a friend who had discovered it at Gyang Yonpolung,[131] near Lhatse Dzong, and close to one of King Trisong Detsen's Yangdul temples. It was this list of hiding places that probably directed him to a power place called Dzengdrag Karpo, beneath the peak of Riwo Trazang, where he found a precise list of treasure texts. At the age of twenty-nine, in the cave of Zangzang Lhadrag, he discovered a blue chest with many partitions that contained the great wealth of Northern Treasure written on yellow parchment, which indicates the dākinīs' hand in the affair. Groups of texts were designated by their position in a mandala of the cardinal directions and their center, and the five groups he called the Five Treasuries.[132] From the dark-brown central cavity he extracted one of the most important of his revelations, the *Kunzang Gongpa Zangtel,* "Immediate Transference to the Dynamic of Kuntu Zangpo." He also discovered various sacred implements and relics there.

Godemchen spent the remainder of his long life disseminating the teaching of his revelation. According to legend it reached every corner of the Tibetan world, and its effects were beneficial in every department of human activity: wars were prevented, all diseases eradicated—particularly those caused by spirits of disease—cattle multiplied, the fields were fertile, men lived in harmony, and peace and goodwill prevailed. It seemed that the Northern Treasure held the key to a buddhafield. In fact, the only further revelation Godemchen made was that of the keys to the hidden valleys that Guru Rinpoche had discovered during his sojourn in Tibet. He ended his life as teacher to the king of Gungthang, who governed a principality north of Kyirong. Godemchen's death is described in terms of his own buddhadynamic dissolving into the reality-continuum. The third incarnation of

Godemchen was forced to move to central Tibet because of some political intrigue, and the hub of the wheel of Northern Treasure Dharma became the *gompa* of Tubten Dorje Drag,[133] which was destined to become one of the two monastic centers of the Nyingma school in central Tibet.

Now *The Wish-Granting Prayer of Kuntu Zangpo* is an epitome of the chapter of the *Dzogchen Kunzang Gongpa Zangtedu Tenpai Gyu*,[134] *The Tantra of Immediate Transference to the Dynamic of Kuntu Zangpo and Dzogchen*, which treats the "involuntary" attainment of buddhahood. This tantra is the principal text in the cycle contained in the volume of treasures called *Immediate Transference to the Dynamic of Kuntu Zangpo*. The tantra itself details the metaphysics of consciousness transference to the Ādibuddha Kuntu Zangpo's mind. What is remarkable and specific to this tantra is the concept of *transference*,[135] which is no-transference because the realm or dimension that is Kuntu Zangpo's mind is ever-immanent insofar as it is inherent in ignorance. There can be no "transference" because there was never any separation from Kuntu Zangpo's mind. Kuntu Zangpo's dynamic is in constant operation and simply needs recognition to be fully functional. So near yet so far!

Thus the *Tantra of the Immediate Naked Clarity of Kuntu Zangpo's Dynamic* is an alternative translation of the title. "All-pervasive" is another connotation of the Tibetan word *zangtel* since it is coextensive with emptiness and total presence. It denotes an existential quality of naked, stark awareness. The word *zangtel* does not appear in the prayer. But since it is a wish-granting prayer, if the transmission *(lung)* from the lama has been received in full awareness, then transference to the mind of Kuntu Zangpo is the amazing result. The prayer is also known as *The Prayer of Great Efficacy*.[136]

Prayer in the context of this title is certainly a supplication—the main verbs have a vocative inflection—but more literal renditions of the Tibetan word *monlam*[137] would give us the "Path of Good Wishes" or "Path of Positive Aspirations of Kuntu Zangpo" as viable translations. The unique difference here is that the words emerge from the mouth of the Ādibuddha—it is as if God the Absolute were uttering the prayer. Thus, not only is the prayer bound to be answered, but there is no error in it. It is the perfect prayer, and if only for this reason it will be fulfilled. It is mantra, and mantra in the mouth of the guru manifests its true meaning. In the dimension of Dzogchen there is no subject/object dichotomy, and true to this verity, the prayer is addressed to its author: the supplicant, disposer, and vision are one. In the very act of expression lies the *immediate naked clarity* of Kuntu Zangpo's dynamic. In a Nyingma school litany containing this prayer, the rubric enjoins the yogin to visualize himself as Kuntu Zangpo before recitation. He should even have performed the guruyoga that unites his mind with the Ādibuddha's mind. If the prayer is recited during times of great danger or radical change, such as during an eclipse, an earthquake, a solstice, or at the end of the year, its efficacy is exponentially increased. At such times the mind's propensities become more fluid, and attachments to one's fixed mental dispensation are loosened. The Nyingma school recognizes a lineage of initiation through prayer.[138] Thus the recitation of these verses can be as potent a skillful means of attaining buddhahood as the practice of difficult yogas, prolonged service to the lama, or maintaining *samaya* with the ḍākinī.

Finally, who is Kuntu Zangpo? He is the Ādibuddha, the Primal, First, Original Buddha. He represents primal awareness of total presence, and that is the universe. His name means All-Good, where his goodness is transcendent and supramoral. He also represents Dzogchen itself in its resultant phase. Kuntu Zangpo's *dynamic* is the power of his mind, or active presence. The word *mind* is rejected because of the danger of conceiving it as a substantial entity. It consists of no more than its motive power or intentionality, and its modes can be defined as primal awareness, communicative vibration, responsiveness, transforming activity, and magical quality.[139] These modes are induced by the prayer.

The prayer of the Ādibuddha Kuntu Zangpo can be analyzed into two parts. The first part explains the nature of ignorance and the vision of Kuntu Zangpo's reality that ignorance veils. The second part describes the meditation upon the five forms of passion that are intrinsically the five aspects of awareness. Each section of this "philosophical" prayer concludes with a vocative statement invoking buddha-awareness.

In the first part, the first section[140] introduces the basic reality of the ground of being[141] that transcends all dualities, including samsara and nirvana, ignorance and knowledge. This is the realm of Kuntu Zangpo. The second section defines buddhahood as total presence of the ground of being. The third section describes the emanation of awareness within total presence of the ground and the qualities of this magnificent vision as it unfolds. Awareness is the radiance of total presence,[142] and out of the undifferentiated union that is total presence arise the five aspects of awareness that are the Five Dhyāni Buddhas. From them the Forty-two Peaceful Deities and from them the Sixty Wrathful Deities arise in turn. The process of emanation from the center of passive total presence to the circumference of active awareness is a function of the increasing scope of pure awareness. Since these buddha-deities are the cognitive essence of the form of the dance of awareness, which is everyman's passionate psychic environment, delusion is precluded.

The fourth section views the dynamics of the previous part from without: the guru-buddha's flow of emanation is motivated by compassion and actually is compassion—ubiquitous compassion. No form whatsoever is not Kuntu Zangpo's compassionate manifestation. The fifth section describes the way in which Kuntu Zangpo's emanation has been misunderstood and perverted through six psychological neuroses, which are produced by karma and which evolved from what in the beginning was our failure to endure the radiance of clear light. When attention lacks focus and concentration is absent, an existential dread of life ("the unknown") is our reaction, and fearful insecurity produces the sense of alienation that is the basis of the wheel of samsara. The wheel is driven by poisonous emotions that create karmas constantly reinforcing the propensities that drive the wheel.

The sixth section restates the twofold ignorance that prevents recognition of Kuntu Zangpo's reality: the innate ignorance that is absence of presence arising with every moment of perception, and conceptual ignorance that locks us into the prison of thoughtforms. Innate ignorance reinitiates the process referred to above in every moment of perception: existential dread, alienation, and passion sustain a vicious circle of constantly reinforced karma. Taking refuge in the alienated ego's thoughtforms, in labeling, structuring, and selecting, the view of subject/object duality is accepted as a god-given verity, and external objects are conceived as discrete substantial entities. The fourth text translated herein, the *Garland of Vision,* lists the most crass forms of this ignorance under "Mundane Vision." The remainder of the prayer provides the specific modes of vision that facilitate recognition of Kuntu Zangpo's reality within the various psychological environments generated by the five fundamental passions.

The deceptive simplicity of language and concept in the second part of the prayer need not induce the belief that a specious technique of mind manipulation is involved. This eminently practicable meditation is essentially contemplation upon the emptiness of the events of daily life. As the Buddha guides us through the various types of mental events, each dominated by a different passion, at each stage he exhorts the yogin to relax and relieve the stress.[143] Thus the Dzogchen precept repeatedly emphasized in this yoga is "Do nothing! Indulge and cultivate nothing! Reject and abandon nothing! Simply be aware and let it be!" To say "Identify the emptiness inherent in simple sensory perception of every situation" would be to cultivate the seeking and striving that precludes attainment. In the first three situations, dominated by desire, hatred, and pride, when the yogin stands back, as it were, from the violent or at least highly intense circumstances, detaching himself from the emotionally charged structures that conceptual ignorance has woven around him, Kuntu Zangpo expresses the result of this in terms of spontaneously arising total presence. In the fourth situation, where jealousy is the dominant passion, the word *total presence* is replaced by *ordinary sensory consciousness,*[144] implying the identity of the two meanings. Pure sensory awareness, free of emotional taint and with the full intensity of mindfulness generated by the high-voltage situation, gives access to emptiness, suchness, the here-and-now-ness, of the event, and total presence is the cognitive aspect of emptiness. Thus the Buddha is urging us to "do" one thing: to relax and allow total presence to assume its rightful primacy. Another way to say it is, "Retrieve the part of mind that has been stolen away by the fascinating or offensive object, and severing all attachment to the object, and bringing it back, stuff it into the heart center—then, no-mind!"

In each case the villain of the piece is dualizing mind,[145] the unconscious process of differentiating subject and object that arises after the loss of total awareness. In the realm of the hungry ghosts, desire for an object is the result of the feeling of insecurity and incompleteness that characterizes the split mind. No desire can arise in the plenum of total presence because total presence is all-encompassing. There is no distinction between self and other, inside and outside, and empathy is so strong that we "know" our object of desire intimately and fully the moment it enters consciousness. Thus desires are only perfectly consummated through the desirelessness of total presence. The Buddha of Wealth, Dzambhala, is the one desireless buddha named to attract aspirants with temporal ambition still in mind. The end of such a "worldly" yogin's path is the same as that of his brother ascetic married to austerity. Both achieve their every desire through emptiness and its cognitive capacity of total presence, which embraces all things and knows all things.

In ignorance, alienated and lonely, we are cut off from the world and other creatures by our belief that we are all separate entities with no connection between us (section 7). Insecure and perplexed, full of doubt and hesitancy, the inner craving for security and certainty becomes transferred to external objects, particularly sexual objects. The more our desire grows the more tormented we become. Our only fulfillment by this route is momentary physical satisfaction. Rebirth as a hungry ghost may be the eventual result of this condition. The Buddha prays that at whatever point we catch ourselves and attain self-recognition in the midst of our desire, we should relax and enjoy the pure sensory consciousness of the moment. Total presence will then assume its natural primacy. Since sensory discrimination is the starting point and indeed the very condition of our desire, it is the discriminating aspect of awareness that remains as the fruit of recognizing the emptiness of the desire situation.

Hatred or aversion is a direct function of the split mind (section 8). Again, due to the fear inherent in "island consciousness," when any event occurs that is not exuding comfort and security, like a dog rolling on its back and wagging its tail, the propensity for hatred can be potentiated. Whenever that initial tremulous vibration of aversion is felt, the primary cause of anger, hatred, and violence is active. If conditioning, particularly childhood conditioning, has been such that a shrinking away from a fearful object has become a hardened propensity, then the tendency to react with aversion will be even stronger. Further, if at any point in life one has been encouraged to express in anger this aversion to an external object, then the conditions for a possible violent confrontation are present.

The Buddha prays that the yogin may catch himself and relax at some point in the progression from the first subtle quiver of aversion to the last blow being struck. If he can, then total presence will spontaneously arise and the radiant aspect of awareness will be attained. This radiance is clarity, or pellucidity of perception. Here, the heat of anger is not at issue: the cold, blue clarity of hatred is the quality to be recognized as the mirror-like wisdom. The mirror itself is the emptiness of mind in which the image appears as illusory gossamer play. The awareness that is like the mirror is the omniscient, omnipresent awareness in which the dance occurs and of which the dance is formed. The protectors of the Dharma are colored blue-black or red-blue.

Less space in the prayer is given to pride (section 9), jealousy (section 10), and sloth (section 11). But in a few lines the psychological mechanisms are explained, the karmic result clarified, the injunction to "relax and release the stress in perception" repeated, and finally the wish that all beings perceive the inherent reality of awareness is expressed. Then in the final section (12), emphasizing the illusory nature of the six karmic predicaments, Kuntu Zangpo expresses the wish that all beings attain buddhahood in order to transform the six types of conditioned being[146] into a dance of awareness. The means by which buddhahood is to be attained, and the means of provoking the recognition by which the transformation is to be accomplished, is this prayer. This is no contrived priestcraft to increase faith and devotion. It is a statement based upon experiential realization supported by a subtle and profound metaphysics that is magnificent in its clarity and simplicity.

The Wish-Granting
Prayer of Kuntu Zangpo[147]

HO! Phenomena and noumena, samsara and nirvana,
    the entire universe has one ground,
    but alternative paths yield different results—
    displays of either awareness or ignorance.
    Through this wish-granting prayer of Kuntu Zangpo
    may all beings attain consummate perfection and buddhahood
    in the palace of the reality-continuum.

(2) The universal ground is unconditioned,
    an unutterable, self-originating, vast expanse,
    where neither samsara nor nirvana are known.
    Total presence of this reality is buddhahood,
    while beings ignorant of it wander in samsara.
    May all sentient beings of the three realms
    attain total presence of the ineffable ground of being.

(3) I, Kuntu Zangpo, also affirm this:
    the ground of being is uncaused and unconditioned,
    and total presence arises spontaneously within it
    free of defiling notions of inside and outside,
    free of boosting affirmation and diminishing negation,
    while no trace of unmindfulness veils it:
    thus our self-manifest display is faultless.

    In pristine intrinsic awareness, abiding in stillness,
    though the three realms are destroyed there is no fear,
    and there is no attachment to the five sensory qualities.
    In self-originating, thought-free perception
    there is no material form and no five poisons.

    As the unobstructed radiant aspect of total presence,
    one substance contains the five aspects of awareness;
    as this fivefold awareness evolves

the five modes of the Original Buddha emerge;
thereafter, fully-awakened awareness
manifests as the Forty-two Buddhas,
and the arising creativity of fivefold awareness
produces the Sixty Blood-Drinking Buddhas:
thus total presence of the ground of being is never deluded.

Through the utterance of this, my wish-granting prayer,
after all sentient beings of samsara's three realms
have recognized self-originating total presence,
may the scope of awareness reach its optimal degree.

(4)   My apparitional emanation, an unceasing stream,
I project incalculable myriads of forms
displaying manifold illusion to convert all beings,
whosoever and whatsoever they may be.
Through this, my compassionate wish-granting prayer,
may all creatures of samsara's three realms
escape the destinies of the six types of being.

(5)   In the first place, deluded sentient beings
lacked attentiveness and were bewildered
because presence did not arise in the ground:
this is the primary cause of ignorance and delusion.
There followed a sudden fainting away,
causing feelings of dread and neurotic vacillation;
"I" was alienated from a hostile "other," "the enemy,"
and with the mind progressively conditioned by this tendency,
samsara was established as a way of life.
The five poisons increasing, defilement resulted,
and karma, five times poisoned, became an interminable stream.

Since the cause of sentient beings' delusion
is unmindfulness and absence of any presence,
through this, my wish-granting prayer, the buddhas' aspiration,
may everyone recognize total presence spontaneously.

(6) Innate ignorance
(accompanying each moment of perception)
implies unmindful, distracted cognition,
and conceptual ignorance
(selecting, structuring, and labeling)
implies dualistic cognition.
This twofold ignorance, innate and conceptual,
forms the basis of all beings' delusion.

Through this, the buddhas' wish-granting prayer,
in all of samsara's sentient beings—
the gloom of their fogged, distracted minds dissolving,
dualistic perception unified in pellucid clarity—
let there be spontaneous recognition of total presence.

(7) The dualizing intellect is doubtful, fearful, and insecure;
it breeds subtle cravings
that gradually crystallize as overt, compulsive desires:
desire for food, wealth, and clothing, home and friends,
for fivefold sensual pleasure and loving companions,
and the tormented yearning of sexual attraction.
These obsessions of temporal, worldly delusion,
the karma of an ego craving objects, are never exhausted.
When the fruit of craving ripens,
tormented by frustrated desire,
there is rebirth as a hungry ghost.
Ah, the misery of hunger and thirst!

Through this, the buddhas' wish-granting prayer,
neither repressing or rejecting the pangs of frustration
nor accepting or indulging obsessive lusts,
may all beings possessed by compulsive desires
be released from the stresses of dualistic perception.
May total presence resume its natural primacy
with the attainment of all-discriminating awareness.

(8) Confronted by appearances of external objects,
     there is tremulous vibration of fear in cognition;
     when the tendency to aversion crystallizes as hatred,
     enmity breeds violent aggression leading to killing;
     when the fruit of hatred ripens,
     ah, the agony of burning and boiling in hell!

     Through this, the buddhas' wish-granting prayer,
     when aggressive hatred erupts,
     neither inhibiting nor indulging it
     but relaxing and releasing the stress,
     may total presence resume its natural primacy.
     May all the six types of beings
     attain the awareness of radiant clarity.

(9) When the mind is inflated with confidence,
     the intellect scornfully contending with others
     breeds a mind full of arrogant pride,
     creating violent confrontation or war
     and all of its consequent suffering.
     When the fruit of such karma ripens,
     a god is born, heir to decay and eventual downfall.

     Through this, the buddhas' wish-granting prayer,
     may all beings prone to inflated confidence
     at its onset relax, releasing the stress in perception,
     allowing total presence to resume its natural primacy,
     attaining the awareness of sameness.

(10) The crystallized tendencies of an alienated mind,
     elevating self and diminishing others,
     breed the karma of contention and violent aggression.
     This leads to rebirth as a murderous titan
     in the antigods' realm of constant conflict,
     where downfall into hell is the final outcome.

Through this, the buddhas' wish-granting prayer,
when contention or violent confrontation arises,
may you break the habit of conceiving of others as enemies
and relax, releasing the stress in perception,
allowing pure sensory consciousness its primacy,
attaining the awareness of unhindered action.

(11) Unmindfulness, apathy, and a wandering mind,
dullness, torpor, and forgetfulness,
languor, laziness, and stupidity
result in rebirth as a wandering, homeless beast.
Through this, the buddhas' wish-granting prayer,
may the radiance of mindful clarity dawn
in the gloom of sloth and depression
to bring awareness of a silent mind.

(12) Every single sentient being of the three realms
remains one with me, the Buddha, the universal ground.
Yet unmindful, they are lost in the ground of delusion,
even now enacting karma that has no purpose.
The six types of karma are all delusory dream,
for I am the Buddha, the Original Buddha.
Transforming the six types of being by emanation
and through this wish-granting prayer, Kuntu Zangpo's prayer,
may all sentient beings without exception
attain buddhahood in the continuum of empty reality.

SECRET INSTRUCTION
IN A GARLAND OF VISION

by Padmasambhava

INTRODUCTION

PADMASAMBHAVA, the tantric yogin from Orgyen who wandered through Tibet in the second half of the eighth century, teaching and practicing exorcism, was no great scholar. However, a vast canon of texts was later attributed to him through the device of the treasure-text doctrine, through revelation of scriptures hidden in the elements or in the samadhis that his meditation instruction induced, or by the kindness of the ḍākinīs of the Orgyen pure land. Such texts are called *terma*. The validity of revealed, or treasure, texts is not to be argued, but treasure finders *(tertons)* do not claim that Padmasambhava himself wrote these texts with his own hand. Tibet's Great Guru is also partly responsible for the *kama,* the lineal, oral teaching of the Nyingma school committed to paper. Again, undoubtedly the guru was a principal link in the transmission of many of these scriptures, but he did not compose them himself. Padmasambhava, the *paṇḍita,* is a mythic form of Guru Rinpoche accounted among the eight names of the guru, and as such he is the embodied inspiration of fully realized adepts of the Nyingma school.

It is difficult to confirm attribution of texts to the historical yogin from Orgyen. It is said that he wrote only four works: a commentary on the Yangdag tantra on the secret level, a commentary on the *Namomanjuśrī-saṅgīti,* instruction on invocation of the Mamo mother goddesses, and the *Garland of Vision.*[148] The last two titles are scripts of discourses. A fifth work, a commentary upon the *Guhyagarbhatantra,* is a text of oral instruction delivered by him, but its scribe, Katog Dampa Desheg, lived three hundred years later. The work is said to have been transmitted verbatim by the lineage during those interim years.[149]

The *Garland of Vision* and the Mamo instruction were given to King Trisong Detsen himself after the king had attained the Dzogchen level, which was at the end of the guru's period in Tibet. Given the somewhat irregular structure of the *Garland of Vision* text, it is easy to see it as the bones of a discourse taken down in note form, although this is not the orthodox view of it. Rongdzom Paṇḍita reports[150] that after singing three songs to the king and the twenty-five disciples at Dragmar Tsomo Gur in Neutang,[151] while the disciples rejoiced the guru composed the two texts and instructed the king in their practice. Perhaps the *Garland of Vision* comprises the notes that the guru used to instruct the king. Whatever its precise origin, in a highly concise, mnemonic form, the levels of human vision are defined therein. Beginning with mundane vision—which hardly deserves the term *vision* in the case of hedonistic perception, for instance—the guru dwells briefly on the Buddhist nontantric levels before treating Dzogchen vision in detail. Thus, despite its unusual form, the *Garland of Vision* is a text describing the *stages of the path (lamrim)*, a genre of literature more rarely indulged in by the Nyingma than later schools. Furthermore, although the *Garland of Vision* has this academic *lamrim* structure, written from a Dzogchen standpoint its accent is still upon experiential vision rather than philosophical view.[152]

However, the *Garland of Vision* is far more than a sketch of the stages of spiritual maturation according to the Nyingma school's ninefold enumeration. This description applies only to the first half of the work, which may be considered as an introduction to the second and more significant half, which consists of an analysis of the Dzogchen path. The first section, entitled "The Mode of the Great Perfection" (iiia, p. 148), is an analysis of vision. The second section with this head (iiib, p. 150) treats meditative vision, while the final section, entitled "Ascetic Practices" (III, p. 155), after noting the respective forms of activity of the lower modes, treats the Dzogchen yogin's activity or conduct. Thus the bulk of the *Garland of Vision* presents secret instruction in Dzogchen vision, meditation, and action. However, the terse comment demonstrating the Dzogchen angle on the "lower" eight approaches and the mundane and non-Buddhist philosophies is also a treasury of precept regarding Dzogchen vision: no perspective created by the human mind is outside the scope of the Dzogchen yogin's ken or beyond his use as a skillful means in service of the bodhisattva vow.

The *Garland of Vision* is well known among Dzogchen initiates. In his short history of the text[153] Jamgon Kongtrul Lodro Taye claims that over the centuries many ordinary yogins gained access to the authentic rendering of the text, and many of the wise among them effortlessly attained their goal. It is surprising, then, that only two commentaries upon it are found in the *kama* canon. One of these is from early times and one is quite recent. The first was written by Rongdzom Pandita, a great eleventh-century scholar and translator, an incarnation of Bairotsana. Rongdzom is known as one of the two "omniscient" Nyingma scholars (Kunkhyen Longchenpa is the other), and his present relative obscurity demonstrates the dominance of the *terma* current in later centuries in the Nyingma school.[154] His scholarship was renowned also in India, where he studied before returning to Tibet to work on translation. His clear, fluent commentary[155] on the *Garland of Vision* is dedicated in part to clarification of logical obscurities through reference to *mādhyamika* metaphysics and basic *abhidharma*.[156] His approach is through *mahāyoga*.

The second commentary was written by Jamgon Kongtrul Rinpoche Lodro Taye (1813–99), the compiler of the *Rinchen Terdzo* and the principal disciple and scribe of Khyentse Wangpo, from whom he received the oral transmission of this work.[157] It is a *word by word* commentary *(tsigdon)* composed in the style wherein the words of the root text, signified by a symbol beneath them, are woven into the fabric of the commentary, which thus becomes a detailed elaboration of the original. This work is also a model of clarity and simple, succinct prose.

Undoubtedly a translation of Lodro Taye's work, or a commentary in English elaborating each paragraph with detailed background, is required for a full comprehension of the *Garland of Vision's* content. Such mnemonic texts as the *Garland of Vision* do assume knowledge of their subject matter, but insofar as the *Garland of Vision* is a metaphysical poem with an inherent mandalic structure, transmitting far more than a body of intellectual knowledge, its principal function here should be as a vehicle for intuitive realization. As the text says, "Absorbing transmission of the root texts of the vehicle of skillful means is to disclose the mandala...and after entering therein, to realize its reality is to attain the supreme power." However, such attainment is only possible if the disciple's mind is prepared, as King Trisong Detsen's mind was prepared, by absorbing Guru Rinpoche's direct transmission. In the paragraph on "Direct and Immediate Realization," the condition for the spontaneous origination of this realization is a falling away of dependence upon the letter of instruction, and rejection of analytical concepts as a source of inspiration. Although we should not hope for the results that can arise from the logical outcome of this parallel, still the principle can be applied. It is beneficial to exercise the intuition on the *Garland of Vision* rather than bring the intellect to bear.

Dzogchen Vision

The *Garland of Vision* first defines starting points on the Dzogchen path, beginning with the most benighted mundane views of reality (section I) and proceeding to the transcendental views, the Nyingma school's nine approaches to buddhahood (section II). Thus the *garland* of the title is a garland of attitudes, views, and visions of the universal fact of being. The word *vision,* as used in the translation, embraces all of these vastly differing perspectives on life, although the four attitudes in the first, mundane category of the text can hardly be considered visions as the word is usually understood. On the contrary, they are perspectives lacking any vision at all. They are ignorant and foolish outlooks where ignorance is "lack of knowledge and awareness"—lack of gnostic knowledge and awareness *(avidyā)*. It would be sectarian bigotry to pretend that in practice Christianity and Hinduism are totally lacking in gnostic vision, but in the Dzogchen yogin's terms, in theory, where nothing but an uncompromising nondual vision is acceptable, certainly the views of the eternalistic schools are imperfect, partial visions. Perhaps a case could be made for the vision of *advaita vedānta* being superior to the vision of some *Hīnayāna* schools, but when the concept of self *(ātman)* is introduced into any Hindu view, that view is immediately suspect. The text is written from the point of view of the Dzogchen yogin's rigorous nondualism, and the Dzogchen vision is defined in every statement.

The *paṇḍitas* of ancient India applied the word *view (darśana)* to their perspectives of reality, so view and philosophy became synonymous. Although these philosophies evolved into formulations of doctrine, or even bodies of dogma, in the first place the view was derived from a vision shared synchronistically by various yogins and sages meditating in jungle solitude or mountain fastness, and insofar as religions and schools of yoga have their foundation in experiential mysticism, at this original point of departure *vision* is the correct word to use. However, even at the moment of vision, in all but a Dzogchen yogin's mind, a process begins that reduces the vision to a mere view, and eventually to dogma. This process is described in the text as the cultivation of any evaluation of reality in the scope between a bloated affirmation giving primacy to existence and the exaggerated negation of nihilism. Any judgmental evaluation of reality is obscured by the twin veils of emotivity and thought, which clothe naked reality with emotionally toned analysis. If the Dzogchen yogin is defined as the yogin who applies the precept "Relax, and let it be," the yogins of the lesser approaches to nirvana, *mokṣa,* or paradise are those who simply cannot leave it alone, but must strive to alter it, stressing existence or non-existence, self or no-self, emptiness or form, male or female principle, inside or outside, the creator or creation, and so on. Regardless of the preferred bias, inevitably there arises a mind-created dichotomy that precludes a perfect vision of reality.

A vision is a subjective phenomenon inseparable from the viewer. It may be as ephemeral as a bolt of lightning or a glimpse of fairie, or it may be a sustained mental penetration of reality that allows the visionary to write it down in mathematical symbols. Our Miltons and Dantes wrote it down in lyrical poetry. A painter or sculptor may sustain a vision for the duration of his creation of a plastic representation of it; but in this instance the content of the vision is also, partially at least, imagined, where imagination is an interpretive and creative faculty manipulating images. On the contrary, the Dzogchen yogin's vision employs an introspective faculty penetrating to the essence, or essences. The visions of both philosopher and poet delve beneath the surface of common dualistic delusion, and in their nature as subjective, unifying vision they partake of the gnostic property of the process, but imagination, whether of an intellectual, metaphysical, or artistic nature, always intrudes. Such vision can be described as a modification of reality on a demi-gnostic plane. Thus there are degrees of mental interference, and the less intrusion of imagination and intellect the greater potential for full gnostic penetration of a nondichotomous reality. The Dzogchen yogin's vision is free of all mental activity. When the mind is silent, when imagination, intellect, and all thoughtforms are still, the vision of indeterminable space arises, empty space full of lightform.

The nature of vision is light, as all things manifest out of a plenum of clear light. The more profound the vision, the more light dominates the perception, and the less concrete the realm of natural objects becomes, until finally the universe is an ocean of light with the form and shape of things delineated merely by their color. This light is the radiance so often spoken of in the Dzogchen texts, and pertaining to the *sambhogakāya* it is apprehended as *inner light*. Its basis is the *clear light,* the light of the ground of being, the universal foundation, which is as invisible as its concomitant emptiness: it is the light of the *dharmakāya*. But since *dharmakāya* and *nirmāṇakāya* are two sides of the same coin, it is nothing but the clear light that we perceive in the pure awareness of sensory perception.[158] Thus the Dzogchen yogin's vision is pure sensory perception with an innate awareness of the clear light of the *dharmakāya*.

If Dzogchen vision is the ultimate vision of buddhahood—the perspective on the highest way of being and on man perfected—then the visions of the lesser approaches to buddhahood, the partial visions of Christians and Hindus, and even the ignorant outlooks of Marx and Epicurus, the *Little Red Book* and *Playboy Magazine,* are not false or untrue. They are the relative truths applicable to their respective levels of karmic maturity. The Dzogchen yogin perceives them as he perceives every intellectual or sensory form that arises into his ken. Without evaluation or discrimination he sees them as emanations of buddha-mind manifest for the benefit of those sentient beings for whom they are worthy ideals. For some beings unable to hear the word of a buddha, the word of Mao Zedong or Hugh Heffner may be the liberating gospel necessary to complete a karmic cycle and reach a level where the Dharma may be heard and understood.

Ultimately, Dzogchen vision is inexpressible. This cannot be stressed too often in case the reader becomes attached to these words as anything but a means to an experiential understanding of ineffable reality. Whatever is said about Dzogchen vision in this and other texts is designed to clear the yogin's way to attainment of it. Thus it should not be classified with the mundane views of reality held by the hedonist and the nihilist. Their vision is fragmented to the point of belief in separate entities, where the *ego* is a discrete person with a consciousness that goes out and apprehends objects out there, alien objects totally independent of the perceiver. Such ignorance is a *view,* a fixed, partial objectification of something that is essentially fluid, mutable, subjective, and holistic. Nor can the Dzogchen view be categorized among the transcendental views held by stream-winners who still believe that reality has some concrete characteristics and a structure that can be expressed in words. The Buddhist atomists, for example, although aware of some of the means by which perfect vision can be attained, still see phenomena as independent of the mind that perceives them. Initiates of the bodhisattva vehicle, with all their knowledge of the means of gathering merit through virtuous conduct and meditative techniques, and with maintenance of the crucial bodhisattva *samaya,* are obstructed even by this very knowledge insofar as it implies a conception of a path with specific attributes: thus their vehicle is called "the vehicle of specific attributes." Dzogchen vision is a vision with no fixed address, a vision of emptiness. Everything perceived is Dzogchen vision, providing the function of perfect insight penetrates to the essential emptiness.

There is no word in English to cover all the forms and levels of perspective described in the *Garland of Vision.* I have used the word *vision* throughout, and its various contexts adduce the different meanings defined above. There is an advantage in using the word that most frequently describes the Dzogchen perspective to describe ignorant views, in that those who lack vision are buddhas in the making, demonstrating the diversity of the creative potency of emptiness. In the meantime they learn the principles of karmic cause and effect, proving the inevitability of karmic retribution, learning the value of the precious human body and the veracity of the four noble truths, particularly the first. In the Dzogchen vision there is no difference between buddhas and sentient beings, between any mental constructs whatever.

Although I do not intend a comprehensive commentary upon the text, there are aspects of the *Garland of Vision* that require elaboration unsuited to footnotes. The remainder of this introduction includes that comment, incorporating extracts from Rongzom Paṇḍita's commentary under relevant headings.

The Lower Tantras (p. 147)

Although the accent in *kriyātantra* is on externals, the essence of practice is visualization of the buddha-deity's mandala and recitation of his mantra. With that in mind we can discuss the peculiarity of *kriyātantra,* the preoccupation with ritual.

"Also of vital importance are the yogin's ritual purity, and his knowledge of propitious and ill-omened times and the movement of the planets and stars. A beneficent environment is established thereby, and through the power of synchronistic conjunctions of objects and mental conditions the *kriyāyogin* attains his goal" (p. 147).

This statement from the *Garland of Vision* introduces many of the elements of ritual magic.[159] Ritual magic is a complex subject, but here it may be defined as application of the interaction between special environmental conditions and controlled mental states. The word *magic* is used here to characterize these effects as forces unrecognized by Western science. They are, however, the ABC's of ritual efficacy, and they are open to the study and understanding of anyone who practices *kriyātantra.* Sympathetic and imitative magic are the most common of such functions. This magic is used in ritual practice for many purposes. Its evocative power provides a method of short-circuiting the Catch-22 implicit in such paradoxical precepts as "concentrate on emptying your mind." The resonance of a highly charged sacred object symbolic of a thought-free mind received on a preverbal level of consciousness may automatically induce a thought-free trance. A beneficent environment is crucial here. Timing must be propitious; the psychic environment must be free from the effects of malevolent planets and stars— the transpersonal web of karmic causality; and ritual purity is required to preclude interference from obstructing spirits.

The dynamic of the ritual event is devotion. Devotion should not be understood as a mindless abandonment of personal responsibility to an external authority but rather as an attitude of total receptivity to a level of purity that glows with a feeling-tone of bliss. Since devotion is alloyed with the devotee's sense of sublime humility in the face of something ultimately supreme, the feeling of the ritual is invariably of worship: in *kriyātantra* the *sādhaka's* relation to the buddha-deity is as servant to master. On this level ultimate purity is the sacred space in which the ritual artifacts hang, as it were, as concrete manifestations of its attributes, such as skillful means (the *dorje*), perfect insight (the bell), emptiness (the skull-cup), aggressive emptiness (the *purbu*), and phenomenal illusion (the mirror). Sense of time and place are systematized in the sacred sciences of geomancy, astrology, and divination of various kinds. These are examples of methods of understanding, which may at times influence the elements of the field of relativity that must be perfectly ordered to create "synchronistic conjunctions" of forces. When the Dzogchen yogin performs this type of ritual, he creates a model demonstrating a holistic, unified, and interdependent field of emptiness and light that is a function of the yogin's primal awareness.

The tantric *kriyāyogin* is also educated in the arts and science of creating *yantras* and mandalas in ink, colored powders, paint, three-dimensional structures, and as visualizations in the mind. He learns the alchemical formulas for producing *torma* (the tantric host) and *chomen* (pills giving longevity), and the geometrical structures of torma. In the ritual environment nothing is out of place, everything is balanced to perfection, and the yogin sees himself serving the buddhas in the pure land of Akaniṣṭha or Orgyen. What in Tibet appeared to the Chinese Marxists as devil worship was this meticulous preparation of the environment for rituals in which the monk-yogins transformed themselves into gods in buddhafields. What may appear to the uncompromising Dzogchen purist, who may practice only formless meditation, as idle manipulation of the realm of aesthetic form, is the *kriyāyogin* performing his meditation.

In *kriyāyoga* the samadhi that is the buddha-deity's mood is a function of simulating the buddha-deity's form and speech through visualization and mantra, which is where the yogin's effort is directed. In *ubhayatantra* equal attention is given to cultivation of body, speech, and mind, while in *yogatantra* the environment is all but ignored. All attention is applied to the cultivation of the buddha-deity's samadhi under the conviction that mind is the leader: if mind is pure, body and speech will automatically be purified. The yogin's samadhi can cut through every hindrance that may arise on the level of ultimate universal sameness. But still, in the outer *yogatantra* the area of attention is the *rūpakāya,* the field of form represented as the body of a god. The rainbow body emanated by the full union of Kuntu Zangpo and Kuntu Zangmo in the *dharmakāya* is accepted as the natural fruit of *samaya,* which is to sustain the basic, innate awareness of ultimate perfection as totally indeterminate, neither existing nor not existing.

The Dzogchen Mandala

The text summarily treats creative *(kyerim)* and fulfillment *(dzogrim)* yogas, which are usually subsumed under the headings of the *mahāyoga* and *anuyoga* vehicles respectively. Creative meditation is the yoga of constructing a mandala from the buddha-deity's seed-syllable mantra by means of visualization. Fulfillment meditation is concerned with detachment from the dance of illusion by creating an illusory body—the nature of which is emptiness—using various other advanced meditations. In anuyoga the yogin also learns control of the vital breath and energies of the body. This facilitates control of the mind and its energies. Ultimately it stops the flow of energies from the psychic centers outward to the gross body, reversing them so that they flow inward to the psychic centers, into the *lalanā* and *rasanā* channels, and finally into the central channel *(avadhūti)*. Both *mahāyoga* and *anuyoga* can be considered as preliminary or supportive practices for Dzogchen.

After the creative and fulfillment yogas, *atiyoga* is treated under the heading "The Mode of the Great Perfection" (section iiia). However, as Rong-dzom's commentary states explicitly, the *Garland of Vision* approaches Dzogchen from a *mahāyoga* standpoint. Thus this first analysis of the Dzogchen mode applies the pure Dzogchen vision to the mandala of peaceful and wrathful Buddha-deities as visualized in *mahāyoga*. The elements of samsara and nirvana that are to be recognized as the buddhas of the five families, the bodhisattvas, the wrathful Buddha-deities, and their consorts—the Peaceful and Wrathful Deities—who comprise the *mahāyoga* mandala, represent those same elements of experience that are to be recognized as already primordially pure in *tregcho* meditation, Cutting Through. Under the second heading "The Mode of the Great Perfection" (section iiib), the analysis treats the dynamic and the shades of meaning of the yoga of spontaneity, which is embraced by *togel*, Immediate Crossing.[160] However, the terms *tregcho* and *togel* do not appear in the *Garland of Vision*.

The Dzogchen mandala, then, consists of the elements of experience, as formulated in Mahayana *Abhidharma,* recognized as primordially pure. By virtue of this recognition, the primal awareness of total presence is informed by the qualities and attributes of the various divine beings that represent the energy and pure awareness inherent in the basic elements of experience. Intrinsic awareness of the psychophysical constituents, the passions, and so forth, is represented by the divine forms of a mandala. The elements of each moment of pure perception are visualized as this Dzogchen mandala called the mandala of buddha-body, buddha-speech, and buddha-mind.

The symbolism of this mandala encompasses the entire gamut of Buddhist psychology, epistemology, and ontology, and employs a vast range of symbolic representation of Buddha-deities, their forms, gestures, and tokens, as developed in Tantra. Although, as the text emphasizes, the individual Buddha-deities of the mandala should not be cultivated sequentially in this context, the assumption is apparent that the Dzogchen yogin has practiced each of them in a context wherein each buddha-deity represents the totality of a single instant of experience. Thus, according to creative yoga instruction, he can visualize the entire entourage in clear, detailed focus. On the other hand, the Buddha-deities are inseparable from total presence and the epistemological attributes of existential awareness that they represent. The visualization is a skillful means of focusing and clarifying the creative efflorescence of total presence.

The nature of total presence, in its simplicity, is the mind of Kuntu Zangpo. The creative efflorescence of total presence is the energy of Kuntu Zangmo. Kuntu Zangpo and Kuntu Zangmo in *yabyum* is the *dharmakāya* origin of this *sambhogakāya* mandala. The five modes of the primal awareness of total presence are defined by the Buddhas of the Five Families,[161] representing the inherently pure nature of the five psychophysical constituents[162] that pertain to the subjective aspect of unitary gnostic experience. The Five Buddhas are Akṣobhya (the name and form constituent and mirror-like awareness), Ratnasambhava (the feeling constituent and awareness of sameness), Amitābha (the perception constituent and discriminating awareness), Amoghasiddhi (the conditioned impulse constituent and all-accomplishing awareness), and Vairocana (the consciousness constituent and awareness of the reality-continuum of all-encompassing space); they belong to vajra, ratna, padma, viśvavajra, and buddha families, respectively. The consorts of the Five Buddhas represent the inherently pure nature of the five great elements, which in their nature as light seed compose the objective aspect, the awareness-ḍākinīs' web of transforming illusion *(māyā)*. The five consorts of the Five Buddhas are Locanā (earth), Māmakī (water), Pāṇḍaravāsinī (fire), Tārā (air), and Dhātīśvarī (space), respectively.

Insofar as the inherently pure constituents of the process of sensory perception belong to the manifest dimension of seemingly dualistic factors, they are represented as bodhisattvas and their goddess consorts. The inner four of the Eight Bodhisattvas (Kṣitigarbha, Vajrapāṇi, Ākāśagarbha, and Avalokiteśvara) represent the inherently pure nature of visual, auditory, gustatory, and olfactory consciousnesses, and their consorts, the Four Beautiful Goddesses (Lāsyā, Gītā, Mālā, and Nṛtyā), represent the inherently pure nature of the objects of those consciousnesses (sight, sound, smell, and taste). The outer four of the Eight Bodhisattvas (Maitreya, Samantabhadra, Sarvanīvaraṇa Viṣkambhina, and Mañjuśrī) represent the inherently pure nature of the organs of perception (eye, ear, nose, and tongue, respectively). The consorts of these "outer" bodhisattvas, four of the offering goddesses (Dhūpā, Puṣpā, Ālokā, and Gandhā), are the inherently pure nature of thoughts and concepts of the four aspects of time (past, present, future, and eternity, respectively). The inherently pure nature of tactile consciousness, the body as the tactile sensory organ, the object of tactile consciousness, and awareness of tactile perception that results from contact of tactile consciousness and object in the physical organ of tactile perception, are the Four Wrathful Guardian Deities (Yamāntaka, Mahābala, Hayagrīva, and Amṛtakuṇḍalī). The consorts of the Four Wrathful Deities (Aṅkuśa, Pāśa, Śṛṅkhalā, and Ghaṇṭā) represent the inherently pure nature of mental concepts of the four extreme ontological views, which are eternalism, nihilism, Brahmanism (the view that propounds a self or *ātman*), and materialism (the view that there is an external substantial reality).

The Dzogchen Mode (pp. 150–55)

As already indicated, the text does not explain explicitly the formal distinction between the first exposition of Dzogchen, which describes the mandala in terms of buddhas and bodhisattvas, and the second, which treats the fourfold intuitive realization,[163] the components of ultimate accomplishment, and the degrees of accomplishment. The interlinear comment in the Tibetan text, interpolated immediately after the second title, is the only clue—the commentaries are also silent. Here it is confirmed that we are now in the ultimate Dzogchen mode of attainment, that the Dharma now operative is the spontaneity of total presence.[164] This is truly the resultant approach,[165] the approach that is so close to final consummation that an assumption of final achievement can be made, allowing the power of conviction to work its own magic and actualize the self-evident potential. This exposition is akin to Immediate Crossing *(togel):* spontaneity is the dominant characteristic of "the final event."[166]

It may appear that the first three of the four realizations (the unitary cause, sacred letters, sustaining grace, and immediate realization) are arbitrarily or fortuitously chosen gates to total presence out of eighty-four potential skillful methods. Rongdzom corrects this error. In the Secret Mantra *(guhyamantra)* approach sacred letters are the principal means of practice and realization, and in the following extract of his commentary treating the fourfold intuitive realization, the relationships of all the elements of the Dzogchen mode of spontaneity are set out in terms of ground, method, and result. These three categories should be seen as aspects of the momentary process of spontaneous manifestation of the final event, a spontaneous manifestation of buddha-body, buddha-speech, and buddha-mind in the Dzogchen mode, rather than descriptive of a process through time. But rather than muddying the waters further, here is the omniscient Rongdzom Paṇḍita explicating the spontaneous, effortless Dzogchen mode.[167]

The relationship of the elements of the Dzogchen mode:

> The four realizations are the ground; the three components are the means; the four degrees are fruition; and the mode of entry into the mandala of spontaneity is the secret instruction in Immediate Crossing. The one cause and sacred letters are the ground; sustaining grace is the method; and direct realization is fruition. In the same way, the cognitive component is the ground; the application component is the means; and the fruition component is fruition. Approach is the ground; close approach and accomplishment are the means; and sublime accomplishment is fruition. Likewise, concerning the three stages of access to the mandala: undivided hearing is the ground; entry into the mandala by constant conditioning is the means; and consummation of conditioning, actualization, and attainment of the great power is fruition. Thus having reached the bottom of the matter, I will now explicate the meaning of sacred letters a little.

An analysis of the heading "The Mode of the Great Perfection":

As it is said, after completing the two forms of accumulation (virtue and awareness) there is completion, which is the *perfection* of the Great Perfection. Then, since there is no progress along the path and no preparation or application by way of support as there is in the lower vehicles, in the final event buddha-body, buddha-speech, and buddha-mind are primordially and spontaneously accomplished, and this feature gives *greatness* to the Great Perfection. In the same way the means of access—the door—is the *mode:* thus "The Mode of the Great Perfection."

Comment on the "Unitary Cause":

Realization of the one cause is realization of unity. There is no cause or conclusion as in the accomplishment of a birth...

Comment on "Sacred Letters":

In the final event *guhyamantra* is intuitive realization of buddha-hood, the three sacred letters being the door to complete liberation. In the final event the spontaneity of body, speech, and mind is complete liberation. *A* is the door of nonorigination; *O* is the door of manifest miraculous illusion; *OM* is the door of nonduality.

Comment on "Immediate Realization":

Direct, immediate realization is the direct, immediate power of perfect insight.[168] There is no other immediacy. Further, in the same way that gold is tested by melting, cutting, and rubbing, the value of realization should be established. By melting it one discovers whether or not a metal is gold; by cutting it one ascertains whether or not a metal contains gold; and by rubbing it on a black stone one tests the quality of the gold. Accordingly, if one's Dharma is in harmony with scriptural transmission, there is, in general, no error in it: this test of Dharma is similar to the proof of gold by melting it. In scriptural transmission there is no explanation of the words, and because it is difficult to extract the meaning of the words of a realized mind from the root texts and to understand their meaning, it is only when there is no conflict with the lama's secret instruction that defects revealed thereby are removed: this test of Dharma is similar to the test of gold by cutting it. In the same way, although there may be no conflict with transmission or with the lama's instruction, still the words may be mere sound, and if no profound experience is transmitted, reliance upon the words of scriptural transmission and instruction should be abandoned altogether in favor of profound confidence and immediate realization, which can be depended upon to remove obscurations and defects: this test of Dharma is similar to the test of gold by rubbing it on a black stone. This immediacy exists coincident with discriminating perfect insight, and when it is actualized through the power of yoga, it is the goal itself.

Rongdzom Paṇḍita has defined the four realizations as the ground and the three components (cognition, application, and fruition) as the means. But again we cannot strive to practice these three elements: as Shabkar Lama says in *The Flight of the Garuda,* it is the paradox of "concentrating on something quite specific" that is indeterminate. These elements originate spontaneously through transmission or initiatory experience, or they do not arise at all. Even the application component must arise spontaneously in a constant stream. The three principles (contingent effect, the imperative, and categorical imperative) demonstrate the necessity of the three components. Then the four degrees, two of approach and two of accomplishment, in Rongdzom's analysis are the fruition of the three components as skillful means with the intuitive realization and confidence of total presence as the ground. The terms *approach* and *accomplishment*[169] belong to *mahāyoga,* where they are used to describe the entire process of visualization and recitation, and then more specifically to define success in the yoga: *approach* refers to progressive clarity in invocation of the buddha-deity, and *accomplishment* to the process of identification with the buddha-deity. In Rongdzom's explanation[170] assumption of *mahāyoga* practice is implicit, but it is still clear that in *atiyoga* there is no progressive development through practice. His analysis of sublime accomplishment is more systematic than that of the root text. These are the three groups, or three aspects, of Dzogchen that are spontaneously accomplished: skillful means, perfect insight, and *bodhicitta;* male and female consorts, and brother and sister emanations; and emptiness—the door of complete liberation, desirelessness, and signlessness.

He then treats the suppression of demon spirits.

Destruction of the four demon spirits in "Sublime Accomplishment":

> In general, each of the various bodies of root texts describes a variant specific method of vanquishing the demons. Here the method involves the four degrees of approach and accomplishment. Accordingly, in *approach* the component of *bodhicitta* cognition [or bodhisattva cognition] destroys the demon lord of death with the samadhi of nonorigination; in *close approach* the component of divine self-identification destroys the demon of embodiment with *māyā*-vision samadhi; in *accomplishment* the component of female-consort generation destroys the demon of passion with the atom-free samadhi; and in *sublime accomplishment* the component of means and insight in tandem destroys the divine prince's obstructive distractions with the samadhi that is coextensive with nonreferential space.

Finally, the ultimate accomplishment, the mode of the Great Perfection, is described in terms of its mandala (p. 154). This is a mandala quite different from *yantras,* the symmetrical designs of colored powder or the three dimensional palaces of the lower vehicles, and no initiation followed by *siddhi*-generating practice is involved. Shabkar Lama's description in song 21 is an excellent metaphor for a mandala whose form is the universe, the six senses giving it six dimensions. The stages of initiation into this Dzogchen mandala are coincident, but Rongdzom Paṇḍita enlarges upon the method as if hearing, contemplation, and meditation are serial events. This should not detract from the essential fact that entry and realization are one hundred percent dependent upon the spiritual friend who transmits the root text and the vital initiatory experience.

Constructing the ultimate Dzogchen mandala:

> Entry [into the Dzogchen mandala] is achieved by means of the three secrets [OM ĀH HŪṂ]. Further, from a spiritual friend who is an unerring exemplar of the Mahayana, first listen to the reading of the root texts with the perfect insight inherent in hearing, and the mandala is revealed to you. Second, intuiting the meaning [of what is heard] through the perfect insight of contemplation, you see the mandala and recognize the absolutely specific nature of the divine being. Third, having realized the nature of the mandala through contemplation, accustom yourself to constant realization through the perfect insight of meditation, and entering the mandala you attain initiation and empowerment. Upon entry and actualization you attain the great siddhi.

"The Great Assembly of Sacred Letter Wheels" (p. 154)

This name, given in Dzogchen to the thirteenth stage of the bodhisattva's path, is fraught with all the mystique of Tantra. In the Mahayana, the highest level, which is that of the Buddha and counted as the tenth level, is called *universal light,* and both names refer to the same reality. In short, the great assembly of sacred letter wheels consists of the infinite number of absolutely specific events that constitute the Dzogchen mandala, each event being, and at the same time symbolized by, a letter or compound letter. Rongdzom again:[171]

> The level of the great assembly of sacred letter wheels: this is spontaneous accomplishment as a great assembly of experiential mandalas that are the consummation of the two types of form— immaculate form and that of some specific appearance—that define the attributes of the effortless, spontaneously originated mandala of awareness and attribute.

But this does not tell us the nature of sacred letters, or even the nature of the alphabet. The meaning of *letters* is one of the deepest mysteries of Tantra, and a subject that only intuition can elucidate, for the intellect is incapable of analyzing objectively what is at its own root. It is impossible for the eyes to look into the head. Here are some conceptual aids:

> Sacred letters are an analogue of the facets of emptiness, the qualities and functional patterns of primal awareness. In the same way that letters give form to the content of expression, the content of all experience gives form to emptiness. Emptiness is never separate from form, and meaning is never separate from syllables.
>
> Letters are the most rudimentary form of expression, the first level of manifestation out of the *dharmakāya*. As such, each focal point of creative energy is represented by a letter. This letter represents the facet of emptiness that is manifested in a specific center.
>
> Insofar as these letters represent the most basic level of manifestation, they are themselves nodal points of power and awareness. It is a mistake to conceive of them as mere symbols, or, indeed, even as intensely potent symbols. We are conditioned to treat letters as a convenient graphic mode of expression. In the tantric view the alphabet is not merely a mechanical aid to speech and memory. The sound and the form arise simultaneously, and because the letter is more definite, it is more miraculous.
>
> The neologism *gnoseme* has been coined to express the specific wonder and mystery of mystic letters or seed syllables. The word *gnoseme* could mean a graphic particle of gnostic awareness, where gnostic awareness is the cognitive function of emptiness. Thus gnosemes are graphic particles, or hologlyphs, of emptiness.

In this Dzogchen context, gnosemes are introduced as an apperceptive mechanism that allows insight into and creates confidence in the self-existent Dzogchen mandala. Should we expect to see Tibetan or Sanskrit syllables in our focal points of energy, or Latin or Greek, if these languages have sacred meaning? Do we see nothing if we are ignorant of these alphabets? The shape of the letter is ultimately immaterial, merely representational. The wonder, the mystery, the potency, and the potential that manifest in increasingly complex, dense, and variegated shapes and colors as letters become words, words sentences, and sentences strings of meanings defining the three realms, these all residing in the fact of being manifest.

Thus gnosemes are transcendental experiences, and they are not to be cat-egorized as *rūpakāya* phenomena. Words belong to the realm of name and form, gnosemes belong to pure-being *(kāya)*. The relative shape of gnosemes indicates conceptual differentiation. As our text informs us, OM indicates the *nirmāṇakāya*, ĀH indicates the *sambhogakāya,* and HŪM the *dharmakāya,* and this differentiation may already have misled us into conceiving of these three *kāyas* as different entities. The pure fact of being of these gnosemes is limited by the distinctions introduced by the various shapes: the crucial nub is the sameness indicated by generic letter, and the distinction is the diaphanous gossamer screen giving the radiance of clear light some defini-tion and specificity.

The Warning (p. 155)

Warning of the dangers of Dzogchen practice is usually included in texts of Dzogchen instruction. In the *Garland of Vision* Padmasambhava's warning is to the preceptor rather than the student: "The preceptor should not initiate the many students who fail in this preliminary work [in the lower vehicles] and prove unworthy." Immature disciples, or disciples without the necessary perspicacity, attempting to practice Dzogchen, even though they are firmly based in practice of the lower vehicles, can become troublemakers and are likely to form a negative view of Dharma in general due to their failure to obtain the intuitive realizations. This is a very different approach to Dzog-chen's dangers from Shabkar Lama's injunction that the yogin beware of the demon that can possess him and turn him into a black magician.

Non-Asceticism (pp. 156–57)

It may not be clear from the passage on the "unsurpassable asceticism" that the discipline involved in no-discipline is the most rigorous and demand-ing. Once the yogin has gained some control over the body and mind through discipline of any kind, whether it be football, gymnastics, or *kriyā-yoga,* will power is developed. If the motivation is strong then determina-tion will be equally strong, and the human machine will be capable of superior feats of discipline, endurance, and accomplishment. Dzogchen is not sought by the hero or the superachiever, the yogi on his bed of nails, or the Scotts and Shackletons of the mundane world. Whatever level of Dzogchen discipline is considered—physical, ethical, or mental—one central precept governs action of body, speech, and mind: no indulgence or abstinence, no judgment or evaluation, no cultivation or rejection. This does not mean that the personality will remain the same under Dzogchen discipline, and neither does it mean that it will change. It is an eccentricity to judge and condemn one's own vices, just as it is to cultivate one's virtues: they are to be left alone. Cultivation of virtue is something that has been perfected in the lower approaches to buddhahood. The preceptor should not give Dzogchen precepts to a student whose accumulation of virtuous qualities is unfinished. In Dzogchen, "Let it be" is the watchword. On the mental level the discipline is the same: the samadhi of universal identity is not attained by mental discrimination of any kind. If a silent mind has been cultivated in another discipline, all the better, but in Dzogchen it is of no greater efficacy than a mind that is constantly chattering. The silent mind is no closer to Dzogchen accomplishment than the chatterer.

Obviously nothing can be said in terms of conventional discipline—physical, moral, or mental—that is relevant to Dzogchen discipline. So here we may have discovered an important indicator: whatever may be said in conventional moral terms has no bearing on Dzogchen conduct. Dzogchen is a nondual discipline, and dualistic analysis is counterproductive. Whenever the temptation arises to posit an antithetical extreme as an antidote to a moral or mental problem, forget it. The middle way cannot be approached through any form of dichotomy; the middle way passes through every extreme whatsoever; the middle way automatically resolves all dualism and polarities; the middle way is beyond dualistic thought and analysis. Look for the source of the unifying power and you have already failed to find it. Want it, and you have locked yourself in a trap from which desirelessness is the only way out. But desire desirelessness and the darkness grows deeper. Thinking about it, you are caught in counterproductive dualistic analysis; but ceasing to think about it, you are at the mercy of passionate reaction. So what is the answer? The true lama and initiatory experience.

Finally, then, we are back to intuitive realization of sustaining grace. As the text stresses, there are many sources of sustaining grace, but experiencing the blessing of the buddha-lama is the most accessible, certain, and potent. The

Garland of Vision does not emphasize the role of the lama, but in *The Flight of the Garuda,* Shabkar Lama's explicit remarks and his implications are clear: the lama is the source of transmission and initiation, and when in doubt take refuge in him.

Secret Instruction in a Garland of Vision[172]

A special condensed memory aid to vision and vehicle

Homage to Mañjuśrikumārabhūta and Vajradharma!

I. Mundane Vision

The innumerable errant visions of sentient beings in the mundane sphere are subsumed under four broadly inclusive heads: hedonistic vision, atheistic vision, nihilistic vision, and eternalistic vision.

1. The Hedonist

The hedonist fails to realize that all events have a cause and an effect. He is totally confused.

2. The Atheist

Blind to past and future lives, the atheist strives for power and wealth in this single lifetime. He depends upon intrigue.

3. The Nihilist

The nihilist is convinced that there is no causal relationship between events. In his rejectionist view he sees everything that happens to him in this lifetime as adventitiously arisen chance events that vanish into the void. In the end, death is ultimate cessation.

4. The Eternalist

The eternalist filters all events through his creative imagination, perceiving an eternal soul. Variously, eternalists see the soul as having a cause but no effect, an effect but no cause, and a confused causal relationship. This is all ignorance bereft of any gnostic insight.

II. Transcendental Vision

There are two ways to travel the transcendental path: on the Vehicle of Specific Attributes (the *Lakṣaṇayāna*), and on the Adamantine Vehicle (the *Vajrayāna*).

A. The Vehicle of Specific Attributes

There are three different approaches taken by the Vehicle of Specific Attributes: the disciple's approach in the *Śrāvakayāna,* the recluse's approach in the *Pratyekabuddhayāna,* and the bodhisattva's approach in the *Bodhisattvayāna.*

(i)[1][173] The Disciple's Vision

The eternalist's vision of an eternal soul and the nihilist's vision of ultimate nothingness, conceived by fixating on the extremes of existence and nonexistence respectively, are like someone's mistaken perception of a rope as a snake. In the vision of adherents to the disciple's approach these extremes are rejected. The disciple views the atoms of the four elements that comprise the five psychophysical constituents, the elements of the sensory process and the sense fields, and consciousness as well, as existing absolutely. Contemplating the four noble truths, the disciple gradually realizes the four aspects of the goal.

(ii)[2] The Recluse's Vision

Adherents of the recluse's approach agree with the disciple in his rejection of the eternalist's notion of an eternal soul and the nihilist's notion of ultimate nothingness, and other such concepts derived from extreme positive or negative interpretations of events. What is specific to the recluse's vision is his realization of the absence of any substantial essence in just the objective aspect of phenomena, the psychophysical constituent of form.[174] Further, while striving for his goal of self-illumination, he employs the insights and habits of mind gained in previous meditation experience rather than relying upon a spiritual friend as does the disciple. Thus equipped, he realizes the true meaning and value of life that underlies events through contemplation of the twelve interdependent elements of the field of relative existence.[175] In this way he attains his goal of self-illumination.

(iii)[3] The Bodhisattva's Vision

In the vision of adherents of the bodhisattva approach, neither passion-defiled experience nor thoroughly purified, immaculate experience has any ultimate existence. On the relative level, insofar as all phenomena are only magical illusion, they are also without any specific attributes. Practicing the ten transcendental perfections,[176] the bodhi-sattva gradually traverses the ten levels leading to accomplishment of unsurpassable enlightenment, which is the goal of his path.

B. The Adamantine Vehicle, the Vajrayāna
There are three approaches in the adamantine vehicle, the *Vajrayāna*: the approach of the ritual-action tantra, *kriyātantra;* the approach of mixed ritual action and internal mind yoga, called *ubhayatantra* or *caryātantra;* and the approach of fully internalized yoga, *yogatantra.*

(i)[4] Kriyātantra Vision
This is the vision of adherents of the ritual-action approach. On the ultimate level the yogin is centered in the space where phenomena neither come into being nor cease to be. On the relative plane the *kriyātantra* yogin's meditation is concentrated upon visualization of the pure-being of a god's form—the representation of the god's being, his archetypal features—and the recitation of mantra and liturgies. Also of vital importance are the yogin's ritual purity, and his knowledge of propitious and ill-omened times and the movement of the planets and stars. A beneficent environment is established thereby, and through the power of synchronistic conjunctions of objects and mental conditions, he attains his goal.

(ii)[5] Caryātantra Vision
This is the vision of adherents of the dual approach, *ubhaya-* or *caryātantra.* On the ultimate level the yogin is centered where there is neither birth nor dying. On the relative level, visualizing the pure-being of the god's form, the *caryātantra* yogin attains his goal through meditation involving four degrees of samadhi relying upon synchro-nistic conjunction of objects and mental conditions. Thus he com-bines ritual action and mind yoga.

(iii) Yogatantra Vision
The vision of adherents of the mind yoga approach *(yogatantra)* has two aspects: the outer *yogatantra* of mastery and the inner *yogatantra* of skillful means.

1.[6] Vision in the Tantra of Mastery
This is the vision of initiates into the outer *yogatantra* of mastery. Denying the primacy of the environment, the yogin of the outer *yogatantra* identifies his mindstream with the union of the ultimately unborn and undying god and goddess. In a samadhi of immaculate being he concentrates primarily upon the yoga of creative visualization of the pure-being of the god's noble form endowed with four seals,[177] and he attains his goal.

2. Vision in the Tantra of Skillful Means
This is the vision of initiates into the inner *yogatantra* of skillful means. This vehicle has three modes: the creative mode, the fulfillment mode, and the mode of Dzogchen, the Great Perfection.

(i)[7] The Creative Mode
In the creative stage with the three degrees of samadhi[178] gradually evolving, the mandala is constructed step by step, and through creative visualization, the goal is attained.

(ii)[8] The Fulfillment Mode
In the fulfillment stage, on the ultimate level, the unborn and undying god and goddess and the essence of the yogin's silent mind do not stir from the central channel, which is a vast plenum of space, the continuum of reality. On the relative plane the yogin visualizes the pure-being of noble form[179] as radiance, accomplishing his goal by meditating upon unalloyed sameness.

(iiia)[9] The Mode of the Great Perfection
The Dzogchen yogin's meditation begins with intuitive realization of the primal mandala of buddha-body, buddha-speech, and buddha-mind, inherent in the indivisible nature of all mundane samsaric events and all transcendental nirvanic events.

The mandala is described in the tantra like this:

The vajra psychophysical constituents—
extol them as the Five Perfected Dhyāni Buddhas;
and the elements of the sensory process and the sense fields—
in truth these form the bodhisattva mandala.
Earth is Locanā, water is Māmaki;
fire is Pāṇḍaravāsinī, air is Tārā,
and space is Dhātiśvarī:
The three realms are immaculate from the beginning.

All experience of the phenomena of samsara and nirvana is ultimately unborn, and since his inherently dynamic, fertile, and provoca-
tive magical illusion[180] *(māyā)* has as its ultimate nature the Five
Sugatas and their consorts in eternal embrace, the yogin's every experience naturally transcends the pain of samsara. The inherent nature
of the five great elements is the Five Buddha Consorts, and the inherent nature of the five psychophysical constituents is the Five Buddhas
of the five families; the inherent nature of the four forms of consciousness is the Four [Inner] Bodhisattvas, and the inherent nature
of the four objects of consciousness is the Four Beautiful Goddesses;
the inherent nature of the four sensory doors is the Four [Outer]
Bodhisattvas, and the inherent nature of the four aspects of time is
the four offering goddesses; the inherent nature of the body as a sensory organ, the consciousness that attends it, the object of tactile consciousness, and the awakened mind that arises from the conjunction
of organ, object, and consciousness are the Four Wrathful Deities, and
the inherent nature of the four extreme ontological notions is the
Four Wrathful Female Deities; the inherent nature of mental consciousness is the awakened mind of the bodhisattva Dorje Kuntu
Zangpo; and the inherent nature of all events in samsara and nirvana,
both simple and compound, is the illusionist of the path, the female
bodhisattva Kuntu Zangmo. Again, from the very beginning, the
inherent nature of all these deities is the manifestly perfected, awakened, and purified mind of the Ādibuddha, and for this reason these
deities are not to be accomplished sequentially.

Thus nothing of the ten directions, the three aspects of time, the
three realms, and so on, all interpreted samsaric experience and all

direct nirvanic experience, has any existence apart from mind. As it is said in the scriptures:

> *The mind differentiated—so many concepts—*
> *these are all buddhas and bodhisattvas,*
> *in actuality the three realms*
> *and the five elements.*

> *All experience of samsara and nirvana is located in the mind;*
> *mind abides in space; space is indeterminate.*

> *All events are empty by virtue of their empty essence;*
> *all events are immaculately pure in their origin;*
> *all events are all-embracing clear light;*
> *all events transcend suffering spontaneously;*
> *all events are manifestly perfect buddhahood.*

Such is the Great Perfection.

(iiib) The Mode of the Great Perfection
Perfection implies complete and perfect attainment of the karmas of virtue and awareness;[181] and the Dharma of spontaneity, which is the result of this completion, is the quality of this mode of being.[182]

The mode of the Great Perfection is a fourfold intuitive realization that progressively quickens profound confidence.

The Fourfold Intuitive Realization
The four modes of intuitive realization are intuitive realization of the unitary cause, intuitive realization by means of sacred letters, intuitive realization through sustaining grace, and direct and immediate intuitive realization.[183]

1. Intuitive Realization of the Unitary Cause
On the ultimate level all events in samsara and nirvana never come into being, and so have no separate existence. On the relative plane

they are illusory figments of mind, so again they have no separate existence. They are unoriginated events appearing in a plethora of magical illusion, which is like the reflection of the moon in water, possessing an inherent acausal dynamic. Since this essentially insubstantial magical illusion also never comes into being, ultimate and relative are identical and their identity is the one cause. Thus intuitive realization [of total presence] arises [with attainment of the unity of the two truths].[184]

2. Intuitive Realization by Means of Sacred Letters

All events in samsara and nirvana, unoriginated, are the sacred letter "A," the actuality of buddha-speech. The unoriginated, appearing as magical illusion with an inherent acausal dynamic, is the sacred letter "O," the actuality of buddha-body. In the same way, the total presence that is the cognitive factor in intuitive realization and the primal awareness without center or circumference that infuses magical illusion is the sacred letter "OM," the actuality of buddha-mind. Intuition of these three sacred letters as buddha-body, buddha-speech, and buddha-mind is intuitive realization [of total presence] by means of sacred letters.

3. Intuitive Realization through Sustaining Grace[185]

Just as red dye saturates white cloth, the power of sustaining grace infuses acts of adoration and praise. Sustaining grace likewise pervades all events in samsara and nirvana, purifying them and awakening awareness. This blissful power that pervades all things, in addition to the power realized through unitary cause and sacred letters, is sustaining grace. Realization of this is intuitive realization [of total presence] attained through sustaining grace.

4. Direct and Immediate Intuitive Realization

Although all events in samsara and nirvana exist from the beginning as pure and awakened being, there must be no conflict [in vision] with either the transmission of the root tantras or the guru's instruction. Dependence upon the literal letter of instruction and transmission must have dissolved. Then, profound confidence gradually arising in the depths of the mind of total presence, direct and immediate intuitive realization is attained.

Progressive Quickening of Confidence

The total presence that is the essential value and objective of the fourfold intuitive realization is the yogin's path whereon confidence is increased. On this path there is no expectant waiting for the time when a goal is reached as a result of accomplishing a cause. Direct, immediate, intuitive realization and confidence arise together spontaneously.

The Three Components

Three absolutely specific components constitute the ultimate accomplishment. The total presence operating as the fourfold intuitive realization is the cognition component; the repetition that inculcates a habitual view is the application component; and actualization through conditioning—by force of habit—is the fruition component.

The Three Principles

These three specific components of accomplishment (listed above) demonstrate the three principles: the cognitive component demonstrates contingent effect; the application component demonstrates the imperative; and the component of fruition demonstrates the categorical imperative.

1. The Contingent Effects of the Cognitive Component

All conceptualization, whether of passion-tainted or utterly immaculate events, is essentially buddha-body, buddha-speech, and buddha-mind, an intrinsically purified and awakened field. Intuitive realization of this field of buddha-nature and intuitive realization of this field as the essential basis of sustaining grace are effects contingent upon the cognitive function. These effects of the cognitive component are the conditions for accomplishing unsurpassable buddhahood.

2. The Imperative Application, or the Practical Component

All conceptualization, whether of passion-tainted or utterly immaculate events, conceptualization of the five panaceas or the five nectars, all is one in the ultimate sameness that is pure and awakened from the beginning. In this universal identity there is no partiality, no judgment, no preference for this more than that, and no cultivation of or indulgence in some things and renunciation or rejection of others. This perfect tolerance is the practical component, which is imperative since it is a necessary condition for accomplishing unsurpassable buddhahood.

3. The Categorically Imperative Fruition Component

All specific conceptualization, such as all passion-tainted or utterly immaculate events, the five panaceas, the five nectars, and so on, is from the beginning spontaneously accomplished, devoid of indulgence or inhibition, in the space of universal identity. For this reason the wheel of existence is from the beginning spontaneously accomplished as nirvana, the actuality of unsurpassable purity and awakened awareness. Thus the fruition component is buddha-body, buddha-speech, and buddha-mind manifest as an inexhaustible wheel of manifest ornamentation. This is the categorical imperative.

The Four Degrees of Practice

To attain the ultimate fruition the yogin must dedicate himself to the yoga in which the essential reality of *approach, close approach, accomplishment,* and *sublime accomplishment* becomes spontaneously existent.

1. *Approach* is bodhisattva-perception. When all events are gradually accomplished as the actuality of ultimate purity and awakened awareness, with the aid of allies and supports, authentic intuitive realization is attained.

2. *Close approach* is perception of oneself as the buddha-deity. As all events, all phenomena, are from the beginning the actuality of purity and awakened awareness, the yogin himself has the nature of a divine being from the first. This is established by the yogin with the intuitive realization that the buddha-deity has no substantial existence.

3. *Accomplishment* is production of the female consort. Out of the field of space that is the great mother, the great mother appears as earth, water, fire, and air, and from the beginning it is she who is the dynamic matrix. *Production of the female consort* is intuitive realization of this great mother.

4. *Sublime Accomplishment* is the conjunction of skillful means and perfect insight. The Five Great Mothers' perfect insight and the emptiness of the feminine space matrix is conjoined with the father of the Five Buddhas of the five psychophysical constituents: they have formed an ineluctable union from the beginning. This conjunction produces brother and sister bodhisattva emanations, whose actuality is mind pure and awakened from the beginning: an illusion dancing with an illusion in a scenario of magical illusion. The blissful situation wherein this illusion of supreme pleasure[186] arises is a reality devoid of marks and signs, coextensive with nonreferential space. When this has become a continuum, there is spontaneous accomplishment. Thus the four demon spirits[187] are vanquished and the ultimate goal attained.

The Spontaneous Dzogchen Mandala

Since all events are immaculate from the beginning, every experience of samsara and nirvana is an immeasurable wish-fulfilling palace, a wheel of limitless dimension. This is the buddha-mandala, primal and unsurpassable. To disclose the mandala is to absorb transmission of the root texts of the vehicle of skillful means *(anuttarayogatantra)*. To see the mandala is intuitive realization of its nature. To enter the mandala is to gain a constant, habitual realization of its nature. To attain the supreme power is to realize its reality after entering therein. By this mode the ultimate reality of the Great Perfection is attained.

Spontaneous Arrival at the Level of the Great Assembly of Sacred Letter Wheels[188]

Highly intelligent people understanding the meaning of *originally pure and awakened from the beginning* as originally pure and awakened from the beginning reject the regular course of study and practice because effective conditioning of the mind in the way of the buddhas is a long and slow process. Common minds listening to the secret teaching, regardless of how they interpret its substance, cannot reach true and profound confidence. Ordinary devotional minds with weak comprehension fail to perceive the true and profound in the teaching, and after experiencing delusory phenomena in their meditation, they believe that other practitioners have experiences similar to their own. They then curse others as liars, reviling superior beings. Adopting disputatious attitudes they insist upon a more secret vehicle to obtain the ultimate secret. Since there are so many obstacles to spontaneous recognition, until the intellect has evolved to intuitively understand the meaning of *pure and awakened from the beginning* as pure and awakened from the beginning, the preceptor should exhaustively teach the student the defects of samsara, the qualities of nirvana, and skill in the techniques of every lower approach to buddhahood, even though the disciple's eventual goal is to go beyond the lower methods. The preceptor should not initiate the many students who fail in this preliminary work and prove unworthy.

III. Ascetic Practices

There is a great diversity of specific ascetic and purificatory practices associated with the various visions. The hedonist and the nihilist have no ascetic practices, but there are four types of asceticism practiced by those who value self-abnegation: the materialists' and the eternalists' mundane asceticism, the disciple's asceticism, the bodhisattva's asceticism, and the unsurpassable asceticism of the Dzogchen yogin.

1. The Hedonist
The hedonist does not practice asceticism because he is confused about cause and effect.

2. The Nihilist
The nihilist has no ascetic practice because of his nihilist views.

3. The Materialist
The materialist practices ritual purity and other such mundane ascetic practices in order to attain specific advantages in this life.

4. The Eternalist
The eternalist practices false purificatory techniques, such as the ascetic rite in which five fires[189] are believed to purify the body, and similar methods, with the intention of purifying the everlasting soul.

5. The Disciple
As it is said in the *Vinaya:*

> *Commit no sin whatsoever;*
> *exercise every excellent virtue;*
> *thoroughly train your own mind:*
> *This is the Buddha's doctrine.*

The disciple believes that all virtuous and vicious events exist independently, as either relative or ultimate entities, so he practices physical disciplines and ascetic techniques to cultivate virtue and eradicate vice.

6. The Bodhisattva
It is said in *The Bodhisattva Vow*[190]

> *Do not act pragmatically*
> *and do not project threatening illusions;*
> *since it is compassionate and loving*
> *there is no fault in a healthy mind.*

When the yogin is governed by transcendent compassion, nothing he does, be it virtuous or unvirtuous, will impair his vow. The bodhisattva's vow, in brief, is to act from the base of transcendent compassion.

7. The Dzogchen Yogin
The unsurpassable asceticism: It is said in the *Sutra of the Great Commitment:*[191]

> *When the yogin has realized the superior method of the buddhas,*
> *even though he indulges constantly in the five passions and sense pleasures,*
> *he remains uncontaminated, like a lotus growing, unsullied, in a swamp:*
> *Here is the most excellent discipline.*

Since all events in samsara and nirvana are ultimately identical, there is no need to cultivate compassion or to reject anger. Similarly, if the mind is merely silent, compassionate responsiveness will not necessarily arise. Depending upon what arises—mental chatter pure from the beginning or a silent mind pure from the beginning—then either ascetic discipline or purificatory transformation is practiced, and action is either immaculate or impure.

This secret garland of vision
is like the gift of sight to a blind man.
If a superior being with skill in wisdom and means exists,
may you meet him.

Thus *Secret Instruction in a Garland of Vision* is completed.

THE THREE INCISIVE PRECEPTS:

THE EXTRAORDINARY REALITY OF SOVEREIGN WISDOM

with a Short Commentary by Patrul Rinpoche

INTRODUCTION

THE ROOT GURU of the Buddhist Dzogchen lineages is Garab Dorje. Born in the seventh century in Orgyen, Land of the Ḍākinīs, he attained buddhahood there. Garab Dorje was a tulku of the bodhisattva Vajrapāṇi, Master of the Tantric Mysteries, and from Vajrapāṇi he received the entire corpus of Dzogchen scriptures, which were then written down by the ḍākinīs. In the early days it was customary for a guru to give a last testament, the quintessence of his teaching, to his principal heart son; Garab Dorje gave his principal disciple, Mañjuśrīmitra, instruction in three incisive precepts that describe the essence of Dzogchen praxis.[192] *The Extraordinary Reality of Sovereign Wisdom*[193] is a short elaboration of these three incisive precepts written by Patrul Rinpoche in the nineteenth century. In sixty-six lines of verse this Dzogchen master created a concise and brilliant masterpiece of instruction that comprises, perhaps, the best known and most frequently practiced precepts in the Longchen Heart Essence (Longchen Nyingtig) lineage. Patrul Rinpoche wrote his own short commentary on *The Extraordinary Reality of Sovereign Wisdom* in a highly succinct but comprehensible style. If Dzogchen texts are difficult to comprehend—and even more difficult to translate—then this work of Patrul Rinpoche is the exception to the rule and deserves its high reputation for clarity and simplicity in elucidating the Dzogchen vision and meditation instruction.

The homeland of Patrul Rinpoche was Dzachukha in the far northwest of Kham in eastern Tibet. The Dzachu River is the name of the reaches of the Yalong above Kandze in the area west of Golog, southwest of the Amnye Machen Range, and to the east of Nangchen. The present-day Sershul

District comprises the western part of Dzachukha. Dzachukha is a region of high rolling pastureland broken by valleys and snow-capped peaks, thinly populated by *drogpa* nomads. Born in 1806, the nomad boy, Orgyen Jigme Chokyi Wangpo, was to be recognized as the tulku Samten Puntsog, the incarnate lama of a small monastery called Pelge Gon in Dzachukha. Later he was to be renowned as Dza Patrul Rinpoche. As a youth he received an excellent education from eminent teachers. Śāntideva's *Introduction to the Conduct of a Bodhisattva (Bodhicaryāvatāra)*, Longchenpa's *Trilogy on Natural Ease (Ngelso Korsum)*, and the *Guhyagarbhatantra* were prominent among the texts he studied. It appears that he was a brilliant student. His formal tulku education was prematurely arrested, however, by murky events that led to his expulsion from the monastery. We have no details of this episode or how old the boy was when it occurred, but it initiated a lifetime of renunciation in the style of a wandering ascetic. Although he became renowned through-out Kham, Dzachukha remained his home.[194]

At the beginning of the nineteenth century the renaissance of the Red Hat schools in Kham was still in its infancy. Kunkhyen Jigme Lingpa (1729–89), who may be considered the inspiration of the nonsectarian movement and who taught in central Tibet, had passed away. His two principal Khampa students, Jigme Gyelwai Nyugu and Dodrub Chen, had returned to Kham, and it was the first of these in whom Patrul Rinpoche found his root guru and master. In the early years of his renunciate practice, Gyelwai Nyugu, shunning even the protection of hermitage or cave, lived on a remote mountainside in a depression in the ground, gathering wild plants for his sustenance. Gradually disciples gathered around him, living in yak-hair tents on the hillside. One of these disciples was Patrul Rinpoche.

The visionary and mystic Kunkhyen Jigme Lingpa was the author of the Dzogchen teaching called the Longchen Nyingtig, which he received in a series of visions from his root guru, Longchen Rabjampa, who had passed away in the fourteenth century. The Longchen Nyingtig lineage was to become the principal vehicle of Dzogchen teaching during the Nyingma nonsectarian *(rime)* movement in Kham as well as in Amdo. It was this tra-dition, above all, that the refugee lamas brought with them from Kham and propagated to their Western disciples in India and Europe, and in America in the late twentieth century. Patrul Rinpoche received the Longchen Nyingtig transmission from Gyelwai Nyugu not just once but many times:

it is said that he listened to the master's exposition of the preliminary practice twenty-five times.

Gyelwai Nyugu eventually founded a monastery in Dzachukha called Trawa or Gyelgon. Patrul Rinpoche spent several years there taking instruction from other Khampa masters, particularly, from Mingyur Namkhai Dorje at the Dzogchen monastery in central Kham, where he spent years in seclusion in the caves of the district. Certainly his meditation practice included the purificatory practice of the Longchen Nyingtig, and indeed he may exemplify, par excellence, the yogin who attains the ultimate Dzogchen goal by focusing on simple purification practice. He also practiced the Longchen Nyingtig *anuyoga* discipline of energy control.

At the age of thirty Patrul Rinpoche began his constant wandering throughout Kham, teaching at the monasteries, writing his inimitable treatises, staying in hermitages and caves, gathering scholarly monk as well as simple nomad and villager disciples. Teaching an uncompromising scorn for mundane concerns, material goods and wealth, and institutional power and its trappings, his name became a watchword for humility and integrity. Offered gold, he would accept it and leave it on the ground like a pile of dung. After he became a renowned lama his lifestyle remained unaltered. Once he met a lama on the road who saw him as an excellent vehicle for the Dzogchen teaching and taught him the *Kunzang Lama,* Patrul Rinpoche's own treatise. Another time he traveled with a widow and her children, doing menial chores for her and carrying her children on his back. Later, at their destination, the woman was amazed to see the beggar who had helped her sitting on a high throne addressing the monastic community.

Patrul Rinpoche's name became a synonym for kindness, though it would be an error to conceive of him as an angelic simpleton, for another side of his personality shows his compassion in an aggressive mode, probing his disciples' minds for hidden personality weaknesses and repressed instincts. Here he demonstrated Jowo Atiśa's maxim, "The best spiritual friend is he who attacks your hidden faults;"[195] and in this process of ego destruction he used wit and humor. While he was in retreat, two monk academics led a crowd of monks and villagers to his hermitage intent on challenging his nonsectarian perspective and publicly humiliating him. Hoping first to establish his lineal roots and thus his doctrinal affiliation, they asked him what his school was, expecting the answer "Nyingma." Patrul replied that he was a disciple of Śākyamuni Buddha. When they asked the name of his root guru, expecting the reply "Gyelwai Nyugu," Patrul replied that the Three Jewels— Buddha, Dharma, and Sangha—were his root teacher. Finally they asked him his initiatory name *(Sangtsen)*, which would certainly reveal his lineage, but in answer Patrul stood up and pulled up his robe and showed them his penis *(sangtsen)*. This vulgar pun reduced the audience to howls of laughter, and the monks slunk away in defeat.

A verse of homage to Patrul Rinpoche characterizes him in his public manifestation as the bodhisattva Śāntideva, in his internal reality as the *mahāsiddha* Śavaripa, and in his hidden reality the exalted Self-Released Suffering.[196] Śāntideva was the *mahāsiddha* who was chastised for eating, sleeping, and general laxity at his monastery when he should have been studying, and who gained the sobriquet Busuku thereby. Is this a veiled reference to the cause of Patrul Rinpoche's expulsion from his monastery? Śāntideva more than redeemed himself by composing and reciting extempore in monastic assembly the *Bodhicaryāvatāra*, the *Introduction to the Bodhisattva's Conduct*, which became a much-loved classic in Buddhist literature and a manual for pursuing the six perfections as the bodhisattva's conduct. Patrul Rinpoche studied this work as a boy, taught it widely and frequently as a man, and characterized Dzogchen action in *The Extraordinary Teaching of Sovereign Wisdom* by the pursuit of the six perfections.

Mipam Namgyel Gyatso was one renowned recipient of Patrul's transmission of the famous ninth chapter of the *Bodhicaryāvatāra* on the perfection of perfect insight. Patrul Rinpoche's standing as a nonsectarian scholar and master of the *Bodhicaryāvatāra* is evinced upon the subsequent request to act as judge in a debate between Mipam Jamyang Gyatso and a Gelugpa master. Mipam was declared the winner, and Patrul Rinpoche thereafter authorized him to write on the topic. Mipam's incomparable commentary on the ninth chapter was the result.

If Patrul Rinpoche's outward behavior was consonant with Śāntideva's ethos, then his internal motivation as a reflection of the yogin Śavaripa's character is more difficult to perceive. Śavaripa was a tribal hunter who was converted from his murderous lifestyle by the compassion of Saraha, the root guru of a mother-tantra lineage who showed him the karmic effects of killing. In the wake of Śavaripa's consequent fear, Saraha gave him initiation and a practice of formless compassion that led to *mahāmudrā* realization. We know Patrul Rinpoche was instrumental in curbing bloody feast rites among some Amdo tribals, but the tantric side of him remains undisclosed.

Self-released Suffering, the name of his secret sublime awareness, indicates Patrul Rinpoche's Dzogchen realization. Suffering is the nature of all conditioned existence, the quality of all pleasure and pain, joy, and sorrow. But when all such suffering is released at the moment of its inception naturally and reflexively, conditioned existence becomes the inexpressible unconditioned nature of the Great Perfection. Like meeting an old friend, like a snake uncoiling its knots, like a thief entering an empty house, whatever arises in the mind is spontaneously released. No trace remains, so the yogin's process is like the flight path of a bird in the sky. This is how Patrul Rinpoche himself expresses the process of self-released suffering in his extraordinary teaching.

The three incisive precepts of Garab Dorje enumerate the three basic imperatives of Dzogchen praxis. The first is a direct introduction into the nature of mind; the second, absolute conviction in the mode of practice; and the third is implicit confidence in release.

The exegetical and didactic traditions of Dzogchen stick fast to the conventional analytic frame of view, meditation, and action. In *The Extraordinary Teaching of Sovereign Wisdom* Patrul Rinpoche attaches the three precepts to an elucidation of view alone. The view, he maintains, is nothing but the meditation itself, and action arises spontaneously out of the meditation. According to this definition, the view is not an integral discursive philosophical system but rather a vision of reality induced by the self-fulfilling precepts that describe it; the vision is like a three-hundred-sixty-degree global gaze into all-pervasive space beyond zenith and nadir. Therefore in this translation I have translated the Tibetan word *tawa* as "vision," implying a holistic existential state, rather than the conventional word *view*, which can denote an intellectual structure.

In the vision of the Great Perfection there is a flawless and seamless reality field that is known through nondual perception. In the vocabulary of Dzogchen such pristine cognition is called *the primal awareness of total presence.*[197] This total presence is the vision itself. Therefore any Dzogchen praxis is predicated upon an introduction to this vision, and Garab Dorje's first precept, his first imperative, is an introduction to the nature of mind. Patrul Rinpoche mentions some traditional ways in which this vision is induced;

each culture surely has its own peculiar methods. The tantric method of ritual initiation provides what is called *illustrative awareness,* of which the essential detached bliss of the climax of sexual union remains the paradigm, and this analogy is realized in the formal, symbolic, but simple word (or *the fourth*) initiation that matures it. But Patrul Rinpoche's extraordinary teaching has at its heart the method of self-introduction to the nature of mind by means of an explosive utterance of the syllable PHAT. In the mental silence that follows immediately upon this expletive, the nature of a deconditioned, deconstructed mind may be intuited, and this is his introduction to the nature of mind.

Existential experience of the nature of mind, which is total presence, is Dzogchen meditation, or rather nonmeditation, which is neither a contrived meditation technique nor a conscientious attempt at quietistic nomeditation. Nonmeditation praxis constitutes Dzogchen vision. Although nonmeditation is a twenty-four-hour-a-day continuum and no technique is allowed to obstruct it, until repeated introductions into the nature of mind have induced a familiarity with it that is irreversible, there is a necessity to include sessions of formal meditation within the twenty-four-hour period.

Within these meditation sessions, *vision* encompasses the entire phenomenology of the mind, beginning with absolute quiescence, stillness, and silence, and including every slight movement of thought, vibration of feeling, and energy expression. In his commentary Patrul Rinpoche makes a salient distinction between desire and hatred and their accompanying waves of judgmental thought, and happiness and sadness as affective states, all of which are realized as the free play of primal awareness. It is this awareness of whatever comes down during or in between formal sessions of meditation as a creative free-form dance, the play of empty form, a phantasmagoric display, that facilitates the second of Garab Dorje's precepts—absolute conviction in the mode of practice.

Within the experience of vision and meditation, the yogin's release from samsara and nirvana is implicit. The nature of this release is described as dissolution of thoughtforms, emotion, and feeling, as each arises, at their inception, *leaving no trace,* like the path of a bird in the sky. The yogin himself is thus the garuda and his process is its flight. The process of release is inherent in total presence of primal awareness and is what distinguishes Dzogchen nonmeditation from other formless modes of contemplation. If this process is absent, then the yogin dwells in the formless realms of the gods bound to sticky essences like love or consciousness. The process of release may be facilitated by gazing at the bare essence of experience, as it arises, which of course is emptiness, and it is confidence in the process of release effected by existential emptiness that is the third of Garab Dorje's precepts.

The most important single thread that runs through *The Extraordinary Reality of Sovereign Wisdom* is *total presence (rig pa)*. The first imperative is an introduction to total presence, which is the nature of mind. Initiatory experience into the Great Perfection is defined by its nature as total presence and the experience of mind in the wake of the mind-shattering PHAT! is all-penetrating, naked, total presence.[198] The conviction that is the second imperative is utter certainty that experience of the nature of mind in an unbroken stream is total presence and that whatever arises is the expression and the play of total presence. Total presence is sustained through the praxis of remaining without inhibiting or identifying with the thoughtforms and emotions that arise. Total presence as natural, intrinsic awareness is recognized as the nature of all experience whatsoever; but it is also seen as the awareness implicit in the introduction to the nature of mind. When these two sources of total presence are recognized as one, the clear light of mother and son have united. The third imperative is implicit confidence in the process of release, which is both a function of total presence and the certain condition of its potentiation. Further, with the certainty that total presence is the natural state, inasmuch as intense thoughtforms are larded with emotion, to that extent is total presence potentiated with clarity and radiance.

Both the laboratory of practice and the natural and authentic reality of total presence are *pure being*, which is *dharmakāya*. It is the free play of pure being, in whatever form it may take, that constitutes total presence, so it is crucial that the intellect make no attempt to control or alter the natural expression of pure being. All appearances arise out of pure being and dissolve back into it through its natural process of release, and thus in total presence there is no carry-through to create miasmic thought trains or deepening shadows of emotional attachment. The natural condition of pure being provides the modality of nonmeditation by which each and every emanation of it is reduced to its original nature. The process of release from the wheel of samsara and the quiescence of nirvana is inherent in the natural condition of pure being.

Although the somewhat abstruse formulation of Patrul Rinpoche's commentary may provide a contrary opinion, Patrul Rinpoche came of nomad stock and was known as a man of the people. He spoke and taught in language that everyone could understand. His most well-known work is an introduction to the Dzogchen tradition, elucidating the preliminary practices, called the *Kunzang Lamai Zhelung* (translated as *The Words of My Perfect Teacher*). This classic text demonstrates his simple and concise expression. A prolific author and commentator, Patrul Rinpoche's teaching is still very much alive today, but nothing is more potent than *The Extraordinary Reality of Sovereign Wisdom*.

THE EXTRAORDINARY REALITY
OF SOVEREIGN WISDOM

THE ROOT VERSES

Homage to the guru-buddha!

Prologue

Vision is Longchen Rabjam, the All-Pervasive Matrix;
meditation is Khyentse Wozer, Radiance of Wisdom and Love;
action is Gyelwai Nyugu, the Aspiring Buddha.
In the experience of such vision, meditation, and action,
without stress or strain, we attain buddhahood in this lifetime,
and failing that—what peace of mind!

Yes, vision is Longchen Rabjam, the All-Pervasive Matrix, and three precepts
penetrate that essential reality.

I. Direct Introduction to the Nature of Mind

First, keep the mind relaxed,
without projecting or concentrating, free of discursive thought,
and in that space of relaxed openness
abruptly utter a mind-shattering PHAT!
forcefully, loud, and short—and there it is!
Nothing at all but wonderment and illumination.
In illuminated wonderment is all-pervading freedom of mind,
and that all-penetrating freedom of mind is inexpressible:
recognize the total presence of singular pure being!
A direct introduction into the nature of mind is the first imperative.

II. Absolute Conviction

Then, whether there is quiescence or flow,
desire or anger, happiness or sadness,

at all times and in every situation,
sustaining direct recognition of pure being,
the familiar son clear light united with the mother light,
remain in the space of inexpressible presence.

Again and again shatter the elation and clarity of quiescence and flow,
abruptly uttering the syllable of means and insight,
and formal meditation and everyday experience are identical,
and meditation sessions and intervals are indistinguishable:
always remain in a state of nondifferentiation.

But while stability is still developing,
renounce entertainment and cherish meditation
and sit in formal meditation in set periods.

At all times and in every situation,
watch the free play of undivided pure being,
convinced that there is nothing other than that:
absolute conviction is the second imperative.

III. Implicit Confidence in Release

In the event of desire or anger, joy or sorrow,
or any fleeting thought,
with direct recognition no trace remains;
intuiting the liberating aspect of pure being,
as with a figure drawn in water,
spontaneous arising and reflexive release are incessant.

Whatever occurs nourishes naked empty presence,
and whatever moves is the creativity of sovereign pure being:
it is traceless natural purity—how amazing!

The manner of occurrence is the same as before,
the crucial difference lies in release;
in the absence of this crux, meditation is delusion;

possessing it, there is the nonmeditation of pure being:
implicit confidence in release is the third imperative.

Conclusion

Vision endowed with these three imperatives
is enhanced by the meditation
that is the melding of wisdom and love
and exalted by the action that is the bodhisattva's praxis.

Though the buddhas of past, present, and future confer,
there can be no precepts superior to these;
the treasure finder of pure being, creative presence,
took this treasure from the All-Pervasive Matrix of perfect insight;
it is not like an extract from stone,
for it is the final testament of Garab Dorje,
the spiritual elixir of the three transmissions;
and it is entrusted with the seal of secrecy to my heart sons.

This message from my heart is the profound truth;
this vital truth is my heart message.
Do not abandon this vital truth!
Do not let these precepts escape you!

A Short Elucidation
of The Extraordinary Reality
# of Sovereign Wisdom[199]

Homage to the gracious root guru, master of peerless compassion!

Prologue

This elucidation of the *Extraordinary Reality of Sovereign Wisdom* explains how to assimilate the essentials of vision, meditation, and action.

First, because the guru is the embodiment of the Three Jewels, by bowing down to him alone we pay homage to every place of refuge simultaneously. So the first line of the root verses is "Homage to the guru-buddha!"

Then to the substance of the explanation: with the perception that the root guru and all the gurus of the lineage are inseparable from our own minds, vision, meditation, and action are experientially assimilated by the mind. Thus the instruction is given initially by associating vision, meditation, and action, these three, with the meaning of the names of my root and lineal gurus.

Vision is the perception that in the All-Pervasive Matrix *(longchen)* that is the womb of the buddhas, its spaciousness-defying conceptualization, all the infinite *(rabjam)* forms of migrating and quiescent consciousness, whatever they may be, through their total sameness are complete and perfect. So, "Vision is Longchen Rabjam, the All-Pervasive Matrix."

This nonconceptual vision is established in its wisdom aspect *(khyen)* by heightened awareness of perfect insight into the nature of all experience as emptiness. Emptiness is inseparable from the skillful means that is tranquil absorption in kindness and love *(tse),* and this unity is sustained in one-pointed equipoise.[200] This is the meditation that is the melding of emptiness and compassion. So, "Meditation is Khyentse Wozer, Radiance of Wisdom and Love."

Then, for whoever is endowed with such vision and meditation, action is to apply the six perfections (generosity, moral conduct, patience, perseverance, concentration, and meditation) to benefit others in accordance with the altruistic practice of the bodhisattva—the Aspiring Buddha (Gyelwai Nyugu). So, "Action is Gyelwai Nyugu, the Aspiring Buddha."

The person who experiences such vision, meditation, and action is blessed with great good fortune. Hence, "In the experience of such vision, meditation, and action."

Further, after retiring to the seclusion of a mountain hermitage, after abandoning the preoccupations of this mundane existence, if we are able to practice one-pointedly in this very lifetime, we will gain release in the ground of primal purity. So, "Without stress or strain we attain buddhahood in this lifetime."

Even if we fail in that, if we so much as turn our minds toward such vision, meditation, and action, in this lifetime we will be able to make adversity into the path itself, mundane preoccupations will generate only slight expectation or anxiety, and in the next life we will proceed from happiness to happiness. So, "Failing that—what peace of mind!"

In the following step-by-step explanation of the vision, meditation, and action possessing such concomitant benefits, primarily I wish to elucidate the manner in which vision is experienced. "Yes, vision is Longchen Rabjam, the All-Pervasive Matrix."

The substance of this process is contained in three precepts that penetrate the core of experience and eradicate the very soul of delusion. So, "Three precepts penetrate that essential reality."

I. Direct Introduction to the Nature of Mind

First, I shall explain the way to lay open the vision that has yet to be revealed to us. In general there are many ways to induce vision, such as establishing it through scriptural authority and logical proof, as in the philosophical approach; or after having become firmly grounded in the illustrative awareness of the third empowerment, receiving experiential introduction to the primal awareness of the fourth empowerment, which is the method of the common tantras. But the method employed here, the established practice of the fearless lineage of *siddhas,* is to receive the introduction through the dissolution of the conditioned mind.

To elaborate, while the rough waves of delusory thought projections persist, gross discursive thought trains engendered by objects of perception cloud the original face of mind; even though we come face to face with the nature of mind, we do not recognize it. So, in order to allow gross thoughts to settle into their natural clarity, "First, keep the mind relaxed."

Insofar as the mind simply let be without contrivance is itself primal awareness of clear light, we cannot realize our natural state of being by means of any artificial technique. In order for innate awareness to reveal itself, "Without projecting or concentrating, remain free of discursive thought."

A beginner may sustain the mind in its authentic space of natural absorption, but it may not be possible for him to escape clinging to the experiences like elation, clarity, and thoughtlessness that are part of this quiescence. Therefore, "In a space of relaxed openness."

Escaping from the cocoon of attachment to these delusory experiences of quiescence, in order to reveal the natural state of all-penetrating naked presence, "Abruptly utter a mind-shattering PHAT!"

It is of crucial importance to interrupt the flow of discursive thought and to destroy any conscientiously structured meditation practice, so the syllable PHAT! should be uttered emphatically, short and sharp: "Forcefully, loud and short—and there it is!"

At that moment, freedom from presumption as to what is mind and freedom from all points of reference is manifest release. So there is "Nothing at all but wonderment and illumination."

In this space of pure being, free of all objectivity, the all-penetrating naked presence that is mind-dissolving awareness stays in the here and now. So, "In illuminated wonderment is all-penetrating freedom of mind."

Further, this all-penetrating freedom of mind is the nub of the inexpressible immanent awareness that transcends the extremes of creation and cessation, existence and nonexistence, and lies beyond the fields of conceptual endeavor of both speech and thought. So, "All-penetrating freedom of mind is inexpressible."

The crucial significance of this experience is that the total presence inherent in the ground of pure being is the true vision of the unelaborated primal purity that is the continuum of the natural state of mind. Until we recognize vision as presence—and only that—in whatever way we try to cultivate the mind through meditation practice we will be confined to a contrived view and to meditation structured by the intellect. The process of natural consummate perfection being more distant than is the earth from the sky, the indispensable circle of clear light of nonmeditation is absent. Because of this imperative to acknowledge total presence at the outset, "Recognize the total presence of undivided pure being!"

The substance of the foregoing is the first of the three incisive verbal precepts. If we lack an introduction to the vision, there is no state to be sustained by meditation, so it is vital first to have vision revealed to us. It is immanent awareness dwelling in ourselves that is to be revealed, so nothing is to be sought elsewhere, and there is nothing to be generated in consciousness that is not already there. So, "A direct introduction into the nature of mind is the first imperative."

II. Absolute Conviction

Now I shall explain in detail the way in which meditation is experienced. Meditation is an incessant stream existing at all times and in every situation, in quiescence or flow, without inhibiting or indulging one or the other. In quiescence lies the original face of pure being, and in flow we watch the natural creativity of primal awareness. So, "Whether there is quiescence or flow."

No matter what is generated by the ingenuity of our conditioned mind's thoughtforms, whether it is emotion, such as anger or desire, pertaining to the truth of the origin of suffering or feelings, such as happiness and sadness, pertaining to the truth of suffering,[201] if we perceive such thought and feelings and emotions just as they are, it is all the free play of pure being. So, "Desire or anger, happiness or sadness."

We may have been introduced to the vision, but if that state is not sustained in meditation and we slip into ordinary habits of delusory thinking, we are tied to cyclical patterns of existence by the uncontrolled stream of thought. When the flow of consciousness has become separated from the modality of vision, there is no distinction between us and any ordinary deluded person. For this reason it is necessary to sustain the involuntary absorption of nonmeditation "At all times and in every situation."

In that way, no matter what state we are in, there is no need to curb each separate thought and emotion with a specific antidote. Whether there is quiescence or flow and no matter what thought or emotion is generated, the universally liberating, ultimate remedy is contained in a single intuition of the vision that has been revealed to us. So, "Sustaining recognition of the primal awareness of pure being."

And again, no thought or emotion can ever escape the primal awareness of pure being. If we recognize the nature of whatever thought or emotion is generated, because the nature of that thought is the real clear light of the ground of pure being, we recognize what is called *the clear light of the mother lode.* The vision of the clear light of intrinsic presence previously revealed to us by the lama and now reflexively recognized is called *the clear light of the path of practice.* The unification of the clear light of the ground of being with the clear light of the path is called *the meeting of mother and son clear light.*[202] So, "The familiar son clear light uniting with the mother light."

Accordingly, giving constant attention to the clear light of reflexively recognized vision, it is of crucial importance to refrain entirely from inhibiting the thoughts and emotions that are the expression of absorption in that state or identifying with them. So, "Remain in the space of inexpressible presence."

When a beginner sustains such a state for a long time, delusory experiences like elation, clarity, and thoughtlessness will surely cloud the naturally pure, original face of his mind. To break out of this cocoon of delusory experience is to reveal the naked face of total presence, primal awareness shining out from within. Someone said, "Precipitous descent increases the ferocity of a mountain stream; disruption improves the yogin's meditation"; so, "Again and again shatter the elation and clarity of quiescence and flow."

How, we may ask, is this disruption or shattering to be done? When the delusory experience of quiescence, elation, or clarity has set in, or when joyfulness and pleasant visions arise and intensify, we must shatter the cocoon of delusory experience to which we have become attached, immediately, with a lightning strike of the forceful expletive PHAT! PHAT is a combination of the glyph of skillful means, PHA, the *Gatherer,* and the glyph of perfect insight, TA, the *Sunderer.* So, "Abruptly uttering the syllable of means and insight."

In that way, sustaining the inexpressible all-penetrating presence that lies at the core of meditation experience at all times and in every eventuality, there is no distinction between the equipoise of formal meditation and the consequent state of mind that is the meditation of perfect insight into daily life. So, "Formal meditation and everyday experience are identical."

Likewise, there is no distinction between the meditation that is the essence of formal sessions and meditation upon the activity between sessions. So, "Meditation sessions and the gaps in between are indivisible."

In this sublime meditation that is no-meditation, in the natural openness of primal awareness that is an incessant stream of the natural state, since there is not so much as a shadow to focus upon, there cannot be even a split second of distraction. That is the significance of the saying, "There is no meditation process, so no falling away from it! How then can we ever lack nonmeditation?" So, "Always remain in a state of nondifferentiation."

For those who are vessels with an innate affinity for the natural Great Perfection, the type who attains sudden release merely by hearing the instruction, all appearances are always spontaneously released into the ground of their arising, and whatever arises is the free play of pure being where there is no meditation and no meditator. But other, less fortunate individuals who are overwhelmed by delusory thoughts must take a gradual path, cultivating meditation until they have gained stability. So, "While stability is still developing."

In such preliminary meditation, when the circumstances that generate concentrated absorption are appropriate, meditative experience will arise; but no matter how much we prolong our meditation in the midst of distractions and entertainment, no meditative experience will be engendered. So, "Renounce entertainment and cherish meditation."

In meditation there is no difference between the equipoise of formal meditation and experiential insight in daily life; but initially, if we have not realized the nature of meditative absorption, we will be unable to integrate meditative experience of primal awareness into postmeditation experience. We may strive to turn the stream of daily activity into the path, but we will keep getting lost in our bad habits. So, "Sit in formal meditation in set periods."

Now that praxis is divided into sessions and intervals of meditation, we may have confidence in the mental focus that sustains the crucial meditative equipoise during sessions. But if we cannot sustain it continuously after integrating it with insight into the emptiness of daily activity between sessions, the antidote will be ineffective, and carried away by contingent thoughts, we will feel like ordinary human beings. So it is imperative to sustain an all-penetrating insight between sessions, "At all times and in every situation."

It is never necessary to employ any other meditation technique. In the space where meditative equipoise is identical to the vision of pure being, every action and thought is to be watched without calculation, just letting it be, without inhibition or indulgence, with an "easy-come, easy-go" attitude. Hence, "Watch the free play of undivided pure being."

Such praxis of inseparable, introversive, tranquil absorption and extroversive, heightened awareness, the yoga of unelaborated, natural purity, is to watch the uncontrived, innate, original face of mind. This is the very essence of every practice of the Guhyamantra Vajrayana tantras; it is the primal awareness that is the actuality of the fourth empowerment; it is the special wish-fulfilling gem of the meditation lineage, and it is the faultless intention of all the adepts of the lineages of India and Tibet and of all the yogis of the old and new transmissions who attained mastery. An open mind should thus be convinced of the validity and efficacy of this instruction. If we are still salivating over further secret precepts, we are like the elephant keeper who, having left his beast at home, looks for it in the jungle: trapped in a cage of fictional constructs we have no chance of release. Total commitment to our practice, and faith in its efficacy, is essential; so we must be "Convinced that there is nothing other than that."

In that way convinced that the immanent, naked awareness of pure being is buddhahood untouched by delusion, constantly sustain the stream of primal awareness. This is the second incisive precept, and it is of crucial importance. So, "Absolute conviction is the second imperative."

III. Implicit Confidence in Release

Now, although the original face of mind has been revealed, and we are convinced that buddhahood is the primal awareness of pure being, if we lack confidence in the process of release, the mere meditation of a resting, quiescent mind will confine us to a subtly deviant existence in the higher realms of the gods. Such meditation cannot dominate the exigencies of lust and anger; it cannot stop the flow of karmically conditioned impulses; and it cannot turn our conviction into confidence. Thus the process of release is all-important.

Whether fierce attachment to an object of desire or fierce aversion to an object of loathing is generated, or whether feelings of pleasure caused by fortunate circumstances such as the acquisition of wealth, or feelings of pain caused by negative conditions like sickness arise,[203] whatever occurs at that time is the creativity of total presence; and recognition of the primal awareness that is the basis of release is vital. Hence, "In the event of desire or anger, joy or sorrow."

Furthermore, if our practice lacks the vital process of release at inception, any reflection produced by subconscious mental processes will reinforce cyclical patterns of behavior. Therefore, whatever thoughts, gross or subtle, are generated, it is essential to watch their release at inception so that no trace remains. Hence, "Or any fleeting thought."

Through this process thoughts cannot become delusive subconscious assumptions about the nature of reality[204] or fixed intellectual ideas; immersed in the space of inherent, natural attention, reflexively recognizing the original face of whatever thought arises, the thought is released at its inception and there is no residue left in the mind. Guard this state in which thought dissolves instantaneously, like a figure drawn in water, so that "With direct recognition no trace remains."

If thoughts do not dissolve in reflexive release at this time and simple recognition of the thoughtform does not interrupt delusory activity, gaze directly at the bare essence at the moment of recognition. Thereby, resting in the intuition of the primal awareness with which we have become familiar, thoughts dissolve without trace. Since this process is of vital importance, "Intuit the liberating aspect of pure being."

When generation of thoughts and their release are simultaneous, analogous to the simultaneous drawing and vanishing of a figure traced in water—now you see it, now you don't—there is uninterrupted arising and reflexive release. Hence, "As with a figure drawn in water."

Therefore, refraining from interference with whatever appearances emerge, allowing whatever arises to arise as it will, consider the core of practice to be a constant process of dissolution of whatever occurs into its naturally pure condition, so that "Spontaneous arising and reflexive release are incessant."

Accordingly, since thought is the creative potentiation of pure being, whatever thoughtform arises occurs to potentiate total presence; and insofar as gross thoughts laced with the five poisons (desire, hatred, pride, jealousy, and sloth) are generated, to that extent the total presence of release is charged with power and radiance. Thus, "Whatever occurs nourishes naked, empty presence."

When each thought that moves occurs as spontaneous creativity in all-penetrating total presence, regarded without acceptance or rejection, released at the moment of its inception, it can never be other than the free play of pure being. So, "Whatever moves is the creativity of sovereign pure being."

Mental concepts, forms of ignorance and delusion, are purified in the All-Pervasive Matrix of pure being as total presence and primal awareness; whatever movement of thought is engendered in the All-Pervasive Matrix of incessant clear light is empty in its original nature. So, "It is traceless natural purity—amazing!"

After a prolonged intimacy with constant practice of purification and dissolution, thoughts arise as meditation. The distinction between quiescence and movement has broken down, and nothing that arises disturbs basic equanimity. Hence, "The manner of occurrence is the same as before."

Now the manner in which thought potentiates joys and sorrows, and hopes and fears, is the same as in ordinary people. But whereas the ordinary person, in whom inhibition and indulgence, affirmation and denial arise compulsively, conditions himself to karmically patterned behavior and is dominated by desire and anger, the yogin whose thoughts are released at the moment of their inception is endowed with the vital process of release. Initially, thoughts are released by their recognition, in the manner of meeting an old friend; as practice develops, thoughts reflexively release themselves like a snake uncoiling its knots; and, finally, thoughts are released harmlessly and profitlessly, as if a thief entered an empty house. Hence, "The crucial difference lies in release."

On that account it is said, "Knowing meditation but not release—isn't that the divine trance of the gods?" If we invest our confidence in the mere concentrated absorption of a quiescent mind, a meditation technique that lacks the dynamic of release, we stray into high trance states. Our belief in the sufficiency of recognizing quiescence and movement as such is not different from ordinary confused thinking, and although our minds are impregnated with intellectual concepts like *emptiness* and *pure being,* when we are confronted by adverse circumstances, the inadequacy of our remedy is exposed and our innate capability is found wanting. So, "Without this vital process of release, meditation is delusion."

Release at inception, reflexive release, direct release,[205] call it what you will, the function of release whereby thought is reflexively dissolved, leaving no trace, is the crux of direct spontaneous release, which is the extraordinary reality and unique feature of the natural Great Perfection. If this crucial function is operative, whatever thought or emotion is generated manifests as pure being; delusory constructs dissolve into primal awareness; adverse circumstances emerge as friendly helpers; and emotion becomes the path itself. Rejecting none of the vicious or pleasant realms through which consciousness migrates, since samsara is intrinsically pure, we are liberated from the chains of attachment to all possibilities of existence and all tranquil states. Doing nothing at all, effortlessly, we jump through. Hence, "Possessing it, there is the nonmeditation of pure being."

If we lack a basic conviction in the process of release, we may boast that our mindstream has the highest and most rarefied vision and most profound meditation, but since the mind does not benefit from it, and it is no antidote to emotion, we have deviated from the path of intrinsic purity. When the crucial function of reflexive release of spontaneously arising thoughts is operative, however, we may not possess the slightest trace of high philosophical view, or even so much as the slightest refuge of deep meditation, yet it is inevitable that we are released from the bondage of the dualistic structure of our stream of consciousness. Reaching an island of gold, even though we search everywhere, it is impossible to find ordinary earth and stones. In the same way, when quiescence and movement and every thought generated arise as meditation (the melding of emptiness and compassion), even though we search for specific delusory projections, we will not find them. Since confidence in the process of release is directly proportional to our ability to hit the core of existential praxis, "Implicit confidence in release is the third imperative."

Conclusion

These three imperatives (introduction, conviction, and confidence) compose the infallible path that alone is sufficient to bring the vision, meditation, action, and goal of the natural Great Perfection within the province of all-penetrating presence. So the three incisive precepts are indeed also the secret precepts of meditation and action. We do not agree with the usual dogma of scriptural traditionalists that the only valid knowledge is mental knowledge tested by reason against textural and logical proof. Realization of the naked direct perception in primal awareness itself is the vision of primal awareness and total presence, and since vision and meditation have a single value, there is no contradiction in explaining the practice of the three imperatives only in terms of vision. Hence, "The vision endowed with these three imperatives."

Such practice is the infallible essential function of the primally pure path that is the natural Great Perfection, itself the apogee of the nine graduated levels of approach to buddhahood. Just as it is impossible for a king to walk in procession without his entire retinue, the essential modalities of all other approaches to buddhahood accompany the natural Great Perfection as bridges or supports.

Moreover, when we see the original face of mind, which is the spontaneous incandescence of the perfect insight of primordially pure presence, creativity blazes up as the perfect insight born of meditation, and wisdom bursts forth like a swollen summer river. The nature of emptiness is actualized as sublime compassion, love's sensibility radiating impartially—this is true reality. Hence, "It is enhanced by the meditation that is the melding of wisdom and love."

Accordingly, when this essential modality of coincident emptiness and compassion is directly manifest, the bodhisattva's activity consisting of the six perfections, vast and deep, arises as its natural expression just as sunlight is an expression of the sun. Since such activity is conditioned by virtue, everything we do will be done for the sake of others, and perfect vision will prevent us from straying into complacency. Hence, "Exalted by the activity that is the bodhisattva's praxis."

This vision, meditation, and action are the crux of understanding of all the buddhas, past, present, and future, so, "Though the buddhas of past, present, and future confer."

Since there is nothing superior to the final outcome of this sovereign peak of all approaches to buddhahood, the essential path of the vajra heart of the Heart Essence,[206] "There can be no precepts superior to these."

The meaning of this secret instruction is truly the core of the secret instruction of the lineage, but even its expression in poor poetry must also have arisen from the creativity of intrinsic presence. Hence, "The treasure finder of pure being, creative presence."[207]

I have gained little experiential understanding of the meaning of these instructions through the perfect insight of meditation; but the perfect insight of hearing derived from the infallible oral transmission of my wise lama completely destroyed my extravagant preconceptions, and after the perfect insight of study and contemplation had confirmed my understanding, I composed these verses.[208] Hence, "Took this treasure from the All-Pervasive Matrix of perfect insight."

Since this text is not like ordinary material treasure that merely removes poverty temporarily, "It is not like an extract from stone."

These three imperatives of vision, known as *The Three Incisive Precepts*, were transmitted to the great master Mañjuśrīmitra by the incarnate buddha Garab Dorje from amid a cloud of celestial light at the time of his passing. They are secret precepts that are inseparable from his mind, "The final testament of Garab Dorje."

By adhering to the vital core of this instruction, the omniscient lord of the teaching (Longchen Rabjampa) realized directly the dynamic mind of primal purity wherein corporeal existence, all concrete substance, and specific characteristics were extinguished, and he attained perfect buddhahood. He revealed his awareness body to the knowledge-bearer Jigme Lingpa, blessing him by way of the symbolic transmission of the knowledge-bearers. Jigme Lingpa gave mouth-to-ear transmission to my gracious root Lama Gyelwai Nyugu, who, having received introduction to these precepts, directly realized the true nature of reality. And these are the precepts that I have heard from that revered lord of beings while he was alive. They are "The spiritual elixir of the three transmissions."[209]

I am reluctant to show such precepts as these, which are like twice-refined gold, the nuclear quintessence, to people who would not take them to heart and practice them; but as to those who will treat them like life itself, and who can experientially realize their vital truth and accomplish buddhahood in one lifetime, I can never refuse them. Hence, "It is entrusted with the seal of secrecy to my heart sons."

This message from the heart is the profound truth;
This vital truth is my heart message.
Do not abandon this vital truth;
Do not let these precepts escape you.

This short elucidation of *The Extraordinary Reality of Sovereign Wisdom* is complete.

JOY! JOY! JOY!

NOTES

INTRODUCTION

I. The Theory and Practice of Dzogchen

1. The introduction is divided into sections under the principal heads of Starting Point, Path, and Goal, a traditional structure of analysis of any method of achieving buddhahood. The material under these heads is designed to provide a kaleidoscopic perspective of Dzogchen.

2. *Lama* is used throughout in the traditional sense of preceptor and exemplar of the buddha's path, rather than in the journalistic sense of Tibetan Buddhist monk.

3. There is no single Tibetan word from which the notion of "simplicity" is derived. *Rnam dag,* usually translated herein as "immaculate," literally "quite pure," is a way of describing the same reality. The adjective *gdod ma'i,* "from the beginning," "primordial," strengthens the sense of purity that is the root of simplicity. *So ma,* "pristine," is another synonym. But what the lama was indicating here was the nature of the *dharmakāya*—emptiness and gnostic awareness.

4. *Rdzogs pa chen po,* contracted to *rdzogs chen* and pronounced "Dzogchen," *mahāsandhi* in Sanskrit, has the sense of completion in its perfection. Thus the word *holistic* is germane to its definition, and Dzogchen could be translated the Magnificent Holistic Perfection.

5. *Gnosis,* and *gnostic awareness,* are employed throughout this work in the general dictionary sense of "mystical awareness," an awareness that in this Buddhist context can only be *ye shes (jñāna),* holistic awareness of transforming illusion *(sgyu ma, māyā).*

6. See Glossary of Sanskrit Terms.

7. *Bya bral* and *dmigs med:* nonaction and aimlessness describe the condition

of the Dzogchen yogin when spontaneity and synchronicity have replaced contrived activity and ambition.

8. If the Nyingma school's nine approaches to buddhahood are conceived as a pyramidal hierarchy, then Dzogchen is the apex, where spatiality and temporality vanish into vast space (or the "cosmic egg"), a realm of pure potential *(skyes med)*. Even the most outspoken ideology of equality and democracy—Marxism—in an age of antihierarchical dogma demonstrates in practice that the archetypal hierarchical mold of mind cannot be recast by political means. Dzogchen at the apex of the spiritual hierarchy is the only means of transcendence of the hierarchy, as the zero inhabits every integer and the point lies all along every line: in Dzogchen this is the only equality and democracy.

9. *Byin brlab, adhiṣṭhana:* see *Garland of Vision,* p. 151, and n.185.

10. Those books in English that did treat Dzogchen included *The Book of the Great Liberation* by W. Y. Evans-Wentz in the short text called "The Yoga of Knowing the Mind" and a section in Dr. Herbert Guenther's *Buddhist Philosophy in Theory and Practice.*

11. See *The Flight of the Garuda,* song 17.

12. See *In Exile from the Land of Snows* by John Avedon (London: Wisdom, 1985) for a factual and highly readable account of Tibet's downfall.

13. *Ma rig pa, avidyā:* literally "the absence of *rig pa.*"

14. *Thar pa, mokṣa/mukti:* the Hindus employ the same word for liberation as the Buddhists, and although their conception of it differs in some radical points—and these concepts are obstacles to its attainment—experientially nirvana is still nirvana.

15. *Sgrib gnyis: nyon mongs pa'i sgrib pa* and *shes bya'i sgrib pa:* the veils of passion and mental concept.

16. See Glossary of Numeric Terms.

17. Desire is eradicated in the *Hīnayāna,* neutralized in the Mahayana, and intensified in the *Vajrayāna* (see *The Flight of the Garuda,* song 13).

18. See n. 3.

19. But see *The Flight of the Garuda,* song 6.

20. The definition of emptiness is disputed between the *Rang stong pa,* who define the buddha-nature as utterly empty in itself, and the *Gzhan stong pa,* who define it as empty of extraneous defilements. Dzogchen, following the latter line, finds emptiness within and inseparable from appearances.

21. *Blo ldog rnam pa bzhi:* the "four mind-benders" provide discursive contemplation upon (1) *mi lus rin po che,* the good fortune of a precious human birth; (2) *mi rtag pa,* the lessons of universal transience; (3) *las rgyu 'bras,* the laws of karma; and (4) the inevitability of karmic retribution.

22. See *The Flight of the Garuda,* song 13.

23. Two Dzogchen terms imply this essential recognition: *ngo sprod pa* means "to be introduced to," "to be initiated into," and by extension "to recognize the nature of the mind"; while *rang ngo shes pa* means "to recognize or understand one's own nature."

24. See *The Flight of the Garuda,* song 16.

25. *Ru bzhi.* See *Khrid ye shes bla ma* of Jigme Lingpa.

26. The terms *vertical* and *horizontal* applied to patterns of causation must be apprehended intuitively. To use the metaphor of the mandala, *vertical effusion* is the acausal manifestation of the circumference out of the center, the emanation of the holistic universe out of the universal ground; and *horizontal causation* indicates the causal relationship between events in linear time and space.

27. See *The Flight of the Garuda,* song 16.

28. *Lta ba, sgom pa, spyod pa, 'bras bu.*

29. Not A; not not-A; not both A and not-A; not neither A nor not-A.

30. *Spros bral:* free of conceptual limitations and interpretive projections, free of all restrictions to a single meaning, and incapable of elaboration.

31. See *The Flight of the Garuda,* song 16.

32. *Āsana,* the third component of Patañjali's *aṣṭāṅgayoga.*

33. See Glossary of Numeric Terms.

34. *Phur bu / kīla, khaṭvāṅga.*

35. *'Gegs* is the substantive derived from the verb *'gegs pa* (hindering, or obstructing).

36. *Bla mtsho:* the sacred lakes whose waters are the spirit of Tibet and its people. *Bla,* life spirit, and *ma,* the feminine definite article, are the two constituent syllables of *bla ma* (lama); *Bla* is a pre-Buddhist, Bon conception.

37. *Rdo rje gya tam, viśvavajra.*

38. See Glossary of Numeric Terms.

39. *Lhag mthong, vipaśyanā.* The technique alluded to here is described in *The Flight of the Garuda,* song 14.

40. *Gcod:* see *The Flight of the Garuda,* song 17.

41. *Bdud bzhi, catturmāra: phung po'i bdud, skandhamāra; nyon mongs kyi bdud, kleśamāra; lha'i bu kyi bdud, devaputramāra; chos rgyal gyi bdud, mṛtyamāra.* The four demon spirits are the powers of embodiment, emotional passion, divine pride, and death.

42. *Srog rlung:* this is not to be identified with sexual energy alone. At the base of the spine, at the lower end of the central channel, is the sexual cakra, the fifth in the fivefold system. Although sexual energy is its primary manifestation, its increasingly subtle and sublimated form is the far-greater life force, an energy that vitalizes the entire being.

43. *Rdo rje myal ba: vajranaraka.* Since no conditioned state is eternal, the everlasting nature of the vajra hell exists as a conviction in the minds of its denizens. But the illusion of eternity feels like eternity itself.

II. The Language of Dzogchen

44. See *Garland of Vision,* pp. 181–82.

45. *Bla med rnal 'byor rgyud, anuttarayogatantra.*

46. See Herbert V. Guenther, *The Royal Song of Saraha* and "From Saraha's Treasury of Songs," trans. David Snellgrove in *Buddhist Scriptures,* ed. Edward Conze (London: Penguin, 1959).

47. *Gnyis med, advaita.*

48. *Zung du 'jug pa, yuganaddha.*

49. *Dbyings, dhātu.*

50. *Rig pa.* The Sanskrit equivalent, *vidyā*, is used nowhere in Sanskrit texts with the sense of *rig pa* as total presence as in the Dzogchen context.

51. *Ye shes, jnāna:* the prefix *ye* means "ultimate," "original," "first," and *shes pa* means "cognition," hence "original or pure awareness," "ultimate cognition."

52. *Rig pa ye shes (rig pa'i ye shes).*

53. *Gsal ba, prabhava.*

54. *Ngo bo, rang bzhin, thugs rje.*

55. *Kun khyab.*

56. *Byams pa, maitrī.*

EMPTYING THE DEPTHS OF HELL

57. *Mchog sprul sku rnam gsum.* The first of the Three Supreme Emanations was Nyang ral Nyi ma 'od zer (1124–92); the second was Guru Chos dbang (1212–70); and the third, Rgod ldem can (1337–1409) (see p. 139). For short biographies of these treasure finders and information about other Nyingma lineage holders, see Dudjom Rinpoche, *The Nyingma School of Tibetan Buddhism: Its Fundamentals and History.*

58. *Mtshan ldan mkha' 'gro ma rnam gnyis dang po.*

59. Grwa pa mngon shes (1012–90) of Mchims, attached to Bsam yas chos 'khor, was the great *gter ston* who discovered the four volumes of medical tantra, the *Rgyud bzhi.* He was a guru of Ma cig Lab sgron, among others.

60. *Rig pa rtsal dbang,* the first and last empowerment into the essence of Dzogchen.

61. The *Padma bka' thang* prophecy states that "the treasure of Gnam skas [and] Mkhar chu will be revealed" by Guru Chos dbang. In the Lcags phur (Iron

Purba) Cave of Mkhar chu, just over the Tibetan border north of Bum thang in Bhutan, Guru Chos dbang discovered a major cache.

62. *Bka' brgyad bsang ba yongs rdzogs* and the *'Khor ba dong sprugs*, which includes the *Bka' brgyad drag po rang byung ba'i zhi khro narag skong bzhags gyi cho ga.*

63. *Nyams chag sdig sgrib thams cad bshags pa'i rgyal po na rag dong sprugs* is the full title.

64. *Guhyamantra*: "secret mantra" language has the power of manifesting its actuality when recited under optimal conditions. This text provides a fine example of mantric language, its meaning realized spontaneously and automatically when repeated by the *sādhaka* with devotion and attention.

65. *Rtsa ba'i dam tshig dang dam tshig yan lag nyi shu tsa lnga.*

66. The Tibetan verb applied to this process is *sgrol ba*, at once "to release" and "to kill."

67. See *The Flight of the Garuda*, song 17.

68. "Point instant" is a synonym of "vast expanse," *klong*, used here in preference to its more vague and yet more literal equivalent to indicate the personal, immediate, existential, nature of the confession. *Klong* is also translated as "matrix."

69. *Bka' brgyad drag po rang byung ba'i zhi khro narag skong bzhags gyi cho ga.*

70. The *Ādibuddha*: Kun tu bzang po is sometimes contracted simply to "Kunzang."

71. *Gyung drung*: the swastika, right- and left-handed, symbolizes immortality and indestructibility.

72. *Bhaga, yum gyi mkha'*: in Tantra the sky is a euphemism for the vagina (*yoni*).

THE FLIGHT OF THE GARUDA

73. The voluminous *Zhabs dkar rnam thar* is a popular masterpiece of autobiography, a source of inspiration for every Dzogchen yogin. The first volume was written by Shabkar Lama himself; the smaller second volume was

partially written by a disciple. It is translated by Matthieu Ricard as *The Life of Shabkar: The Autobiography of a Tibetan Yogin.*

74. A mdo Reb gong, known as Gser smug ljongs, the Golden Valley, is located in Mdo smad A mdo region to the northeast of the Ma chen Pom ra range.

75. For Sngags kyi dbang po's secular genealogy and spiritual lineages, see *The Life of Shabkar*, table 1, p. 559 and table 3, p. 566.

76. The *Rta phag yid bzhin nor bu* was a *gter ma* of the treasure finder Kun bzang Bde chen rgyal po (b.1736) of Snye mo Ka rag, transmitted to Zhabs dkar by Bla ma O rgyan bstan 'dzin. See *The Life of Shabkar*, app. 4.

77. Snow lion (earth), tiger (air), dragon (water), and horse (space) complete the symbolism of the five elements in the prayer flag.

78. *Thabs dang shes rab, upāya* and *prajñā.*

79. *Gnas lugs.*

80. *Gnas 'gyu rig gsum:* this is a vital Dzogchen precept, one that can be given as the sole meditative support to Dzogchen practice. See songs 15 and 18 and n. 112.

81. In the Tibetan legend of the origin of Rudra, it was this same error that gave birth to the lord of demons. Rudra is the Tibetan vision of the Hindu Bhairava, based in undeniable metaphysics rather than in experiential practice.

82. Longchenpa reduces to absurdity the notion that mountains, for instance, are merely figments of the mind. He distinguishes clearly between our perception of the mountain, which is like a dream, a hallucination, the reflection of the moon in water, etc., and the mountain "out there" (see *Yid bzhin rin po che mdzod kyi 'grel pa,* chap. 1). Nowhere does Shabkar make this distinction in *The Flight of the Garuda*, the reason being, presumably, that the ontological status of the mountain is irrelevant to the yogin, who at this stage in his progress must be absolutely convinced that all phenomena, such as the shape and color arising in his visual sense field, are creations of his mind. It is useful to bear in mind Saraha's *mahāmudrā* assertion that no concept is valid but that its efficacy in its own context makes it so. In this context the concept of all things as mind is a sharp-edged sword to destroy attachment to phenomena.

83. *Chos thams cad mnyam pa nyid du rdzogs pas: mnyam pa nyid (samatā)*, literally, sameness, is synonymous with *chos nyid (dharmakā)* and *stong pa nyid (śūnyatā)*.

84. *Rang rig pa'i ye shes.*

85. *Lam rim ye shes snying po* of Bde chen chos rgyal gling pa, pp. 204–5. Compare the song of Ye shes mtsho rgyal in *Sky Dancer* (Dowman, 1996), pp. 45–47.

86. *'Od gsal rdzogs pa chen po'i khregs chod lta ba'i glu dbyangs sa lam ma lus myur du bgrod pa'i rtsal ldan mkha' lding gshog rlabs.*

87. See p. 87 for identification of Shabkar Lama's principal teachers.

88. Titles to the songs have been added by the translator to facilitate reference to the content.

89. *Sa (bcu) dang lam (lnga):* the ten levels of the bodhisattva path and the five stages of the path to realization. As a vehicle, Dzogchen is defined as neither sudden nor gradual in its approach to buddhahood. *Khregs chod* is taken to precede *thod rgal,* but both are complete and perfect in themselves.

90. Tibetans point to the heart as the seat of the mind; occidentals point to the brain.

91. *Sems nyid, cittatā:* in the previous verses the object of examination was mind *(sems)*. Now the object is the nature of mind or mind in itself *(sems nyid),* but since our examination has established that mind and its nature are identical, the distinction between *sems* and *sems nyid* is academic.

92. *Gzhi yi sems nyid gnas lugs kyi rang bzhin gtan la phab pa'i ngo sprod do.* This is an introduction to our original nature by way of mind: the nature of mind is our original nature. See song 6. The list of synonyms of "I" at the beginning of song 6 mix epistemological with ontological terms.

93. *Sku dang ye shes:* this mandala is a field of infinitesimal mandalas of light *(thig le)*—light seeds—emanating from the heart of Kuntu Zangpo.

94. The *Theg mchog mdzod* and the *Zab don rgya mtsho'i sprin phung* are the two texts mentioned here. But the first chapter of the early work of Longchenpa, the *Yid bzhin rin po che mdzod,* and his autocommentary upon it treat the origination of samsara in detail. See also *The Wish-Granting Prayer of Kuntu Zangpo,* p. 148.

95. *Nga; bdag (ātman); gang zag bdag med; sems (citta); shes rab pha rol tu phyin pa (prajñāpāramitā); bde gshegs snying po (sugatagarbha); phyag rgya chen po (mahāmudrā); dbu ma (madhyamaka); thig le nyag gcig; chos kyi dbyings (dharmadhātu); kun gzhi (ālaya); tha mal shes pa.*

96. *Rig pa.*

97. *Dngos gzhi'i gnas lugs do:* discursive examination of mind constitutes preparatory practice in *khregs chod,* and direct realization of our existential condition *(gnas lugs)* is the main practice.

98. *Sku (kāya).*

99. *Rig pa'i rtsal.* See song 22.

100. The three buddhas of past, present, and future are Dīpaṅkara Buddha, Śākyamuni Buddha, and Maitreya Buddha. Here the 108 Peaceful and Wrathful Deities are implied: see *The Prayer of Kuntu Zangpo,* p. 149.

101. *Rang snang:* this difficult concept is best understood by identifying with the all-pervading cognitive principle *(rig pa)* and then conceiving one's own body and the environment as a holistic gestalt, or hologram, projected within it.

102. *Gzhan 'phrul dbang byed lha.*

103. Shabkar Lama uses the term *phyi rol mu stegs,* which applies only to Hindu yogins. Although the Nāths are probably most renowned for such miraculous practices, many stories exist of Buddhist *siddhas'* achievements of this kind. In particular see Lawapa's *siddhi* in *Masters of Mahamudra,* p. 179.

104. *Thod rgal:* see p. 81.

105. *Rnam rtog, vitarka,* is the process of thought, and *rtog pa, vicara,* are the concepts underlying thought. These two terms describe the mental veil that conceals total presence.

106. *Lhun gyis grub pa'i dgongs pa:* this is the dynamic of *thod rgal,* the fruit of *thregs chod* practice, and the final level of *atiyoga.*

107. In song 7.

108. *Dkyil 'khor:* in Dzogchen *mandala* has a special signification. Since the *atiyoga* Dzogchen mandala has no center or circumference, rather than

signifying a symmetrical *yantra,* it indicates the patterning of the formal gestalt of the *nirmāṇakāya* level. This patterning is the asymmetrical patterning of nature, the perfect asymmetry of a tree or the asymmetry of the structure of a complex molecule, for instance. See also *Garland of Vision,* pp.185–86, for the *mahāyoga* Dzogchen mandala.

109. In this verse first mention is made of the apogee of Dzogchen attainment—the rainbow body *('ja' lus).* Thus "the end of the path" *(mthar thug)* implies what appears to be death to deluded observers, but what in reality is a dissolution of the individuated *dharmakāya,* which manifests as the *rūpakāya* in the universal ground of being, and dissolution into the *dharmakāya* that is synonymous with the ground of being. The macrocosmic chalice and elixir manifest for the sake of all beings out of the ground of being.

110. *Rtsal byong.*

111. *Adornment* does not imply that mental quiescence is merely a secondary, decorative state of mind, but rather that it is an immaculate mode of mentality, and is, therefore, like a rare jewel.

112. *Gnas 'gyu rig gsum:* this phrase indicates the important Dzogchen precept devised to accelerate the process of integrating one's experience of the active and the contemplative modes into the continuity of consciousness with equal value in every sense. Cultivation of this aspect of nondual meditation removes the Buddhist bias toward the contemplative mode, which defines meditation as formal sitting meditation, and the dangerous assertion that a quiescent mind is inherently superior to a dynamic mind. See song 18.

113. *Glu dbyangs snyan mo:* Sarasvatī, the bodhisattva goddess of learning, music, and poetry, and consort of Mañjuśrī.

114. *Theg pa'i yang rtse:* if the nine approaches to buddhahood, beginning with the Śrāvakayāna, are conceived in a pyramidal hierarchy, then the nontemporal, nonspatial apex of the pyramid is Dzogchen.

115. At this stage reflexive recognition of the nature of mind has become a habit. Examination of the mind is now an obstacle to the spontaneous arising of total presence. No-meditation indicates a state where even the notions of meditation and meditator are absent, free of both meditation and nonmeditation when both states are self-conscious. This double negative

has the same meaning as Nāropa's *mahāmudrā* statement of simple negation, the oft-quoted lines:

Without thought, deliberation, or analysis,
without meditation and without action,
without doubt or expectation,
mental constructs and dualities spontaneously dissolve
and the original face of reality shines forth.

The mendicant pilgrim is best placed to recognize anonymous, unlearned (or learned) realized beings whose attainment has arisen in spontaneous no-meditation.

116. *Go ldog 'gros:* the paradox of discovering immutable samadhi in relaxed, carefree, no-action—framed in the previous verse—is restated in this verse as the paradox of no-meditation as sustained meditation.

117. *Bya bral:* this is an epithet with significant outer and inner meanings. As an epithet it indicates "a religious mendicant without any responsibilities," a "vagrant" or "wastrel." The outer meaning is "duty-free," "workless"; while the inner meaning is "nonaction," the achievement of spontaneous, acausal action.

118. *Rdzogs chen snying thig:* Refers to a category of lineages, foremost among them the Klong chen snying thig, a tradition established by the fourteenth-century yogin and sage Klong chen rab 'byams pa (Longchenpa), who fused the *gter ma* and *bka' ma* teaching into a unitary, systematized corpus of theory and practice. The term also indicates a metaphysical reality, the all-encompassing *bindu* at the heart center, the *thig le nyag gcig,* the cosmic seed.

119. *Khregs chod.*

120. See songs 3, 8, 9, and 13.

121. *Thig le, bindu.* The same term is used in the following verse.

122. This expletive is employed in Patrul Rinpoche's *Mkhas pa shri rgyal po khyad chos.* It creates a state of shock that empties the mind and allows the space for recognition of mind's original face to arise. See p. 122.

123. This practice is classed as an "internal, extraordinary preliminary practice" in Dzogchen. It is one of the *ru bzhi.*

124. See the second part of song 7 for an identification of the Five Dhyāni Buddhas.

125. Red and white are the colors of female and male, solar and lunar energies, the blending of which give rise to the mandala.

126. *Rig pa gcer mthong gi ngo sprod; Mdzod bdun; Shing rta gsum; Rdzogs chen rgyab chos nam mkha' skor gsum: Zab don rgya mtsho'i sprin phung; Rdzogs chen mkha' 'gro snying thig; Sangs rgyas lag bcangs.*

127. Śrī Siṃha was the disciple of Mañjuśrīmitra and the guru of Vimalamitra and Jñānasūtra. He was also the guru of Bairotsana who first brought Dzogchen to Tibet. Śrī Siṃha's native place, So khyam, was probably in central Asia, but he taught Bairotsana in Orgyen.

THE WISH-GRANTING PRAYER OF KUNTU ZANGPO

128. *Byang gter.*

129. *Khyung, Garuda:* see p. 68.

130. *Mchog sprul sku rnam gsum.* See n. 57.

131. Rgyang Yon po lung was a major place of *gter ma* concealment *(gter gnas)* in its own right. The cave still exists today in a small grassy valley opposite the Yang 'dul temple and close to the great 'Bum pa of Rgyang near Lha rtse Rdzong in Gtsang.

132. *Mdzod lnga: Vajrakīla—las rgyu 'bras, bsnyen sgrub, rten 'grel; Bgegs thal bar rlog pa'i chos;* and *Kun bzang dgongs pa zang thal* were the five categories.

133. Thub bstan rdo rje brag lies on the north bank of the Tsangpo River between its confluence with the Kyichu and Samye Chokhor.

134. *Rdzogs pa chen po Kun tu bzang po dgongs pa'i zang thal du bstan pa'i rgyud* is the principal text of the cycle of texts contained in this volume of *gter ma.*

135. *Zang thal:* there is no known Sanskrit equivalent to this term, the etymology of which is unclear. In contrast to *pho ba,* which is often translated as "transference," *zang thal* implies a preexistent existential base at the location to which the transference shifts full awareness.

136. *Smon lam stobs po che.*

137. *Smon lam:* literally, "path of good wishes."

138. *Smon lam brgyud.*

139. *Thugs, gsung, sku, 'phrin las, yon tan:* otherwise, buddha-mind, buddha-speech, buddha-body, buddha-activity, and buddha-quality.

140. The versification and verse or part numbers are the translator's interpolation.

141. *Kun gzhi.*

142. *Rig pa'i gsal ba.*

143. This stress refers to the gross tension of competitive and demanding lifestyles, but it also indicates the subtle stresses that accompany dualistic vision, varieties of which are listed verse by verse in *Emptying the Depths of Hell*, pp. 59–61.

144. *Shes pa,* or *lta da shes pa:* consciousness of the here and now, which means nonreferential awareness *(dmigs med ye shes).*

145. *Gnyis 'dzin blo* or *gnyis 'dzin btas pa'i bag chags.*

146. See "six realms" in Glossary of Numeric Terms.

147. *Kun bzang smon lam.*

SECRET INSTRUCTION IN A GARLAND OF VISION

148. *Yang dag gsang 'grel; 'Jam dpal mtshan mdzod; Ma mo rgyud 'grel; Man ngag lta ba'i phreng ba.*

149. *Rtsa rgyud gsang ba snying po'i 'grel ba nyi ma'i snying po zhes bya ba gu ru padma rgyal po'i gsungs rgyun man ngag snyen brgyud chos rje ka thog pa chen po'i bshad srol bzhugs so.*

150. *Lta phreng Rong zom,* p. 176, 50b ff. See n. 155.

151. *Brag dmar mtsho mo mgur kyi Ne'u thang: Brag dmar* probably refers to the valley above Samye.

152. For a more philosophical and less practically oriented Nyingma *lam rim,* or

philosophical perspective, of the various Buddhist schools, see Mi pham Rinpoche's *Grub mtha' sdus ba,* translated into English with commentary in *Buddhist Philosophy in Theory and Practice* by H. V. Guenther.

153. *Lta phreng 'grel ba,* 2a ff. See n. 157.

154. Rongdzom's revealed texts did not survive him. See *Gter ston lo rgyus* of Blo gros mtha' yas, 97b ff.

155. *Man ngag lta phreng gi 'grel pa Rong zom pandita chen po Chos kyi bzang pos mdzad pa Lta phreng Rong zom, Rnying ma Bka' ma,* vol. 'A, text PA, pp. 177–279, 50 ff.

156. See Glossary of Sanskrit Terms.

157. *Man ngag lta ba'i phreng ba'i tshig don gyi 'grel zin mdor bsdus pa zab don pad tshal 'byed pa'i nyi 'od (Lta phreng 'grel ba), Rnying ma bka' ma,* vol. BA, pp. 279–360, 41 ff.

158. *'Od gsal, gsal ba,* and *snang ba* are the degrees in progression of light's emanation. The "clear light" *('od gsal)* is the basis of all lightform, of all color and shade, identical to the "ground of being" *(kun gzhi),* and unobjectifiable. We know the clear light only as the radiance of the spectrum.

159. *Mthu* is the Tibetan word that implies magical power. This is the "power" of synchronistic conjunction.

160. Primordial purity *(ka dag)* is the key word of *khregs chod,* as spontaneity *(lhun grub)* is the key word of *thod rgal.*

161. See also *The Flight of the Garuda,* pp. 93 and 132, and *The Wish-Granting Prayer of Kuntu Zangpo,* pp. 149–53.

162. See Glossary of Numeric Terms.

163. *Rtogs pa bzhi.*

164. *Rig pa.*

165. *'Bras bu'i theg pa, Phalayāna,* as opposed to *rgyu'i theg pa, Hetuyāna.*

166. *'Bras bu'i chos* is the phrase used in the interlinear note and also in Rongdzom's commentary.

167. The following excerpts are from *Lta phreng Rong zom,* 39b–40b ff.

168. *Shes rab, prajñā:* insight into the continuum of illusion as emptiness.

169. *Bsnyen pa dang sgrub pa.*

170. *Lta phreng Rong zom,* 42a ff.

171. *Lta phreng Rong zom,* 44a ff.

172. *Man ngag lta ba'i phreng ba (Lta phreng).*

173. Numbers in square brackets indicate the number in the nine vehicles, or approaches, to buddhahood of the customary Nyingma school enumeration.

174. *Gzugs kyi phung po, rūpaskandha:* this consists of color and shape and also all things that have names. Thus it includes both visible and invisible objects, but excludes the internal processes of mind that are subsumed under the heads of the other four, the internal, psychophysical constituents.

175. *Rten 'grel bcu gnyis, pratītyasamutpāda:* the analysis of the interaction of man and his environment in terms of the "twelve elements of coemergent origination," which is another translation of the phrase, is complete and satisfying; but greater significance is extracted from this Mahayana contemplative technique with the realization that this function of manifestation is understood as synchronicity in Tantra.

176. *Pha rol tu phyin pa bcu, daśapāramitā:* the ten perfections represent an admirable, saintly ideal of life that any Christian could practice in his imitation of Christ; but the adjective *transcendental* is of crucial importance. Without the detachment inherent in the view of emptiness that *transcendental* implies, the bodhisattva merely accumulates a wealth of merit through virtuous activity; the detachment implies insight into the nature of all things as emptiness and thus cultivates the ultimate awareness that leads to buddhahood. To the bodhisattva, perfect action and perfect awareness are the two wings of the bird that soars into the buddhafields.

177. *'Phags pa'i gzugs kyi sku phyag rgya rnam bzhi dang ldan pa:* "the *rūpakāya* with four *mudrās—mahāmudrā, dharmamudrā, samayamudrā,* and *karmamudrā.*"

178. *Māyā*-vision samadhi, wherein all is seen as magical illusion; *vajra*-vision, or imperturbable, samadhi; and the samadhi of universal sameness.

179. *'Phags pa'i gzugs kyi sku, aryarūpakāya.*

180. *Bya ba byed pa'i nus pa'i sgyu ma:* the fundamental characteristic of the

feminine principle is receptive, open, and responsive, but at the same time the awareness-ḍākinī is a dynamo of uninhibited activity. This dynamic power that drives her and provokes activity is called *śakti* among the Hindus, and here we find the same term applied to the feminine aspect in Buddhist Tantra: *nus pa* is the Tibetan equivalent of *śakti*.

181. *Tshogs gnyis kyi tshogs rdzogs.*

182. This commentary on the title is found in the original text in an interlinear note, the origin of which is uncertain. See Rongdzom's commentary.

183. It is only by inference that we grasp that the object *(don)* of intuitive realization *(rtogs pa)* is total presence *(rig pa)* until the first line of the paragraph entitled "Progressive Quickening of Confidence" states it explicitly. The fourfold intuitive realization of total presence is contingent upon the four supports, or doors, but the relation between the cognitive factor and the support varies: in the first and last case, realization of total presence is coincident with actualization of the support (indicated by an adverbial particle, although in the first case the genitive was necessary in the translation), while in the second and third the supports produce the realization (indicated by the instrumental case).

184. *Lta phreng 'grel pa,* 26b ff. The two truths are absolute and relative truth.

185. "Sustaining grace" is a rendition of the Tibetan *byin brlabs,* more often translated as "blessing."

186. *Bde mchog, Saṃvara.*

187. *Bdud bzhi:* see pp. 36 and 175.

188. *Yi ge 'khor lo tshogs chen gyi sa.* This is the thirteenth stage of the bodhisattva's path. According to some, it is the final stage, the stage of the Buddha, the *dharmakāya* stage. According to another system, there are three further stages: *ting nge 'dzin chen po, rdo rje 'dzin chen gyi sa,* and *ye shes bla ma'i sa.*

189. This alludes to the ancient Vedic ascetic rite of sitting in the center of a circle of four fires, preferably at noon in summertime, with the sun above being the fifth fire.

190. *Byang chub sems dpa'i sdom pa.*

191. *Dam tshig chen po'i mdo.*

THE THREE INCISIVE PRECEPTS

192. "The three incisive precepts" is a translation of the *Tshig gsum gnad brdegs (tsigsum nedeg)* which literally translates as "the three words that strike the essential point" or "the three phrases that strike home." For the *gter ma* that elaborates these points according to Garab Dorje, see *The Golden Letters,* John Myrdhin Reynolds, pp. 129–37.

193. *The Extraordinary Reality of Sovereign Wisdom* is a translation of the *Mkhas pa sri rgyal po'i khyad chos (Khepa srigyelpo khyecho).* Other translations of this text, including Patrul Rinpoche's commentary, may be found in *The Golden Letters,* John Myrdhin Reynolds, pp. 43–63; *Simply Being,* James Low pp. 101–14; and *The Crystal Cave,* Eric Pema Kunzang, pp. 143–60.

194. Patrul Rinpoche's root guru, Rgyal ba'i nyug gu, founded Rdza rgyal dgon (also known as Phra ba dgon) in Rdza chu kha. Further south, in Amdo, is the Mdo grub chos sde founded by Mdo grub chen, Rgyal ba'i nyu gu's fellow disciple of 'Jig med gling pa.

195. *The Words of My Perfect Teacher* by Patrul Rinpoche, p. xxxi.

196. *The Words of My Perfect Teacher,* p. xlvi.

197. *Rig pa'i ye shes.*

198. *Zang thal rig pa rjen pa.*

199. *Mkhas pa sri rgyal po'i khyad chos cung zad brkal pa.*

200. Dzogchen meditation combines the two forms of meditation that are the genius of Buddhism—*vipaśyanā (lhag mthong)* and *śamathā (zhi gnas).* In nonmeditation, heightened awareness *(vipaśyanā),* which is perfect insight into the nature of experience as emptiness, is combined with the one-pointed absorption in a state of tranquillity *(śamathā),* which is love and compassion. Thus *vipaśyanā* provides the wisdom *(prajñā, shes rab),* and *śamathā* is the compassionate skillful means *(upāya, thabs),* and these two are inseparable.

201. The truth of the origin of suffering refers to the fundamental positive and negative reactions of attachment and aversion to objects of consciousness; these are known as emotional states. Happiness and sadness are the moods or feelings that are produced consequent upon desire and anger.

202. The "mother light" is the clear light of the ground *(gzhi gnas ma'i 'od gsal)*, and the "son light" is the clear light of the path of practice *(nyams len lam gyi 'od gsal)*.

203. See n. 201.

204. *'Og 'gyu 'khrul 'byams:* this phrase indicates basic metaphysical notions about the nature of being as well as delusive assumptions about inter-dependent circumstances that turn our perception of a rope into a snake or a snake into a rope, for example.

205. *Shar grol, rang grol, cer grol.*

206. *Snying thig rdo rje snying po'i lam.* This is the sole indication in the text that it belongs to the *Klong chen snying thig* lineage.

207. *Rig rtsal chos sku'i gter ston gyis.* Here Patrul Rinpoche attributes the Mkhas pa shri rgyal po to the *dharmakāya* treasure finder, creative presence, the natural creativity of intrinsic awareness personified.

208. The three sources of perfect insight *(shes rab)* are meditation *(bsgoms pa),* hearing *(thos pa),* and contemplation *(bsam pa).* Out of conventional humility Patrul Rinpoche denies any perfect insight of meditative attainment, but nevertheless the threefold all-pervasive matrix *(klong)* of perfect insight was the origin of this treasure text.

209. The three transmissions are buddha-mind-to-mind transmission *(rgyal ba'i dgongs brgyud)* that Patrul Rinpoche received from Longchenpa; the symbolic transmission of the knowledge bearers *(rig 'dzin brda brgyud)* he received from Jigme Lingpa; and the aural mouth-to-ear transmission he received from Gyelwai Nyugu.

GLOSSARIES

1. SELECTED TIBETAN DZOGCHEN TERMS

N.B. The terms in square brackets are used in *Extraordinary Reality* only.

ka dag: primal or primordial purity, primally pure, pure from the beginning.
kun gzhi: universal ground, (original) ground of being.
klong: spaciousness, immensity, vast expanse, point instant, [matrix].
klong yangs: vast expanse.
skal ldan: beloved.
sku, kāya: pure-being, buddha-body.
sku gsum: three existential modes, the three modes of being.
skyes med: unborn (inchoate); pure potential.

khregs chod (tregcho): Cutting Through.
'khrul pa: delusion, bewilderment; delusive, deluded.

'gyu: movement, active.
sgom pa: meditation.
sgyu ma, māyā: illusory enchantment, magical display.
bsgoms, bhāvanā: meditation, discursive contemplation, fixation upon an external or internal object, nonreferential meditation, creative visualization according to context.

ngo bo: essence.
ngo sprod pa: to be introduced to, to be initiated into.
dngos po mtshan ma: nominal delusion.

chos sku, dharmakāya: the existential mode of emptiness and clear light, [pure being].
chos thams cad, sarvadharma: all phenomenal and noumenal experience, all elements of experience, all experience or all events in nirvana, all phenomena and noumena.

chos dbyings, dharmadhātu: plenum of pure space, continuum of pure space, reality-continuum, [field of reality].

'ja' lus: rainbow body.
rjen ne ba: naked and pristine.

mnyam pa nyid: sameness, identity.
bsnyen sgrub: "approach and identification."

rtog pa: mental constructs, conceptualization.
rtog med: thought-free, thoughtless.
rtogs pa: intuitive realization.
lta ba, darśana: vision, philosophical view.
stong pa nyid, śūnyatā: emptiness.
brtags pa or *rtags pa, lakṣaṇa:* mark, token, sign.

thig le, bindu: seed-essence.
thig le nyag gcig: sole seed, cosmic egg, cosmic seed.
thugs rje: responsiveness, compassion, (spirituality).
thod rgal (togel): Immediate Crossing.

bde chen, sukhāvatī: pure pleasure.
bde gshegs snying po: buddha-nature, buddha-essence.

gnas: quiescence.
gnas lugs: original nature, original existential condition.
rnam rtog, vitarka: discursive thought.
snang ba: appearances, lightform, phenomenal appearances, light, vision.
snang srid: phenomena and noumena, phenomenal existence.

spyod pa: action, conduct.
sprul sku, nirmāṇakāya: the existential mode of constantly transforming illusion.
spros bral: indeterminable, indeterminate, unelaborated.
spros med: formless, unformed and inconceivable, beyond conception.

phyag rgya chen po, mahāmudrā: magnificent stance.
'phro: diffused; diffusion, movement.

bya bral: nonaction.

'bras bu: goal, fruit, result.

dbyings, dhātu: space, plenum of space; = *chos dbyings q.v.*

ma bcos: unstructured, uncontrived.

ma rig pa, avidyā: literally, "absence of any presence," ignorance.

rtsal ba: creativity, efflorescence, skill, creative power, potency.

'od gsal: clear light.

gzhi: ground; also = *kun gzhi,* ground of being.

zang (nge) tel (le): (zangtel): all-pervading freedom of mind, "transference."

ye shes, jñāna: literally, ultimate cognition; pure, pristine, or primal awareness; nonreferential awareness; gnostic awareness as the nondual cognitive mode.

yi ge 'khor lo tshogs chen gyi sa: the stage of the great assembly of sacred letter wheels, denoting the thirteenth level of the bodhisattva path.

rang grol: spontaneous release, reflexive release, natural freedom.

rang ngo shes pa: reflexive recognition, spontaneous recognition; to recognize one's own nature; self-liberation.

rang gdangs: natural radiance or glow.

rang snang: self-manifest display, one's own natural manifestation.

rang byung: self-originating, spontaneously arising, (self-existent).

rang bzhin: nature.

rang rtsal: spontaneous efflorescence, self-expression.

rang rig: intrinsic knowledge, self-existing knowledge.

rang sa glod la zhog: compose yourself in the natural state, relax.

rang gsal: natural radiance or glow.

rig pa: total presence; see Introduction, p. 36.

rig pa ye shes = *ye shes kyi rig pa:* total presence or awareness, gnostic cognition.

ro gcig: one taste.

lam: path, method.
longs spyod sku, sambhogakāya: the existential mode of instructive vision.

shes rab, prajñā: perfect or penetrating insight (into the nature of all elements of experience as emptiness).

sang rgyas: pure and awakened being.
sang nge ba: secret fullness.
sal le ba: brilliance; brilliant, vivid.
sems, citta: mind.
sems nyid, cittatā: the nature of mind.
gsal ba: radiance, clarity.

hrig ge ba: intense vigilance of the awakened state, wakefulness; alert.

lhun grub: spontaneously originated/accomplished; spontaneity.

2. SANSKRIT TERMS

abhidharma: the psychological theory of Buddhism.
Ādibuddha: the Original Buddha, Kuntu Zangpo.
anuttarayogatantra: the supreme, nondual, tantric vehicle.
anuyoga: the eighth vehicle to buddhahood.

bodhicitta: the all-embracing compassion of the bodhisattva.
bodhisattva: aspirant devoted to the enlightenment of all beings.
buddha: "the one taste of the *dharmakāya.*"

caryatantra: see *ubhayatantra.*

dākinī: the dynamic female archetype; the awareness-dākinī is the guru-buddha's consort, mahamaya as empty awareness.
Dharma: enlightened spiritual praxis.
dharmadhātu: the reality-continuum of pure space, [field of reality].
dharmakāya: the existential mode of emptiness and clear light, [pure being].

gaṇacakra: the tantric sacrament of samaya reaffirmation.
garuḍa: the bird symbolic of the Dzogchen vehicle.

Hīnayāna: the approach to buddhahood first taught by Śākyamuni.

jñāna: primal awareness of the *dharmakāya*.

kriyātantra: the fourth, ritual vehicle to buddhahood.

Lakṣaṇayāna: the vehicle to buddhahood utilizing attributes.

madhyamaka: the philosophical method of maintaining the middle way.
mahāmudrā: "magnificent symbol," a synonym of buddhahood.
mahāsiddha: a great master or adept in *mahāmudrā*.
Mahāyāna: the vehicle of the bodhisattva Dzogchen yogin.
mahāyoga: the seventh vehicle to buddhahood.
maṇḍala: a symmetrical *yantra* representing the nature of mind.
mantra: a euphonic representation of a buddha-deity.
mudrā: a gesture of hand or body indicating a buddha-attribute.

nāga: an elemental spirit of water; a treasure protector.
nirmāṇakāya: the existential mode of compassion and constant transformation
of illusion.
nirvāṇa: the perfect reality of peace and bliss.

paṇḍita: a Sanskrit scholar.

rakta: blood, symbolizing the nature of the *ḍākinī*.
rūpakāya: the buddha-body of form.

sādhaka: a practitioner of Dharma.
sādhana: the form of existential praxis.
śakti: the dynamic energy of the *ḍākinī*.
samādhi: a degree of absorption in emptiness.
samaya: union with reality and the commitment or pledge thereto.
sambhogakāya: the existential mode of luminosity and clarity.
saṃsāra: the round of suffering and rebirth.
siddha: a master or adept in *mahāmudrā*.

siddhi: the *siddha's* powers of ultimate and relative attainment.
sugata: a buddha.
sūtra: scripture of the Buddha's teaching.

trikāya: the three modes of being, the three buddha-bodies.

ubhayatantra: caryātantra: the fifth vehicle to buddhahood.

vajra: "thunderbolt," symbol of immutable power and awareness.
vajrayāna: vehicle of the *tantrika* and the Dzogchen yogin.
vidyādhara: bearer of Dzogchen knowledge.

yantra: a graphic aid to understanding or compassionate manifestation.
yogatantra: the sixth vehicle to buddhahood.
yogin: a practitioner of meditation.

3. NUMERIC TERMS

two truths: absolute and relative truth.
two veils: passion and mental concepts; emotion and intellect.
twofold ignorance: innate and conceptual.
three aspects of time: past, present, and future.
three components: cognition, application, and fruition.
three degrees of samadhi: *maya*-vision, *vajra*-vision, and the samadhi of universal sameness.
three doors: body, speech, and mind.
three emotional poisons: desire, aversion, and ignorance.
three lower realms: of animals, hungry ghosts, and denizens of hell.
three modes of buddha-being: the three *kāyas*—*dharmakāya, sambhogakāya,* and *nirmāṇakāya.*
three principles: contingent effect, the imperative, and the categorical imperative.
three realms: the sensory realm and realms of aesthetic form and formlessness.
three realms of samsara: of gods, humans, and subterranean spirits.
three sacred letters: OM, ĀH, HŪM.
four aspects of time: past, present, future, and eternity.

four continents: the major island continents in the cardinal directions of Mount Meru in Indian cosmology.

four degrees: approach, close approach, accomplishment, and sublime accomplishment.

four demon-spirits: *skandhamāra, kleśamāra, devaputramāra,* and *mṛtyamāra*—of embodiment, the passions, divine pride, and death.

four elements: earth, water, fire, and air.

four extreme ontological notions: eternalism, nihilism, Brahmanism, and materialism.

four forms of consciousness: visual, auditory, olfactory, and gustatory.

four infallible guiding stars: vision, meditation, action, and the goal.

four mind benders: discursive contemplation of four topics, *i.e.,* the precious human body, impermanence, the laws of karma, and karmic retribution.

four noble truths: suffering, origin of suffering, nirvana, path to nirvana.

four objects of consciousness: sight, sound, smell, and taste.

four seals: the four seals of the *rūpakāya.*

four sensory doors: eye, ear, nose, and tongue.

four unshakable bolts: unchangeable vision, meditation, action, the goal.

fourfold intuitive realization: unitary cause, sacred letters, sustaining grace, and direct intuitive realization.

five (great) elements: earth, water, fire, air, and space.

five aspects of (primal) awareness: mirror-like awareness, awareness of sameness, discriminating awareness, all-accomplishing awareness, and awareness of the reality-continuum.

Five Buddha Consorts: Locanā, Māmakī, Pāṇḍaravāsinī, Tārā, and Dhāthīśvarī.

Five Buddhas: Akṣobhya, Ratnasambhava, Amitābha, Amoghasiddhi, and Vairocana; the Five Dhyāni Buddhas or Five Sugatas.

five colors: blue, white, yellow, red, and green.

five families: *vajra, ratna, padma, viśvavajra,* and *tathāgata* (or *buddha*).

five fires: four built around the Hindu ascetic in the summer, plus the sun.

Five Great Mothers: see Five Buddha Consorts.

five modes of the Original Buddha: the Five Buddhas (of the five families).

five modes of being: *nirmāṇakāya, sambhogakāya, dharmakāya, svabhāvikakāya,* and *vajrakāya.*

five passions: desire, aversion, sloth, pride, and jealousy.

five paths: five stages of the bodhisattva's path.

Five Perfected Dhyāni Buddhas: see Five Buddhas.

five poisons: see five passions.

five psychophysical constituents, *pancaskandha:* name and form, feeling, perception, motivation, and consciousness.

five sensory qualities: sight, sound, smell, taste, and touch.

fivefold sensual pleasure: see five sensory qualities.

Five Sugatas: see Five Buddhas.

five types of precious stones: gold, silver, turquoise, coral, and pearl.

six realms: of gods, titans, humans, animals, hungry ghosts, and denizens of hell.

six sense fields: of sight, hearing, smell, taste, touch, and mind.

six types of sentient beings: see six realms.

six types of karma: karmas of the six types of sentient beings.

seven-horsed mandala: the sun.

eight worldly obsessions: praise and blame, ignominy and fame, loss and gain, and pleasure and pain.

nine approaches to buddhahood: the nine yānas: *śrāvaka, pratyekabuddha,* bodhisattva, *kriyātantra, caryātantra, yogatantra, mahāyoga, anuyoga,* and *atiyoga.*

ten directions: four cardinal, four intermediate, nadir, and zenith.

ten levels or stages: the ten stages of the bodhisattva's path.

ten transcendental perfections, *daśapāramitā:* moral conduct, generosity, patience, endeavor, concentration, perfect insight, skillful means, aspiration, inner strength, and primal awareness.

Forty-Two Buddhas: the Peaceful Deities.

Sixty Blood-Drinking Deities: the Wrathful Deities.

SELECTED BIBLIOGRAPHY

Dargyay, Eva. *The Rise of Esoteric Buddhism in Tibet*. New Delhi: Motilal Banarsidas, 1977.

Dowman, Keith. *Sky Dancer*. Ithaca, NY: Snow Lion Publications, 1996.

————. *Masters of Mahamudra*. Albany, NY: State University of New York Press, 1985.

————. *The Divine Madman*. Clearlake, CA: Dawn Horse Press, 1980.

Dudjom Rinpoche. *Perfect Conduct*. Boston: Wisdom Publications, 1996.

————. *The Nyingma School of Tibetan Buddhism: Its Fundamentals and History*. 2 Vols. Trans. Gyurme Dorje and Matthew Kapstein. Boston: Wisdom, 1991.

Evans-Wentz, W. Y. *The Tibetan Book of the Dead*. Oxford: Oxford University Press, 1957.

————. *The Book of the Great Liberation*. Oxford: Oxford University Press, 1954.

Guenther, Herbert V. *The Creative Vision*. Novato, CA: Lotsawa, 1987.

————. *Matrix of Mystery*. Boulder, CO: Shambhala Publications, 1984.

————. *Kindly Bent to Ease Us*. Parts 1–3. Emeryville, CA: Dharma Publishing, 1975, 1976.

————. *Buddhist Philosophy in Theory and Practice*. London: Penguin, 1960.

Gyatso, Janet. *Apparitions of the Self: The Secret Autobiographies of a Tibetan Visionary*. Princeton, NJ: Princeton University Press, 1998.

Karmay, Samten Gyaltsen. *The Great Perfection*. Leiden: Brill, 1988.

Longchen Rabjam. *The Practice of Dzogchen*. Trans. Tulku Thondup. Ithaca, NY: Snow Lion Publications, 1995.

_____. *The Precious Treasury of the Way of Abiding*. Trans. Richard Barron. Junction City, CA: Padma Publishing, 1998.

Longchenpa. *You Are the Eyes of the World*. Ed. Kennard Lipman and Merrill Peterson. Novato, CA: Lotsawa, 1987.

Low, James. *Simply Being*. London: Vajra Press, 2001.

Namkhai Norbu. *Dzogchen: The Self-Perfected State*. Ithaca, NY: Snow Lion Publications, 1996.

_____. *The Cycle of Day and Night*. Trans. John M. Reynolds. New York: Station Hill, 1987.

_____. *The Crystal and the Way of Light*. London: Routledge Kegan & Paul, 1986.

Namkhai Norbu, and Adriano Clemente. *The Supreme Source*. Ithaca, NY: Snow Lion Publications, 1999.

Namkhai Norbu and Kennard Lipman, eds. *Primordial Experience*. Boston: Shambhala Publications, 1987.

Nyoshul Khenpo and Lama Surya Das. *Natural Great Perfection: Dzogchen Teachings and Vajra Songs*. Ithaca, NY: Snow Lion Publications, 1995.

Patrul Rinpoche. *The Words of My Perfect Teacher*. Trans. the Padmakara Translation Group. London: Shambhala Publications, 1998.

Pema Kunzang, Erik. *The Crystal Cave*. Kathmandu: Rangjung Yeshe, 1990.

Reynolds, John M. *Golden Letters*. Ithaca, NY: Snow Lion Publications, 1996.

_____. *Self-Liberation through Seeing Everything in Its Nakedness*. New York: Station Hill, 1988.

Ricard, Matthieu. *The Life of Shabkar: The Autobiography of a Tibetan Yogin*. Albany, NY: State University of New York Press, 1994.

Tenzin Namdrak. *Heartdrops of Dharmakaya*. Ithaca, NY: Snow Lion Publications, 1993.

Tenzin Wangyal. *Wonders of the Natural Mind: The Essence of Dzogchen in the Native Bon Tradition of Tibet*. New York: Station Hill, 1993.

Thinley Norbu. *The Small Golden Key*. Boulder, CO: Shambhala Publications, 1993.

Tsele Natsok Rangdrol. *The Heart of the Matter*. Kathmandu: Rangjung Yeshe, 1994.

Tucci, Giuseppe. *The Religions of Tibet*. London: Routledge Kegan & Paul, 1980.

Tulku Thondup. *Masters of Meditation and Miracles: The Longchen Nyingtig Lineage of Tibetan Buddhism*. Ed. Harold Talbott. Boston: Shambhala Publications, 1996.

_____. *The Tantric Tradition of the Nyingmapa*. Marion, MA: Buddhayana, 1984.

Tulku Urgyen Rinpoche. *As It Is*. Vols 1 & 2. Kathmandu: Rangjung Yeshe, 2000.

INDEX OF TIBETAN NAMES AND TERMS

(WITH TRANSLITERATION)

ABOUT THE AUTHOR

 KEITH DOWMAN has been involved in the arena of Buddhism for more than forty years, living and raising a family in India and Nepal and in Tibetan refugee society. He received lay ordination in the Nyingma school of Tibetan Buddhism and is the author of more than a dozen books on Tibet and Tibetan Buddhism, including *Natural Perfection, Sky Dancer*, and *Original Perfection*.

WISDOM PUBLICATIONS

WISDOM PUBLICATIONS, is the leading publisher of contemporary and classic Buddhist books and practical works on mindfulness. Publishing books from all major Buddhist traditions, Wisdom is a nonprofit charitable organization dedicated to cultivating Buddhist voices the world over, advancing critical scholarship, and preserving and sharing Buddhist literary culture.

To learn more about us or to explore our other books, please visit our website at www.wisdompubs.org. You can subscribe to our eNewsletter, request a print catalog, and find out how you can help support Wisdom's mission either online or by writing to:

Wisdom Publications
199 Elm Street
Somerville, Massachusetts 02144 USA

You can also contact us at 617-776-7416 or info@wisdompubs.org.

Wisdom is a 501(c)(3) organization, and donations in support of our mission are tax deductible.

Wisdom Publications is affiliated with the Foundation for the Preservation of the Mahayana Tradition (FPMT).

ALSO AVAILABLE FROM
WISDOM PUBLICATIONS

Natural Perfection
Longchenpa's Radical Dzogchen
Keith Dowman
336 pages | $17.95 | ebook $13.08

"*Natural Perfection* is a translation of a key work by Longchenpa, the most important exponent of Dzogchen. Dowman offers the reader the essence of Dzogchen stripped of any cultural trappings. Dowman's radical Dzogchen is—like Alan Watts's Zen—distinguished by its transcendence of the other aspects of Buddhist practice."
—*Buddhadharma: The Practitioner's Quarterly*

Original Perfection
Vairotsana's Five Early Transmissions
Keith Dowman
Foreword by Bhakha Tulku Pema Rigdzin
128 pages | $16.95 | ebook $12.35

These five texts are the root of Dzogchen practice, the main practice of the Nyingma school of Tibetan Buddhism. Vairotsana, a master among the first generation of Tibetan Buddhists, reveals here a truth that is at once simple and deeply profound: that all existence—life itself, everyone one of us—is originally perfect, just as is.

"A major contribution to the exciting spread of Dzogchen in modern times."
—James Low, author of *Simply Being*

Nyingma School of Tibetan Buddhism
Its Fundamentals and History
Dudjom Rinpoche
Translated, edited, and annotated by
Matthew Kapstein and Gyurme Dorje
1,584 pages | $90.00 | ebook $39.99

"Every once in a while there comes a work which, by its breadth of vision and attention to details, becomes the standard and classic in its field. This is such a work."
—*Tricycle: The Buddhist Review*

"A landmark in the history of English-language studies of Tibetan Buddhism."
—*History of Religions*

Perfect Conduct
Ascertaining the Three Vows
Nagari Panchen, Pema Wangyi Gyalpo
Commentary by His Holiness Dudjom Rinpoche
192 pages | $21.95

"This book fulfills a crucial need for serious students of Buddhism. At last we have a handbook in English that explains the full code of discipline [pratimoksa, bodhisattva, and tantric vows]...along with an elucidation of...philosophical principles and historical background."
—from the preface by Tulku Thondup, author of *Hidden Teachings of Tibet*

Creation and Completion
Essential Points of Tantric Meditation
Jamgon Kongtrul
Translated and introduced by Sarah Harding
Commentary by Khenchen Thrangu Rinpoche
208 pages | $16.95 | ebook $12.35

A classic practice text becomes even more useful: the inclusion of Rinpoche's commentary makes the terminology experientially alive. These are powerful meditation instructions, of immense value to aspiring and experienced practitioners alike. Includes Tibetan root text.

Natural Liberation
Padmasambhava's Teachings on the Six Bardos
Padmasambhava
Commentary by Gyatrul Rinoche
Translated by B. Alan Wallace
360 pages | $18.95 | ebook $13.81

Padmasambhava, the great ninth-century Indian master who established Buddhism in Tibet, describes in detail six life-processes, or bardos, and how to transform them into vehicles for enlightenment. This most extraordinary teaching is here accompanied by meditation instructions and edifying anecdotes in a lucid commentary by Gyatrul Rinpoche, an esteemed teacher of the Nyingma tradition.

Mipham's *Beacon of Certainty*
Illuminating the View of Dzogchen, the Great Perfection
by John Whitney Pettit
592 pages | $32.95 | ebook $22.99

"Lama Mipham Rinpoche was a great Nyingma scholar of the nineteenth century, who wrote a prodigious number of works on all subjects, as well as brilliant commentaries on both sutra and tantra. His work translated here by John Whitney Pettit as *Beacon of Certainty* was particularly famous and one of his most beneficial for clearing away the doubts and confusions on the view, path, and meditation. This is a valuable work indeed."
—Penor Rinpoche

Journey to Certainty
The Quintessence of the Dzogchen View
Anyen Rinpoche
Translated by Alison Choying Zangmo
248 pages | $17.95 | ebook s$13.08

"Anyen Rinpoche takes us into the mind of Mipham Rinpoche, one of the greatest teachers of nineteenth century Tibet, to discover in our own experience Mipham's deep integration of philosophy and contemplative awakening. Remarkably accessible, this book is essential reading for anyone attempting to understand or practice Dzogchen today."
—John Makransky, author of *Awakening Through Love*